PETER & PIERRE

THE LIVES, BATTLES, AND POLITICAL VISIONS
OF PETER LOUGHEED AND PIERRE TRUDEAU

by

JACK MARTIN

Peter & Pierre

Jack Martin
Delta, British Columbia

978-0-9937793-2-9 (Hardcover)
978-0-9937793-3-6 (Paperback)

Cover design, lettering and illustration by Kara Eade
Printed and bound in Canada by Blitzprint Inc.

Contents

Acknowledgements

I thank Robin Barrow, Wyn Martin, Jeff Sugarman, Jim Sanders, Brigitte Kappel, and Kara Eade for their willingness to read and comment on various drafts of the chapters of this book. Kara also contributed the front cover design and graphic, which I think nicely capture a central theme of the book.

Chapter One: The Premier and the Prime Minister

They were "golden boys"—athletic, popular, highly capable, and successful, seemingly born leaders. They dominated Canadian politics from 1965 to 1985. One was gregarious, sometimes with a touch of shyness; the other shy with a cultivated social presence. But, either could rise to almost any situation. They were medium-sized men, about 5' 8" in height and 170-180 pounds in weight for most of their adult lives. Yet, they seemed larger, possessed of formidable and charismatic personalities. They were unusually confident and determined, with considerable familial resources and contacts at their disposal—mothers who adored and helped them, and fathers whose models, for better and for worse, challenged them. Both were well educated, with graduate degrees from Harvard University, although only one was professorial. Both aspired, from a surprisingly early age, to be leaders in their home provinces and the Canadian federation, although the more federally oriented one (in his youth) became famous and admired as quite possibly the best provincial premier in Canadian history, while the more provincially oriented one (in his youth) became one of the most famous, perhaps the most famous (albeit, controversial and divisive), prime minister in that same history. Both burst onto the political scene in the mid-1960s, one initially modeling himself on the American President John F. Kennedy's call to citizenship ("Ask what you can do for your country"), the other motivated by abstract, deeply religious, and philosophical ideas concerning the sanctity and protection of personal freedom and dignity. However, both governed as secular humanists, located near the middle of the political spectrum, although one veered more to the left, the other more to the right. Both were proud Canadians committed to the ideal of a strong Canadian federation in which people of all backgrounds and circumstances could participate fully as valued citizens. Both wanted to make Canada an ideal democratic society.

The Premier was Peter Lougheed. The Prime Minister was Pierre Trudeau. Both men often projected a supreme self-assurance in their opinions and arguments that would brook no interference. Yet both were possessed of a disarming boyishness, which hinted at a basic decency and willingness to engage, that lay behind their steely resolve. They could be hot-tempered if insulted—Trudeau's ire frequently manifesting as a sharp-tongued barb accompanied by a shrugging aloofness; Lougheed's as a "don't mess with me" aggressiveness, containing a hint of defensiveness. Nonetheless, both exuded a potential for concerted and concentrated thoughtfulness once their tempers cooled. Neither was a bully, but both hated to be bullied, preferring civility and honest exchange. Both were driven, often blunt, and not entirely comfortable in the roles in which they occasionally found themselves enmeshed. Despite their differing visions for Canada, their strong wills, and their deep aversion to losing, they were well-matched adversaries who respected each other and their differences. They fought hard and sometimes angrily, but maintained a genuine regard for each other.

This is their story—a story that considers their political and personal outlooks, loyalties, battles, and legacies within the overall contexts of their lives and political careers. Despite sometimes seen as representing their home provinces of Alberta and Quebec, both Lougheed and Trudeau were committed federalists who desired to speak for Canada as a whole. When Lougheed fought for what he regarded as a fair share of revenues generated by Alberta's non-renewable oil and gas resources, he understood himself to be fighting a larger battle for the rights of provinces and their citizens within the Canadian federation. When Trudeau insisted on attaching a Charter of Rights and Freedoms to the Canadian Constitution during its patriation from Britain, he believed he was fighting for the rights and freedoms of all Canadians and an ideal of Canada as a just society. Committed to the wellbeing of their home provinces, both nonetheless aimed to speak for Canada as a united nation. What divided them and roused them to battle were basic differences in their visions of what Canada could and should be.

The story begins with the childhoods of our protagonists and ends with their combats over resources and the constitution, contests undergirded by deep differences concerning the nature of the Canadian federation. These disagreements focused on the extent and nature of provincial powers in relation to those wielded by the federal government. Any federal system of governance divides political and legal authority across different, more or less autonomous, levels comprised of national and subnational bodies. In Canada, this separation is between the federal government and the ten provincial governments. The primary reason for the adoption of a federal system is to accommodate and reflect linguistic, economic, and cultural differences that exist across different regions of a nation. Canada's federal system dates from its founding in 1867—an undertaking that brought together English residents (in Upper Canada or Ontario, New Brunswick, and Nova Scotia) and French residents (in Lower Canada or Quebec) to form the new nation of Canada. Throughout its history, the distribution of powers between the federal and provincial levels of government has been the country's most continuously contested political concern. [Territorial governments in Canada operate under the political and legal authority of the federal government, while municipal governments operate under the authority of the provincial governments.]

Some Canadian prime ministers, like John A. Macdonald and Pierre Trudeau, have exercised greater federal or central authority than others, while some provincial premiers, like René Lévesque and Peter Lougheed, have demanded and attempted to exercise greater levels of provincial authority. The political lives of Pierre Trudeau and Peter Lougheed unfolded mostly in what has been called the era of Canadian conflictual federalism, from 1970 to 1984. Intergovernmental conflicts during this time reflected the differing political visions and personal styles of these two leaders, although René Lévesque's contributions to this same period of "federation stress" also were significant.

How much of history, including political history, is a function of the visions and actions of individuals and how much is a result of broader social and cultural factors is one of the more enduring questions in the social sciences and humanities. Nonetheless, it is a question that, on reflection, seems to attempt an impossible separation of individuals from their life contexts. There can be no denying that all historically important events arise within a context of ongoing cultural, sociopolitical, economic, and religious interactions, exchanges, and conflicts. Consider the Yom Kippur War of 1973, which started on October 6, when Syrian and Egyptian forces attacked Israel in an attempt to retake territory that had been claimed by Israel during the Arab-Israeli war of 1967. Israel's counter attack, aided by an airlift of arms from the United States, beat back Arab forces and resulted in the loss of significant portions of Arab controlled land in the Sinai Peninsula, Gaza Strip, West Bank, and Golan Heights. In economic retaliation, the Organization of Petroleum Exporting Countries proclaimed an oil embargo, and ceased shipments to the United States and other countries that had supported, or expressed support for, Israel during the conflict. The embargo caused significant oil shortages and price increases, particularly in the arms-supplying United States. By the time the embargo was lifted in March of 1974, the price of oil had increased by 300 percent world wide, with American prices significantly higher.

In Canada, with the outbreak of the 1973 Yom Kipper War, a combination of high inflation coupled with a rise in oil prices convinced Pierre Trudeau and members of his federal Liberal Cabinet to slap a 40-cent tax on every barrel of Canadian oil exported to the United States from the oil fields of Western Canada. The amount of the tax was linked to the difference between Canadian domestic and international oil prices. For the most part, the revenues generated by the tax were used by the federal government to subsidize the cost of oil and gas, thus offsetting the financial pain caused by the oil embargo to the citizens of central Canada, who elect a large majority of members to the Canadian federal Parliament.

In his capacity as Premier of Alberta, Peter Lougheed and his Provincial Progressive Conservative Cabinet responded to the added federal tax on Alberta oil with outrage. Lougheed's own family, like many Albertan households, had been hit hard by the Great Depression of the 1930s, and the federal government in Ottawa had shown little concern for their wellbeing, as eastern financiers and bankers enforced foreclosures on Albertans' homes and farms. At no time in the memories of most Albertans had the Feds acted to alleviate the impact on them of price hikes on essential eastern Canadian goods and services exported to Alberta. With such thoughts running through his mind, Lougheed described the tax levelled by the Trudeau government as "the most discriminatory action taken by a federal government against a particular province in the entire history of Confederation."[1]

In retaliation, Lougheed and his government announced an increase in Alberta's royalty rate on oil production and export that would be linked to international oil prices—a royalty hike that would increase Alberta's oil and gas revenues and be used to protect itself and its oil sector from further federal intrusion. All of this eventually led to the enactment in 1981 of the federal government's *National Energy Program*—the *NEP*, a set of initials guaranteed to this day to set Albertans' teeth on edge, shorthand, as it became, for once again being mistreated by "The East."

Given such examples, it seems obvious that both individual actions and social, cultural (including economic and political) contexts play significant roles in human affairs. Individuals always act within contexts that influence the course of events. Yet these events could not possibly occur without the actions of the people involved. The extent to which individuals like Lougheed and Trudeau were able to achieve their goals for themselves, those they represented, and the provinces and nation they governed depended greatly on their abilities to read situations as they arose, recruit others to their causes and visions, and work together toward common ends. In their interactions and exchanges with colleagues and others, both Lougheed and Trudeau often displayed uncanny abilities to motivate and inspire, see situations as opportunities to act, and adapt strategies and purposes quickly when contexts changed and such openings occurred. Some of this, of course, can be attributed to luck. But, as the life and political stories of our two protagonists attest, a goodly part of what makes for success and failure comes down to a combination of clarity of purpose, gritty determination, talent, and good timing. The acquisition of such capabilities often is a life-long undertaking.

Yet, all individual attributes and capabilities must be deployed with a keen understanding and appreciation of the situations in which individuals find themselves. Such insight requires familiarity not only with matters as they currently stand, but with events and occurrences that led up to them. A brief sketch of the history of relations between Alberta and Ottawa prior to the political debuts of Trudeau and Lougheed during the mid-1960s provides a useful background to their life stories, stories that help to explain at least some of their convictions and capabilities as political leaders.

◆◆◆

Alberta became a province of the Canadian federation in 1905. Prior to that, the area out of which the province was carved belonged to the vast Canadian North West Territories, and for more than 10,000 years before that, it was inhabited by Indigenous groups that included the Dene, Blackfoot, Cree, and Stoney Nations. The first Europeans in the area were explorers and fur traders associated with the Hudson Bay and North West Companies, who arrived around 1750. With the merger of the two companies in 1821, the enlarged Hudson Bay Company controlled and managed the area until it was transferred to the Dominion of Canada in 1870.

After 1870, farmers, ranchers, and early prairie entrepreneurs joined Indigenous Peoples, Métis, fur traders, and missionaries. These early settlers were anxious to grab low-cost homesteads, made available through the Dominion Lands Act of 1872. The Canadian Pacific Railway reached Calgary in 1873, and in 1874, the North-West Mounted Police established Fort McLeod as a base from which they administered Canadian law enforcement. Immigration to the province increased dramatically during the first decade of the twentieth century, ballooning the provincial population to 78,000 by 1905.

The sale of public land was over in the United States as the twentieth century approached, with the result that the Canadian prairies became, for many, the "Last Best West." Immigrants who previously had sought American homesteads, now flooded into western Canada. At the same time, western Canadian wheat found a world market and prairie farmers began to take advantage of cheap shipping costs. The Klondike gold rush in the Yukon also drew many to the Canadian northwest and provided a considerable economic stimulus for the area. Clifford Sifton, Minister of the Interior in Wilfred Laurier's federal Liberal government, presided over and encouraged the entrepreneurial aspirations of the newcomers with enthusiasm and flair, declaring that "One of the principal ideas western men have is that it is right to take anything in sight provided nobody else is ahead of them."[2] Sifton sent his minions to Britain, Europe, and the US to distribute pamphlets and give talks, supported with magic lantern slides, extolling the virtues of independent western life (unencumbered by rules and regulations of existing bureaucracies) to "stout, hardy peasants in sheepskin coats,"[3] willing to endure hardships that would make them and the prairies prosper. Between 1896 and 1911, more than a million newcomers settled into their new western Canadian lives. Pre-existing Indigenous traditions and practices of land use were entirely ignored by Sifton and the Government of Canada.

In 1905, Laurier authorized the establishment of the provinces of Alberta and Saskatchewan and encouraged their provincial governments, in cooperation with the North West Mounted Police and federal authorities, to bring greater order to western development. Such actions included curbing dishonest grain market manipulators and elevator operators who were creating a bonanza of "heartless robbery by the big 'vested' interests,"[4] named after the size of their owners' vests, presumably overflowing with bills and coins. With the new governments in place, Laurier hoped to secure federal control of land and resources, a greater number of free homesteads for immigrants, and a guarantee of peace and prosperity that encouraged an investment friendly and more controlled environment. Laurier had decided to create two new provinces against the wishes of many prominent westerners because he feared the concentration of too much power in a single province, which potentially might rival that of Ontario and Quebec. Sole federal control of Alberta's resources persisted until 1930. At that time, a series of Natural Resources Acts was passed by the Canadian Parliament, which transferred control of natural resources and much of the crown lands within their boundaries to the four western provinces.

One significant fly in Laurier's ointment was his promise to the Catholic Church to ensure greater minority rights for western Catholics, a promise that led a furious Sifton to resign. In response to Sifton's resignation and western anger more generally, Laurier relaxed provisions promised to Catholic officials, only to enrage Henri Bourassa and other Quebec MPs who objected strongly to Laurier's seeming willingness to treat western French Canadians as "equal in rights and privileges to the Doukhobor or the Galician who had just disembarked," thus opening "a gulf between eastern and western Canadians which nothing will fill."[5] Nonetheless, Liberal provincial governments in Alberta continued uninterrupted from the province's founding in 1905 to 1921. Conservatives like future Canadian Prime Minister R. B. Bennett, the legal partner of Peter Lougheed's paternal grandfather Sir James Lougheed, preferred to pursue their political ambitions at the national level.

By 1914, the population of Alberta had skyrocketed to 470,000, creating tremendous needs for educational, health, and municipal facilities and services. These unmet requirements combined with a continuing sense of grievance by farmers against the Province's elevator and railway operators, falling grain prices, and a general distrust of eastern interests and politicians, to encourage Albertans to ignore both Liberal and Conservative parties in their 1921 provincial election. At that time, Albertans handed a landslide victory to a loosely knit group of farmers' lobby groups that coalesced into the United Farmers of Alberta (UFA) political party. Throughout the 1920s and early 1930s, the UFA passed a succession of bills and legislation intended to help indebted farmers and other workers with loan adjustments, financial assistance, and progressive wage codes. A highlight of the UFA's reign in Alberta from 1921 to 1935 was a series of lengthy negotiations with the federal government of Canada that eventually resulted in Alberta gaining control of its own resources in 1930. But by then, the Great Depression of the 1930s had begun to create widespread economic and sociopolitical havoc in Alberta and elsewhere.

Sir James Lougheed, Peter's paternal grandfather, was born in 1854 in Brampton, Ontario, the descendent of a Scottish family that had fled Scotland for Ireland in the mid-1700s when, as supporters of Bonnie Prince Charlie, they found themselves on the wrong side of the Battle of Culloden in 1746. For reasons unknown, the Lougheeds immigrated to Canada in 1815. Upon graduating from Toronto's Osgoode Hall, James articled with a Toronto law firm, and was admitted to the Ontario bar in 1881. In 1883, James Lougheed traveled to Medicine Hat, Alberta, where he wrangled a job as a lawyer for the Canadian Pacific Railway. His future and fortune were secured through informed speculation and investment in parcels of

Calgary land, soon to benefit from close proximity to the new Calgary station of the CPR.

James further solidified his status as a prominent Calgarian through his marriage in 1884 to Isabella ("Belle") Hardisty, of English and Métis ancestry, whose uncles included Lord Strathcona and Senator Richard Hardisty. Born in Fort Victoria in Canada's Northwest Territories, Belle grew up and was educated in Ontario. After the death of her father, she returned to the Canadian West with Senator Hardisty. It was through the Senator that she and James Lougheed met. When her uncle died in a wagon accident in 1889, Prime Minister John A. Macdonald appointed James to take Hardisty's place. At 35, James was the youngest person in the Senate, the Upper House of the Government of Canada.

Senator Lougheed became known as an avid booster of Calgary and the Canadian West. In his private life, he was the patriarch of an expanding family, supported by income from his rapidly growing law practice, which increasingly was being managed by his partner Richard Bedford Bennett, who joined James in 1897. With Bennett handling most of the firm's legal work, James shrewdly added petroleum to his investment portfolio and the Turner Valley oilfield to his promotion efforts. When Alberta and Saskatchewan became provinces in 1905, Senator Lougheed declared, on the floor of the Senate: "Their natural resources and the various possibilities which are to be found within the boundaries of those provinces are calculated to make them more important ... than any of the older provinces."[6]

Soon thereafter in 1906, for his work on behalf of western Canada, Senator Lougheed was elevated to Conservative leader in the

Senate. In discharging his senatorial duties, Sir James was guided by his loyalties to the federal Conservative Party and the CPR—loyalties that worked to the disadvantage of the fledgling Canadian Northern Railway (CNR) and the Liberal Party of Canada. As further reward for his continuing efforts on their behalf, Lougheed was granted a seat in the cabinet (as Minister Without Portfolio) of newly elected Conservative Prime Minister Robert Laird Borden. With the outbreak of World War I, James Lougheed was named Acting Minister of the Militia, an appointment that subsequently led to his receipt of a knighthood in June 1916 from King George V of the United Kingdom and Dominion of Canada, whose coronation James had attended in 1911.

When Arthur Meighen succeeded Borden as Prime Minister in July 1920, Sir James became Minister of the Interior, effectively making him the government leader for western Canada. Also chairing the Natural Resources Commission, James' energies turned more fully to the strengthening of government control over what he regarded as a neglected area of government policy. Here, it is relatively easy to draw a connection between James and his future grandson Peter, for the neglected area in question was the development and implementation of federal oil regulations affecting western Canada. Anxious that Canada should not lose control of its natural resources, in 1921 James moved quickly to rescind exploration and drilling rights that had been given to US Oil Companies in the Mackenzie River Valley. He also placed 49 sections of the Athabasca tar sands in federal reserve to protect them from exploration, experiment, and development. Although lauded for his efforts by many who declared that protecting the interests of Canada in this way was exactly what a

Minister of the Crown should be doing, Sir James' efforts in this direction were cut short by the defeat of Meighen's Conservatives in the autumn of 1921 by Mackenzie King's Liberals.

With the federal Conservatives out of power, James refocused his energies on his Senate job and his Calgary law practice, where he found himself locked in a struggle for control of the practice with his partner R. B. Bennett—an extremely acrimonious affair that eventually saw Lougheed ousted from the firm he had established, despite his somewhat humiliating last-ditch efforts to reconcile with his former partner. Shortly thereafter, Sir James succumbed to pneumonia and died on the night of November 2, 1925. Two years later, Richard Bedford Bennett became leader of the federal Conservative Party, and went on to serve as Prime Minister of Canada from 1930 to 1935. Sir James left his extensive estate to be divided between his wife Belle and his five surviving children. His two oldest sons, Clarence and Edgar, who three years later was to become Peter's father, were named as Sir James' executors.

At noon on July 1 of 1867, the Dominion of Canada was formed when the British Parliament passed the British North America Act (now referred to in Canada as the Constitution Act of 1867). The act authorized a joining together of the colonies of Upper and Lower Canada, Nova Scotia, and New Brunswick. In the process, Upper Canada was renamed Ontario; Lower Canada became Quebec. The founding of Quebec was an attempt to accommodate the existence of a French-Canadian nation in what had become by that time, through immigration and shifting population, a predominantly English-speaking country. Confederation acknowledged Quebecers as a minority, but a minority with its own provincial government to safeguard its cultural and social development. The 1867 Constitution Act also conferred the right of Quebecers and other Canadians to access and interact with all federal governmental institutions and services using either the French or English languages.

In the years that immediately followed Confederation, Quebec could be considered a traditional agrarian society, focused inward and mostly ignoring events outside its borders. Nonetheless, the development of Quebec and Quebecers was inevitably affected by the widespread industrialization and urbanization that typified the last half of the 1800s. Although a massive wave of immigration ended in the early 1870s, a high birth rate continued to increase the province's population, in both urban and rural areas. As rural land became increasingly coveted and less fertile holdings with poorer soil (mostly north of the St. Lawrence River) were added to the land register, many Quebec farmers endured challenging lives that required supplementing their incomes with part-time work as lumberjacks or hunters. Their older children often helped cover expenses by putting in long hours in nearby factories. Between Confederation and 1930, over a million French Canadians immigrated to the United States in search of better opportunities. By 1900, a third of Quebec's once almost entirely rural population was to be found in towns and cities, especially in Montreal, now home to half of the province's industrial activity and a quarter of its citizens.

With greater financial and industrial growth in Montreal, a new commercial class, consisting mostly of English speakers (with connections to sources of wealth in Ontario, Britain, and the United States), controlled powerful economic engines like the Bank of Montreal and the Molson Brewery. Large numbers of French-speaking and Roman Catholic citizens found themselves increasingly alienated from economic and political power. During the first half of the twentieth century in rural and small-town Quebec, the Catholic Church, large landowners, and outside capitalists benefited from what some have called a "peasant society," presided over by the Liberal Party of Quebec and later by the Union Nationale Party of Maurice Duplessis. It was to the transformation and amelioration of such circumstances that Pierre Elliott Trudeau was to dedicate himself. Despite his devout Catholicism and Jesuit education, Trudeau came to believe that Quebec's church hierarchy and politicians constituted a corrupt elite who fostered a repressive ideology of backwardness that prevented any genuinely democratic reform or collective social justice in the province. This was a state of affairs made worse by the failure of Quebec's federal members of parliament to represent the interests of all Quebecers.

The almost two decades of the twentieth century preceding Pierre Trudeau's birth in 1919 had been difficult ones for Francophone Canadians, despite the hope that surrounded the election of Quebecer Wilfrid Laurier as Prime Minister of Canada in 1896. Laurier presided over a rapidly growing Canadian population, economy, and industrial sector. Unfortunately, in Quebec, by the time Laurier was voted out of office in 1911, the distribution of the benefits of such advances had funneled increasingly into the pockets of Montreal's mostly Anglophone, wealthy citizens. So opulent were their Mount Royal life styles, and so out-of-touch with those of the much poorer denizens of the lower east end of Montreal spread below them and those in the villages that dotted the rest of the province, that Stephen Leacock opined, "The rich in Montreal enjoyed a prestige in that era that not even the rich deserve."[7] City life for Quebec's French population became spiked with resentment.

Throughout the province, a growing sense of maltreatment and offence grew into an increasingly strident nationalist reaction, one that had the effect of further alienating Francophone Quebecers from the English ways of life that seemed to them responsible for their plight. Such resentment was fanned further when Laurier's successor Robert Borden introduced conscription in 1917, forcing Quebec's young men to risk their lives in the Great War that Francophones regarded as another testament to the British imperialism of which they considered themselves to be victims. Quebec journalists like Henri Bourassa and the province's Catholic bishops had muted any criticism of the war effort because Borden had promised there would be no conscription. When Borden broke his promise and was re-elected as Prime Minister over Laurier who opposed conscription, riots and deaths followed in Montreal and Quebec City.

Pierre Trudeau's ancestry was a complex mixture of French and English, and rural and urban. His father's family was French Canadian—ten generations of rural farmers initiated by Etienne Truteau, a French carpenter who came to New France (later to become Lower Canada, and later still to be known as Quebec) in

1659, to farm near Longueuil, south of the St.. Lawrence and Montreal. Truteau (later changed to Trudeau) is remembered by historians for his part in turning back an attack on Montreal by Iroquois warriors, soon after his arrival in the new world. Surviving this and other adventures to father fourteen children ensured a productive beginning for the Trudeaus of Quebec, some of whom eventually spread to other areas of North America.

Trudeau's paternal grandfather, Joseph, was an uneducated, but well-heeled farmer south of Montreal near the land initially settled by Etienne Truteau. However, Joseph's wife set higher expectations for their sons. Daughter of the local mayor, Malvina Trudeau insisted that Joseph send them to some of the best schools in the province—the Collège Ste. Marie, Loyola, and the University of Montreal. Thus, bootstrapped out of rural agrarianism, Charles Trudeau, Pierre's father, took his law degree and established himself as a highly successful and well-connected businessman in Montreal, making his fortune (one that would support his wife and children throughout their lives) by selling his string of full service garages and service stations to Imperial Oil in the autumn of 1932.

Trudeau's maternal grandfather, Philip Armstrong Elliott, was a prosperous Montrealer who had benefited from the money that poured down the hill from Mount Royal. He owned the Captain's Saloon in downtown Montreal and had a talent for making money through real estate speculation. Philip's family were British loyalists who had fled the United States, but his wife, Sarah Suavé, was a French Canadian Catholic. Their daughter Grace, Trudeau's mother, although raised by her mother as a Catholic, was sent to Dunham Ladies' College, a finishing school for many daughters of Montreal's Anglo-Protestant establishment. Her marriage to Charlie Trudeau ensured that their children would be fully embedded in both the French and English cultures of Montreal.

With the foregoing sketches of our two protagonists in place (together with bits of the history of their respective provinces prior to their births, and short glimpses of their immediate ancestries), the stage is almost set for the unfolding of our story of their lives and political battles, the outcomes of which continue to shape contemporary Canadian life and politics. Only one additional, and critically important, matter remains to be articulated before launching into the full story that awaits us. Like so much else in the lives and life contexts of Peter Lougheed and Pierre Trudeau, this is a matter that bears both striking similarities and striking differences when compared across our leading men and their home provinces. It concerns the unusual fact that during their development as individuals and would-be politicians, both Alberta and Quebec were dominated politically by lengthy reigns of powerful men who headed uniquely autocratic and populist movements—William Aberhart, Ernest Manning, and the Social Credit Party in Alberta; Maurice Duplessis and the Union Nationale in Quebec. These leaders commanded their respective parties and provinces as near demagogues, presiding over them as quasi-religious patriarchs. When they eventually were rejected by voters, they and their parties never to return, these rejections were experienced as revolutionary— Quebec's Quiet Revolution of the early 1960s and Alberta's derivatively-named, quiet revolution of the early 1970s, each occurring when our protagonists were in their early forties, Trudeau being nine years Lougheed's senior.

To grasp more firmly the significance of the Social Credit and Union Nationale regimes as fodder for the political aims and visions of Lougheed and Trudeau respectively, it is worth exploring these movements a bit further. By the mid-1930s, the populations of both Alberta and Quebec were experiencing the worst of what was to be a decade long economic depression, following the 1929 world-wide stock market crash, for which none of the existing provincial or federal political parties in Canada appeared to have a solution. In these circumstances, economically frightened Albertans and Quebecers, like many Canadians in other parts of the country, could be persuaded to cast their votes for almost anyone confidently proclaiming easily understood solutions to, and relief from, their troubles. Enter William Aberhart in Alberta and Maurice Duplessis in Quebec.

In Alberta, the United Farmers of Alberta, the party that had governed Alberta (with the support of the Canadian Labour Party) since 1921, suddenly found itself experiencing a schism between its leadership and its rank and file members. Many of the latter were being radicalized by the dire effects of the Depression, which hit the prairie provinces especially hard. In contrast, their leaders were trending in a more conservative direction. With its members passing resolutions proposing that the provincial government take over companies vital to the province's wellbeing, such as those that sold farm machinery and financed farming operations, UFA leader Jack

Brownlee and his cabinet allowed both industrialists and financiers to seize farms and houses when payment of bills was in arrears. With him and his cabinet facing public animosity for their refusal to curb what was widely regarded as the heartless greed of moneyed interests, Brownlee was forced to resign over allegations of a forced affair made by a young government stenographer. Things then fell apart quickly for the UFA. Since most Albertans had roundly rejected the more established Liberal and Conservative Parties during the previous decade, Brownlee's and the UFA's downfalls created a vacuum that William Aberhart and his newly formed Social Credit Party were anxious to fill.

"Bible Bill" Aberhart was an outspoken Calgary educator and Baptist preacher who attributed much of Albertans' suffering during the Depression to the obvious fact that they had little money to spend. Aberhart was well known to most Albertans through his highly popular Sunday morning radio broadcasts delivered on the Calgary Prophetic Bible Institute's *Back to the Bible Hour*. In these broadcasts, Aberhart mixed his religious and political convictions and promised a solution to the current economic disaster. The way out was based on his rather limited understanding of the radical economic prescriptions of Scottish engineer Clifford Douglas, who was not an economist. At the heart of Douglas' *social credit* beliefs was the distribution of debt-free credit, over and above wages earned, to all citizens, so as to bridge the gap between purchasing power and prices, using a mechanism based on the idea of a "just price" to control inflation. Unfortunately, Douglas' economic ideas were mostly untested, and Aberhart's grasp of them, and the workings of Canadian politics in general, uncertain.

Nonetheless, the well-known and popular Aberhart gained control of the political arm of Alberta's social credit movement and was able to direct a winning campaign in the 1935 provincial election. During that campaign, he promised to give each Albertan $25 a month in addition to their income from their regular jobs, if they had them. Aberhart claimed this would revitalize not only the fortunes of individual Albertans but stimulate the province's economy. He also proposed a variety of other anti-poverty and debt reduction policies and programs, including the Alberta Treasury Branches as a Crown corporation of the Alberta government. The treasury branches were intended to compete with eastern financiers and banks by offering Albertans relief and survival funding that the easterners would not. On the day of the election, Aberhart and his social creditors won a landslide victory.

Although there seems to be little reason to doubt Aberhart's sincerity, once elected many of his plans were predictably thwarted by the federal government of Canada, which had jurisdiction over Canadian currency and banking, a fact that incumbent Premier and UFA leader Jack Brownlee had pointed out repeatedly during the build-up to the election. The basic problem Aberhart faced in implementing his attempts to reform Alberta's economy was that he had no constitutional authority to do many of the things he had promised. His apparently fuzzy understanding of federal powers, coupled with his misunderstanding of Douglas' theory, meant that no $25 monthly payments ever materialized.

Another Aberhart election promise, his "prosperity certificates," fared only slightly better. These were intended to work as a kind of provincially-backed "money substitute," supported by a government-proposed bartering system that allowed Albertans who owed money to other Albertans to pay in certificates, rather than cash. Although wholly redeemable, at least if kept in constant (i.e., weekly) circulation, the owners of uncirculated certificates were required to purchase government stamps to attach to their certificates to signal that these retained their value. Since the federal mint continued to produce Canadian bills and coins, most businesses and individuals in the province found it more convenient, and more prudent, to forego the certificates and continue to use the currency of the realm.

Yet another Aberhart initiative, eventually blocked by John Bowen, Alberta's Lieutenant Governor, hinted at a darker, more authoritarian side of Aberhart (one well known to many teachers and parents who had interacted with him during his time as a teacher and principal in the Calgary school system). Frustrated by what he regarded as interference by Alberta newspaper editors and journalists, Aberhart's government passed a bill that would have forced newspapers, such as the *Calgary Herald* and *Edmonton Journal*, to print government rebuttals to stories deemed to be inaccurate by the provincial Cabinet, and not to use sources without the approval of the government. Another indication of Aberhart's autocratic tendencies and over-reaching was his personal assumption of the portfolios of Minister of Education and Attorney General in addition to that of Premier.

Nonetheless, Aberhart received considerable public acclaim for freezing some debt collections and thereby blocking related foreclosures on mortgages. On another front, his moves to protect

Alberta's natural resources from being taken over by U.S. oil companies received mixed reviews, including the attempt by some Alberta oil workers to invoke another election promise of Aberhart's that allowed the recall of elected officials—legislation that was quickly withdrawn with the party leader in peril.

When Aberhart died unexpectedly in 1943, following his re-election in 1940 with a significantly reduced mandate (in both seats and popular vote), his long-time right-hand man, Ernest Manning, took control of their party's fortunes. Manning continued Aberhart's tradition of weekly religious radio broadcasts and maintained the Social Credit domination of Alberta politics until 1971, when its long reign, of 36 years, finally was ended by Peter Lougheed and his Progressive Conservative Party.

Manning was acutely attuned to the economic and political workings of the province in relation to the federal government. Nonetheless, in the middle of his first of six terms as Alberta Premier, he attempted to enact an "Alberta Bill of Rights Act" that would give the provincial government much greater control of the chartered banks. When this was disallowed for infringing on federal jurisdiction, Manning stopped all attempts to tie his administration to social credit monetary reform, put such theories behind him, and moved on to the business of governing the province with what most Albertans regarded as a fair and steady hand, thereby maintaining the strong support of his citizens. For the rest of Social Credit's life in Alberta, with Manning in charge, there were no signs of the chaotic reformist struggles that had beset Aberhart's social creditors.

Manning governed in a style that fit and flowed from Manning himself. He exercised a cautious financial conservatism, accompanied by equally conservative initiatives at social reform, which included carefully considered expansions in education, health, and transportation services and facilities. In doing so, he was aided greatly by abundant revenues that flowed into provincial coffers following the discovery of the Leduc oil field in 1947. Manning was a straight-talking advocate for what he regarded as the best interests of Alberta and Albertans. His caution and rectitude, in combination with low provincial taxes, which did not include a sales tax, seemed like a steady and sensible path to most Albertans, who rewarded him with 25 years of uninterrupted stewardship of their province.

However, in the 1967 Alberta election, the last that Manning contested, it was clear that the Alberta electorate was changing. Support for Social Credit was down in the big cities of Edmonton and Calgary, where its rural and religious roots were losing traction. Perhaps seeing the writing on the wall, Manning retired from political life in 1968, effectively ending the long reign of Social Credit as the major political force in the Province of Alberta. Three years later, Peter Lougheed and his Conservatives ushered in a new phase in Alberta's political history. Their election strategy was based on demonstrating that social creditors had become complacent and stagnant, locked in an inertia that was preventing the province, especially in its urban areas, from reaping the benefits that ought to accompany its financial strength and youthful energy. It was time for Alberta to transform itself by broadening its politics. It was time to join a wider world of commerce, cosmopolitanism, and opportunity, which included seeking a better deal with Ottawa for the management of its own resources and endowments, natural and human, for the benefit of all Albertans.

The Union Nationale Party of Maurice Duplessis governed Quebec from 1936 to 1959 (with a one-term interruption from 1939 to 1943). Duplessis easily eclipsed whatever autocratic tendencies might be attributed to the Alberta social creditors. The Depression had caused general discontent amongst Quebecers who had loyally supported a succession of Liberal provincial governments since 1897. As leader of the peripheral Conservative Party of Quebec, Duplessis was destined to stay on the fringes of Quebec politics. However, as young Liberal members of Quebec's National Assembly, unhappy with increasing charges of corruption that linked their party to powerful English-dominated enterprises like Quebec's electricity trust, fled the Liberal ranks, Duplessis adeptly scooped them up to create a new party ostensibly committed to social reform and nationalism ("Quebec for Quebecers"). However, once the newly formed Union Nationale was elected, Duplessis soon abandoned the liberal newcomers and their ideas, and reverted to priorities of his own. These included aligning himself with the Catholic Church and its authorities to rigorously combat communists and unionists. Most galling for the former Liberals, who now fled the Union Nationale, Duplessis also courted American investment and Montreal's Anglophone business communities, amidst new charges of corrupt dealings.

Although Duplessis temporarily relinquished power to the Liberals in the 1939 Quebec election, Quebecers' anger at the federal and provincial governments for introducing conscription of the province's young men to serve in what most Francophones regarded as a British imperialist war, returned him and the Union Nationale to power in 1943—power he did not relinquish until his death in 1959. Under Duplessis, it was business as usual for powerful church and corporate interests. Duplessis appealed to traditional values of church and state to flaunt his power and induce fear in his opponents. He ridiculed the progressive ideas of Francophone intellectuals and, with the Church's help, vetoed university appointments of professors who were not practicing Catholics or who opposed his regime. Duplessis also passed laws that enabled locking up buildings and resources he claimed were being used for the purposes of communist enemies of the state. He stood by as provincial police attacked picket lines of striking workers. He attacked Ottawa for standing against Quebec's interests, even as he welcomed foreign investors and developers.

In the words of André Laurendeau, Duplessis "defended provincial autonomy to make Quebec the paradise for monopolies, the kingdom of low salaries, and the land of slums."[8] In courting businesses he favoured, he rented out the province's natural resources in exchange for the modest income tax paid by their corporate and out-of-province renters. During his time in office, Maurice Duplessis maintained a status quo that did nothing to improve the lives of Francophone Quebecers, especially those in the vast rural areas of the province, or to prevent money flowing out of the province to foreign interests. In consequence, he did little to develop Quebec's natural and human resources for the benefit of most Quebecers.

By the time of Duplessis' death, the extent and effects of his traditional alliances with Church conservatives and outside entrepreneurial interests had become painfully obvious to many groups who spent most of the 1950s mobilizing and encouraging dissent and calls for change to social, political conditions and directions in the province. Such unrest was significantly expedited by the Asbestos strike of 1949, which for the first time frayed the alliance between business and church that ensured the dominance of the Union Nationale. Several outspoken clerics openly expressed sympathy for the workers in reaction to the brutal tactics of the provincial police in breaking the strike. A few years later, some of those who had actively supported the strikers launched the magazine, *Cité libre,* which became a forum for dissent and opposition to the Duplessis government.

Amongst those who volunteered to help the Asbestos workers during the strike of 1949 and who subsequently established, edited, and contributed many articles to *Cité libre* was Pierre Elliott Trudeau. Trudeau was one of those intellectuals who had been unable to gain a tenured position at the Université de Montréal because of Duplessis' interference with university hiring practices. Yet, he and others who had the enormous benefits of independent wealth and social standing did not suffer under the Duplessis regime like many more impoverished and powerless Quebecers. Although Trudeau had flirted with Quebec nationalism as a university student, he later became bitterly opposed to nationalism and separatism of any kind. However, several others associated with *Cité libre* and the more general resistance to the Union Nationale during the 1950s were much less attached to Canadian federalism than Trudeau and became instrumental in the rise of Quebec separatism during the early 1960s.

Trudeau was initially enthusiastic about the Quiet Revolution of Jean Lesage's Quebec Liberals, who succeeded the Union Nationale after its long reign under Duplessis and devoted themselves to dragging Quebec into the modern world. However, his enthusiasm faded quickly to disenchantment as several members of the new Lesage Government displayed more centrist and left-wing versions of nationalism and separatism that eventually led to the formation of the Parti Québécois toward the end of that same decade.

What follows is a detailed examination of different stages in the personal development and political lives of Peter Lougheed and Pierre Trudeau—their childhoods, education, adult lives before they formally entered politics, their early political careers before they were elected to the positions of Premier of Alberta and Prime Minister of Canada respectively, and their later battles about the division of powers and resources between the provinces and the federal government. These were nation-changing clashes over the *National Energy Program* and the *Canadian Constitution and Charter of Rights and Freedoms*, during the early 1980s, before they retired from political life in 1984 (Trudeau) and 1985 (Lougheed). Particular emphasis is given to their personal development, personalities, political visions and strategies, relationship with each other, and to their respective legacies. It is no exaggeration to suggest that the Canada we know today would probably not exist as it does were it not for their contributions to their home provinces and to the Canadian federation as a whole.

Pierre Trudeau and Peter Lougheed were confident, powerful men who were not prone to self-indulgence, but who understood themselves as having obligations to their country that only they could discharge. Their different visions of Canada, to which they devoted their enormous talents and energies, and the ways in which they strove to advance those visions, continue to command our attention and remain central to our future and that of our nation. Contemporary debates and frictions concerning federal versus provincial powers with respect to the management of Canada's natural resources and the constitutional rights and freedoms of Canadian citizens are historically and politically linked directly to their visions, contests, and legacies.

Chapter Two: Early Lives and Education

There is much debate about the effects of childhood experiences on the lives and actions of prominent individuals, or any of the rest of us for that matter. However, we begin our lives as children and whether, as adults, we are more or less able to alter our earlier experiences of life, it is indisputable that the child precedes the adult and in that sense begins what comes after. As put more metaphorically by William Wordsworth, in his poem *My Heart Leaps Up*, "the child is father to the man." One of the things that stands out most in the lives of our protagonists is the surprisingly early age at which each of them was perceived by others, and declared by themselves, to be marked for political leadership. Like many others of their precocious and ambitious ilk, Trudeau and Lougheed were encouraged and supported by parents who were demonstrative in challenging them and mothers who were perhaps even more demonstrative in their love and support for them. These relationships are best understood in the context of knowing something about their parents, their homes, their communities, and their education, all of which inevitably contributed to the forging of their early experiences and their characters.

Pierre Trudeau's parents were social, cultural, and characterological opposites. Charles-Émile Trudeau, a Catholic Francophone, was "a dynamo, gutsy, gregarious, extravagant, and loud,"[1] "an extrovert who loved games, gambling, and the high life."[2]

"He spoke loudly and expressed himself vigorously."[3] Grace Elliott was "contemplative, devout, frugal, forbearing, and resolutely refined."[4] She was of French-Canadian and Scottish ancestry (British loyalists who had come to Canada from New England), whose businessman father had sent her to be educated at Dunham Ladies' College in the Eastern Townships, with daughters of the Anglo-Protestant establishment. However, she, like her mother and her husband, was Catholic.

Charlie's Québécois family had farmed land on the south shore of the St. Lawrence for nine generations before his semi-literate father had sold the land at the urging of his mother (whose brother was a physician) so that their boys could be schooled at the eminent classical college of Sainte-Marie in Montreal. After winning many academic and athletic prizes and earning a reputation as a troublemaker at Sainte-Marie, Charlie studied law at the Montreal campus of Laval University (now the Université de Montréal) and established a successful, three-person law firm.

Energetically driven to succeed, Charlie quickly grew bored with his legal practice. He founded what he called the Automobile Owners' Association, a string of garages selling gasoline and maintenance services, which he expanded into a club for car owners who paid an annual fee. By the time Pierre entered adolescence, his father owned thirty garages, which he sold to Imperial Oil in 1932 for the then extravagant price of $1.2 million. He invested these funds wisely in enterprises like the Sullivan Mines, Belmont Park, and the Montreal Royals baseball team, for which he served as vice-president. He "became a member of the Cercle Universitaire, the Club Canadien, and several golf clubs."[5] Although a political conservative, his circle of friends contained both conservatives and liberals, including the mayor of Montreal, Camillien Houde, who Pierre, in his memoirs, recalled as "incredibly portly ... which made a big impression on such a little guy as I was then."[6] The Trudeaus "became and remained members of the *haute bourgeoisie* of Quebec, with financial resources that ensured security for Grace and her children for the rest of their lives."[7]

The Trudeau family (Suzette, Pierre, Charles Jr. or Tip, and their parents) first resided modestly at 5779 Rue Durocher, just inside the boundaries of the new middle-class suburb of Outremont. From there, Pierre attended the Académie Querbes, a few blocks away, for his early schooling—first in the English section and then in the French, once his English was up to the standards demanded by his father. At home, the family spoke mostly French. The Durocher house was in a somewhat mixed neighbourhood of primarily French Canadians, but also included some Irish Catholics and Jews. Querbes was an exceptionally modern and well appointed school, complete with swimming pool, bowling alley, and a progressive curriculum that included sports, augmented by other extracurricular clubs and activities. With the windfall from the sale of Charlie's garages, the family moved to a new three-story building of brown brick on McCullough Street in the heart of Outremont. At twelve, Pierre was enrolled at Collège Jean-de-Brébeuf, the elite Jesuit classical college within walking distance of his home, to continue his schooling and eventually to obtain the equivalent of a University undergraduate degree.

Throughout his childhood and early education, young Pierre lived with a mostly absent, but when present, domineering father, who was simultaneously loving and demanding. It was his mother who maintained the home and cared for the children. At eight pounds four ounces, Pierre was a well-sized but colicky baby, who when he turned one had an operation on his adenoids that stopped most of the crying. From his birth, his mother kept meticulous records and mementos of his development and accomplishments. Having just turned two, "Pierre made the sign of the cross" and could say his prayers alone. Precociously bilingual, little Pierre already knew many children's songs in both languages. During his absences, Charlie wrote frequent letters to Grace and the children, reminding her to observe their character and correct their faults, because such correction was important and for their own good. Both Suzette and Pierre found their father strict, intense, and dynamic when he was present. He taught Pierre to box, wrestle, and shoot, encouraging him to become strong and independent. Biographer, George Radwanski describes a typical day when Charlie was at home.

> Promptly at 5:15 every day, he would drop whatever he was doing at work and go home to spend at least an hour giving his three children ... his undivided attention. Then he would usually go out and spend the evening with friends. ... Though he was severe when disobeyed, he preferred to encourage his children with incentive... he would offer a quarter to whoever could jump the highest or run the fastest or hang by his legs the longest, or he

would promise to buy a canoe when his children could swim a certain distance.[8]

In Suzette's words: "He wasn't with us an awful lot, but when he was there he was very much present. He was interested in our schooling ... he always wanted to see our homework and see what kinds of marks we were getting."[9] In Trudeau's own words:

He was basically a very good father, because he didn't punish very often; he rewarded much more than he punished. ... He was a successful man. ... He was a leader, he had wit ... He wielded some authority; that made me respect him and, during the last years of his life, probably also challenge him from time to time as adolescents do. But he died before I ever got into any open conflict with him. ... He had demanding standards, which didn't consist of saying, 'You must be more like me,' but did consist of saying, 'You must do whatever you are doing properly.' ... He gave me a taste for life; he was much more exuberant than I and I wanted to imitate him. But he was stern. He had principles: when we were fooling, we were fooling; but when it was serious, it was serious. ... I felt so inferior to him in all respects ... But he gave me the means to be like him: He taught me boxing, to shoot a rifle, he taught me to talk, to read ...[10]

By contrast, Pierre's mother Grace was refined and cultured, often frequenting museums and concerts—intelligent and charming, even adventurous, though quiet. Like her husband, she had many friends. She possessed a good sense of humour and was not prone to criticize. As described by Trudeau:

> She was a good mother, spent a lot of time with us. … my mother was more discreet and withdrawn, didn't loom so large. But in terms of love and presence, of course, she was always there. … I remember spending a lot of time with her. … She loved liberty perhaps more than my father did. She never gave me the impression of an overly protective mother. … She wasn't always off to parties, didn't break down and weep, never took things too tragically, never imposed her wishes on us. She left her children free. What I most admire about her was her lack of possessiveness: I never felt held back in any way.[11]

When he was twelve, Trudeau was enrolled in the Jesuit Collège Jean de Brébeuf, a mile away from his family home. At Brébeuf, he was encouraged by the priests, with the approval of his father, to counteract his shyness and sensitivity by cultivating his reason and assertiveness over his emotion and reticence. Brébeuf traditionally emphasized rational argument and cogent debate through a classical curriculum that combined the usual academic subjects taught in junior and senior high school with extensive forays into the arts, philosophy, and politics. Trudeau proved to be an outstanding student, usually at or near the top of his class. The school's emphasis on personal development fit his father's desires. Trudeau became determined to assert his individuality. At school, he cultivated an aggressive mix of mischievousness, playfulness, aloofness, flair, and pugnacity that made him a leader of a group of similarly minded Outremont adolescents, often referred to by other students as "the snobs." However, Pierre himself never paraded his affluence and privilege or bragged about his family travels to Europe or anything else in his family life. As a day student, he typically walked to and from school.

While at Brébeuf, the adolescent Trudeau excelled as a student, athlete, and editor of the student newspaper. In these roles he encouraged his fellow students to shake off their inertia and assert themselves: "If you are right to have your ideas, you are wrong to keep them to yourself. If you are wrong to have your ideas, you would be right to expose them to correction."[12] In his own life, Trudeau now was consciously cultivating an "international accent that most students must have considered alien or pretentious" and "developing his own style, writing in terse, pithy sentences" and seeking "to stimulate debate, arguments, or at least expression of personal viewpoints,"[13] without fully realizing that there were strict limits to what he was asking students to do—limits that were imposed by the pedagogue priests. Although seeing himself as independent and sometime rebellious, Trudeau mostly kept well within the bounds of what the priests would tolerate. Much of Pierre's time at Brébeuf was spent in developing his intellect, capabilities, and personal style. He was learning how to stand out from the crowd as he studied and experimented in how to lead it.

After his father's premature death from pneumonia in 1935, the 15-year-old Trudeau confined any rebelliousness and "acting out" to his life at school, while adopting a calm, obedient, and increasingly responsible and helpful demeanour at home, in support of and respect for his mother in her new role of single parent. By occasionally pushing the limits at school, Trudeau "came to know the difference between a sally that would throw the teacher off his stride, bringing down his anger, and one that would get the class laughing without provoking the teacher's wrath."[14] Counterbalancing the strong Francophone atmosphere at school, his home environment began to reflect the more English culture favoured by his mother. English replaced French as the domestic language of choice and his father's boisterous and emotive Gallic presence began to fade.

Clarkson and McCall claim that Charlie's death left the adolescent Pierre in a "state of psychic imbalance": "The day would never come when he could successfully challenge the 'lickings' he describes his father as having given him when he disobeyed, when paternal dominance would be replaced by the father's acknowledgement of the son's achievements as a grown man."[15] Adopting ideas about psychological development advanced by Jung, Erikson, and Freud (as synthesized by David Levinson), Clarkson and McCall opine that his father's sudden, unexpected death disrupted Pierre's "emotional formation, turning him into the kind of man who evolves outside the normal patterns of growth," forcing "him to develop great strengths but at the same time leaving him prey to crippling weaknesses." His father's death prevented Trudeau, as an older adolescent and adult, from resolving conflicts between the different values and characters of his mother and father—pushing such resolution into middle-age, at a time when most men made life-shaping commitments related to occupation, marriage, friendship, and a family of their own. As it turned out, there can be little doubt that Trudeau did not decide such matters until much later than most adult men. Whether or not these delays were occasioned by the kinds of psychological conflict suggested by Clarkson and McCall is, of course, a much more speculative matter. What is more certain is that in the aftermath of Charlie's death, and without the excitement engendered by his presence in their lives, the remaining Trudeaus settled into a more muted, restrained, and refined way of life.

In his father's absence, Pierre readily accepted his mother's authority and gradually took on increased responsibility in assisting her to manage the family finances. Somewhat consistent with Clarkson and McCall's speculations, Radwanski suggests that after his father's death, Trudeau's "transfer of hostilities from the domestic to the public arenas may well ... have helped freeze him into an almost lifelong posture of resisting authority,"[16] causing him to develop a mild form of what psychologists call a double personality. However, his later biographers Max and Monique Nemni reject this thesis as overly and unnecessarily dramatic, arguing that Trudeau, after an initial period of shock, coped quite well with his father's death, just as his father would have expected him to do. The Nemnis also believe that Radwanski, and other biographers, like Clarkson and McCall, accept too readily Trudeau's own frequently repeated claim to have been constantly challenging authority during his adolescence. They acknowledge that "he sometimes acted the clown," but argue that his "breaches of discipline through pranks, teasing, and deliberate provocation, were met with indulgence because they were perpetrated without malicious intent" and that "if the adolescent experienced his father's death as a great emptiness, that did not come out in his behaviour or in his academic results."[17]

Radwanski and the Nemnis also disagree somewhat about the nature of the education the adolescent Trudeau received at Brébeuf. For the most part, Radwanski extolls Brébeuf's classical education as serving to broaden his intellectual horizons, selecting Father Jean Bernier, a young French Canadian Manitoban, as a stellar example of the kind of teacher and education Brébeuf had to offer. Citing a 1969 interview and profile of Trudeau by Edith Iglauer that appeared in the *New Yorker*, Radwanski indirectly quotes Trudeau as saying that "Father Bernier [who taught French Literature] was the most highly cultivated man I had met," teaching "me to like beautiful things, poetry or books or art; he really set standards of appreciation which have never left me." Bernier himself is quoted as saying "Literature, philosophy, music, painting—all went together. ... All this was a bit cut off from the atmosphere of daily life, but these were the sons of bourgeoisie and didn't have money troubles, so they could throw themselves into art and beauty. It was an atmosphere of elation, where everything was beautiful ... I taught them French, Greek and Latin literature."[18]

Recognizing the elitism that characterized a Brébeuf classical education, Bernier qualifies by remarking that "although all of this was a typical modern French culture, it was open to other streams of thought," including "Tagore, the Indian poet ... [and] what Thoreau said about the wilderness, which was very appealing to Canadians ... Our little life gave the boys respect for the rational, an instinctive repulsion against the rising Fascism and Nazism. I insisted on a respect for man-made beauty. They had to understand that real men are not destroyers but builders—of society, of poetry, and of beauty. ... I used to give the boys Plato as a model of intellectual courage. ... You could feel that Pierre had this kind of courage; even as a boy, he would say what he thought any place."[19]

Both Radwanski and the Nemnis credit Brébeuf as being decisive in acculturating Trudeau as "a French Canadian who speaks impeccable English, rather than a French-speaking Anglophone." [20] However, whereas Radwanski credits Brébeuf with keeping the adolescent Trudeau "at a skeptical distance from the Quebec nationalism of his classmates and thereby providing the first major channel for his urge to swim against the prevailing currents of thought,"[21] the Nemnis insist that whatever the merits of Brébeuf, such an education also included indoctrination into a nationalist worldview stereotypical of Quebec during the 1930s, one that was both anti-English and sympathetic, or at best neutral, about events in Europe at that time, in direct contradiction to the claims of Father Bernier.

The Nemnis reject "the fabrication that his father's death had a crippling effect" on Trudeau and support the portrait "of a youth who was well adjusted to his surroundings" at Brébeuf—an educational environment that was carefully constructed to "fulfill its divine mission" of preparing its students "to save the people" of Quebec from the oppressive practices of English Protestant liberalism, which were understood as threatening their culture and religion. They go on to say that "Pierre Trudeau accepted that he personally had such a mission. He believed that a good student who was a good Catholic had a duty also to be a nationalist." Indeed, according to the Nemnis, "Nationalism and religion together constituted the fundamental values that infused all the life of the college. Brébeuf even developed a reputation as a bastion of separatism." They point directly to what they regard as a core hypocrisy: "At Brébeuf, it seems, every effort was made in the 1930s to develop free spirits who, remarkably, would then agree to promote the two fundamental values of their Jesuit teachers: Catholicism and French-Canadian nationalism." "Almost all the students, including Trudeau, ended up with identical values ... and they were convinced that they reached these values of their own free will."[22]

As for Father Bernier's claim to have instilled in his students an appreciation for democracy, federalism, and pluralism and "an instinctive repulsion against Fascism and Nazism," the Nemnis are disparaging, attributing such a view to a "memory lapse."[23] They back their critique with a careful reading of Trudeau's student essays, notebooks, and editorials for the Brébeuf student newspaper. "In Trudeau's notes from the period, when he was the Jesuits' student, we found no trace of the promotion of federalism, democracy, or a pluralistic society." Instead, they found ample evidence, which included a 1998 interview with Trudeau, that the Brébeuf curriculum to which Trudeau was exposed marched in time to the common Québécois chorus of the day—i.e., "that Pétain was a hero and de Gaulle a traitor, [that] Mussolini, Salazar, and Franco were admirable corporatist leaders, [that] the democratic leaders were sell-outs."

Trudeau "adopted the notion that he must develop all his capacities to the fullest degree so as to join the ranks of the elite," thus supplementing his father's faith in the virtues of self-reliance and self-discipline, convictions to which Trudeau added what became a lifelong commitment to asceticism, especially as expressed in physical challenge and endurance. Throughout his life, Trudeau "would take pleasure in pushing his body and mind to their utmost limits."[24] In remembering an essay assigned by Father Bernier, requiring students to write about how they envisioned their future, Trudeau recalls that he "wanted to know everything and experience everything, in every realm. Maybe the essay even envisioned that some day, at the end of my life, I might want to become an important figure such as governor general or a prime minister. But first I would have explored the world."[25] "Trudeau wanted to succeed by himself, owing his success to no one but himself,"[26] not recognizing the extent to which he was being influenced by the fathers, both his own and the priests. For example, Trudeau thought nothing of requesting the permission of the Catholic Church to read books on the Church's Index of books judged to be morally dangerous, a practice he continued into his twenties.

By the time he left Brébeuf to study law at the University of Montreal, Trudeau was an exemplary Catholic Québécois who was purposefully preparing himself to pursue a political career through which he would ensure a place and role for a vibrant Québécois society. Questions concerning how such a Québécois society should be, or even if it should be, part of Canada were largely ignored by Trudeau while he was attending Brébeuf. This was to change rather dramatically during Trudeau's legal studies at the University of Montreal.

◆◆◆

Radwanski[27] describes Trudeau's decision about what to study at the University of Montreal in Pierre's own words: "One fork in the road was law, and another was all the area of the mind—I'm thinking of psychology, philosophy, and so on. What interested me was to know what makes a society tick, what it was that produced order or disorder … either in the mind through psychological derangement … or in society itself by legal or monetary troubles." Such a linking of the personal and the societal was typical of Trudeau's thought at the time and subsequently. In Trudeau's mind, his private, personal development was yoked closely, and strategically, to the development of his public, social persona. Unable to leave Canada because of the Second World War and unwilling to leave Montreal and Quebec, Trudeau's decision to study law was an easy one because UM then offered no programs in psychology. However, Pierre never was particularly interested in the study of legal practice. Instead, he "studied it [the law] as one would study economics or political science, to understand how a society works, how it governs itself, how it controls itself."[28] He detested his courses, although he did develop further his interest in law as an instrument of justice, especially against abuses of authority. It was the social process of how the law worked in relation to society and its governance that fascinated Trudeau and subsequently led him to continue his studies in economics and political science at Harvard and abroad.

Freed by his relative disinterest in his legal coursework, Trudeau used his years at UM to test his mettle through demanding and dangerous outdoor adventures by canoe, motorcycle, or on foot, during which he demonstrated stamina, courage, and careful calculation. Such adventures allowed him to "project the image of a breakneck type" when being "actually very careful," in the words of his good friend Gérard Pelletier.[29] Perhaps so, but, there is no doubt that 100 mile hikes and remote trips through churning, freezing waters, accompanied only by canoe and paddle, sleeping bag, fishing rod, rifle, knife and a few canned provisions, were arduous in the extreme. For Trudeau, such adventures combined his deep love of nature with ascetic, almost mystical self-discovery. "It is a condition of such a trip that you entrust yourself, stripped of your worldly goods, to nature."[30]

In a more frivolous but perhaps equally revealing way, Trudeau also spent substantial extracurricular time during the early 1940s honing a peculiar penchant for pranks and teasing. His sister Suzette told George Radwanski that Pierre liked "to tease" her and his younger brother Tip, to "see how far we could stand being teased before we broke out,"[31] something that later staffers in the PMO would describe as giving "you a good shot now and again, just to see how you'll react."[32] More elaborately and obnoxiously, while at UM, Trudeau, who also enjoyed a bit of acting (both on stage and off), impersonated a German soldier wandering about in the Quebec country side, apparently just to witness the reactions and possible upset of locals. Even more cruelly, after losing a public debate at the University, he pulled a pistol on a fellow debater, rigged to fire with smoke and a bang, saying "That will put some stuffing into your head."[33]

The German soldier stunt hints directly at how disconnected Trudeau was from the actual events that took place in Europe during the Second World War. He avoided conscription by being enrolled in his legal studies at UM and taking his unenthusiastic part in the Canadian Officers Training Corps. Like many French Canadians of his generation, he wanted nothing to do with what was widely regarded in Quebec as an imperialistic war of Britain and her allies, of which they were not part. According to John English, "The war made Trudeau into a Quebec nationalist ... He increasingly regarded his heritage as primarily French."[34] He saw the Canadian government's Defence of Canada Regulations as an imposition that not only invoked conscription, but that also limited the free speech and cultural expression of French Canadians. He became increasingly and "deeply concerned about the fate of his 'French self.'"[35]

The Nemnis provide comprehensive and compelling evidence that Trudeau in the early 1940s, while a law student at UM, devoted himself to the study of writings that espoused forms of corporatism entailing a rejection of capitalism and liberalism in favour of the Catholic authoritarianism and self-sufficiency espoused and practiced after 1940 by Pétain's Vichy government in France. Like historian Esther Delisle, they argue that Trudeau became a member of a secret revolutionary cell (Les Frères Chausseurs) and actively participated in enacting plans to overthrow the government of Quebec, and by implication that of Canada. Trudeau never, in his memoirs or elsewhere, responded to or refuted this charge. It is remarkable that no journalists of the day, either English or French, probed deeply into this matter, allowing Trudeau's later attempts to conceal his wartime activities to go mostly unchallenged. A typical later day concealment of his nationalist days in the early 1940s was to blithely dismiss them "as something of a lark, just another attack on authority,"[36] typical of anyone in their late teens and early adulthood. Nonetheless, given that his political stance at this time was in stark opposition to his strident and forceful denunciations of all forms of Quebec separatism after he entered federal politics, that he got away with it, and was allowed to get away with it, seems amazing.

To help explain Trudeau's behaviour in his last years at Brébeuf and during his law school days at UM, John English resorts in part to the developmental psychology of Jerome Kagan. Adolescents and very young adults, according to Kagan, "become focused on their personal identities. In doing so, they struggle to reconcile discontinuities, tensions, and oscillations that they perceive in their character and conduct, as well as tensions and disjunctions they perceive in their existing beliefs and understandings, when set against what their education and life experiences seem to indicate."[37] "Adolescents, who are beginning to synthesize the assumptions they will rely on for the rest of their lives, are unusually receptive to historical events that challenge existing beliefs."[38]

For Trudeau, who already was contemplating and planning a successful career in politics, a major personality and psychological hurdle was to reconcile his ambition with his timidity, his love and need for solitude and escape with his desire for celebrity. Such tensions, in part, reflected divergent perspectives to which he was exposed in his childhood and early adolescence, such as those between his Francophone and Anglophone cultures, as personified in his interactions with his father, mother, and on the streets and playgrounds of Outremont.

At Brébeuf, in a more consistently francophone and nationalistic environment, Pierre displayed his intellectual brilliance, athletic skill, and combativeness. At home, in his father's absence and after his death, young Trudeau embraced greater solitude and escape from the demands of the classroom, athletic fields, and peer interactions. When studying law at UM, Trudeau assuaged his boredom with more aggressive pursuits in which he could test his leadership mettle and hone his rhetorical abilities in ways that appealed to his ever-present penchant for drama and danger, but from which he always thought he could escape, given his familial and personal resources. In developing this ability to be different and act differently in different contexts, Trudeau could be mistaken for perhaps showing signs of a "double personality," but Kagan likely would see such shifts as ways of coping with and resolving the differing demands and expectations that others placed on the young Trudeau and that he placed upon himself—a kind of compartmentalization that allowed him to focus all his energies on the tasks at hand, without concern for any overall coherence, so long as his purposes of the moment and his image of himself were served.

As an aspiring politician, an ambition he most often concealed, he reveled in developing charismatic, adventurous, and semi-mysterious ways of presenting himself. By taking on the beliefs and sociopolitical views of many of his Jesuit teachers at Brébeuf, even to the point of involving himself in subversive political games, which he apparently took quite seriously, he was exploring possibilities for political action and allegiance. In short, he was getting to know different aspects and sides of his society and himself. Through all of this, the individualism he internalized from his father, suited his oscillating desires for solitude and celebrity, allowing him to reveal and conceal himself as he found it advantageous to do one or the other.

Knitting it all together, young Trudeau saw himself as a romantic spirit in the manner of Cyrano de Bergerac. In his late teens and early twenties, Pierre found in Cyrano "an expression of who I was and what I wanted to be: I don't care if I don't make it, providing I don't need anyone else's help, providing what I do make I make alone, you know, without begging for favours."[39] Even when the immaturities and excesses of this period of Trudeau's life began to fade, "the assertion of individuality" remained "a major priority in both his life-style and his philosophy. So long as what seemed to others like contradictory aspects of his character and undertakings fit his Cyrano-like persona of presentation and disguise, he was happy to ignore how these others regarded him. The important thing, he decided, was not to compete against others or to seek outside approval, but constantly to test himself and improve:

> I guess I was competing against myself all the time, which contains an element of immaturity. Just look at sports. When I was in college, there were no other sports but team sports. I played them, hockey and lacrosse, but as soon as I was out of college, I didn't stay in team sports. I went into solitary things like skiing or cycling or skindiving or canoeing or things that you do alone or with very few people. You're testing yourself."[40]

This was a sentiment Trudeau repeated in a letter of March 1941 to his first serious girlfriend, Camille Corriveau (described by John English as "a student at Smith College ... very pretty, with a full figure, in the manner of Vivien Leigh and Jean Harlow, actresses he admired"), in which he states he was "still aiming to be accomplished in every field" but that his first task was to "master Pierre Trudeau."[41]

Nonetheless and despite his dominating individualism, throughout his life Trudeau maintained a small circle of close and carefully chosen friends, whom he cultivated with purpose, yet with obvious enjoyment. Even Pierre, the rugged individualist, realized that you can't fight and succeed entirely on your own. One of these was Jean de Grandpré, a Brébeuf classmate and long-time friend, who subsequently became a major figure in legal and business circles in Quebec. De Grandpré, in an interview with Trudeau biographers Stephen Clarkson and Christina McCall, reminds us of the importance of Trudeau's independent wealth in his development as a would be politico. Given the heavily psychological leanings of some of his biographers, it is important to keep in mind that "In those days … three million dollars was a lot of money. … It set Pierre apart. It meant he had choices the rest of us didn't have. He could afford to search for his identity. … As a rich bachelor, Pierre was able to spend years 'finding himself'."[42] Indeed, Trudeau's life-long oscillation between periods of solitude and celebrity and his attendant strategies of being alternatively sociable and reclusive, revealing and concealing, would have been impossible without the ready financing that always was available to him. It was this important fiscal circumstance and reality that allowed him to play "the reluctant groom" and enter into games of "cat and mouse" with both his supporters and detractors, stratagems that served him and his interests extremely well in the years to come—entering the limelight when it served his purposes; withdrawing from it when he required solitude to collect himself and consider his circumstances, inner strengths, and ambitions.

By 1943, Trudeau had completed his law school requirements, graduating at the top of his class, and had become a lawyer with the firm of Hyde and Ahern on St. James Street in Montreal (at an apprentice wage of $2.50 a day). His days as a revolutionary had passed. He remained active in, and supported financially, the Bloc Populaire Canadien, which included Jean Drapeau and others who had opposed conscription, the Union Nationale, and Maurice Duplessis. As the war neared its end and travel once again was permitted for students pursuing their studies outside of Canada, Trudeau, having narrowly lost a bid to become a Rhodes scholar at Oxford, now planned the next stop in his program of self-development, this time at Harvard University. In his application to the graduate program in Political Economy and Government, Trudeau (who had so aggressively and passionately opposed Canada's involvement in the Second World War) wrote about "men of sciences and of letters who will honour Canada in peace, even as her soldiers will have honoured her in war," before concluding that "I shall make Statesmanship my profession and, if God permit, I shall know my profession well."[43]

Upon his arrival at Harvard in the Fall of 1944, Trudeau hung a sign on his Harvard door that read "Pierre Trudeau, citizen of the world." But it did not take long for him to realize that his Jesuit education, though commendably concentrated and deep in certain areas, was much too narrow, parochial, and provincial to support such a claim. Realizing he needed to "up his game," Trudeau devoted the intensive and sustained concentration of which he was so capable to mastering those aspects of the social sciences that had escaped Brébeuf speculation and debate concerning the nature of truth, beauty, and the existence of God. He was soon pulling top marks in many of his courses. Pierre was now exposed to new arguments and positions that challenged his previous understandings and perspectives. Economics as taught and practiced in his legal studies in Montreal was completely inadequate. His law degree from UM included almost nothing relevant to the disciplinary studies of law, economics, and political science as he experienced them at Harvard.

Of course, Harvard itself had been reconstituted during and after the war. It transformed from a Protestant American preparatory school for the political and economic elite to a major site of active debate surrounding the latest currents in twentieth-century thought. Displaced and progressive Jewish, Russian, and German-Austrian professors joined their American and British counterparts, part of the great academic migration of the 1930s and 1940s, and represented a wide array of doctrines and opinions. Future Nobel laureate Wassily Leontief had just developed input-output tables for the US economy, using computerized techniques, even as John Kenneth Galbraith, who described Trudeau as a "first rate economics mind of postwar vintage,"[44] advocated his post-Keynesian pragmatic and liberal approach to state spending.

Trudeau's study of the economic positions available to him at Harvard made him skeptical of economics as a science, perhaps explaining, in part, why in his subsequent political career he never paraded his knowledge of academic economics, even when pillared by Canadian university economists for his inattention to economic matters. Trudeau came to regard both economics and political science as highly questionable: "The more you read ... the more you realize that respectable political scientists can also indulge in pseudo-science."[45] In consequence, both disciplines were prone to special interests related to political positions, economic circumstances, and individual and collective psychologies.

At Harvard, Trudeau also was brought face to face with his own ignorance (shared by his Brébeuf and UM teachers) about the Second World War. Works like Franz Neumann's *Behemoth* gave Trudeau a full portrait of Nazi atrocities, militarism, and exploitive capitalism. From such readings and related discussions, together with his formal courses, he was forced to re-examine what he previously had learned and done. In a letter to his new girlfriend Thérèse Gouin, Pierre expressed regret about the dismissive attitude he had held towards the Second World War: "Will this be my great regret? Never to have raised my eyes ... when the greatest cataclysm of all time was occurring ten hours away from my desk."[46]

Thérèse was the daughter of a powerful political family in Quebec, and at the time a student of psychology, who later became a professor of psychology at UM. She was an important source of support for Trudeau, who although immersed in his studies at Harvard, never developed any real affection for the place itself, did not involve himself in its extracurricular activities, and frequently suffered from bouts of loneliness during his time there. They exchanged many intensely intimate letters and became life-long friends. In describing their relationship, English opines "Their caution and Catholicism mixed oddly with the Freudian psychology that Thérèse studied and Pierre found intriguing."[47] Nonetheless and despite his attachment to Thérèse, by the time Pierre received his MA from Harvard in 1946, and passed his "General Examination for entry to the PhD in Political Economy and Government" on May 16th of that year, he was ready to move further afield. He began to apply to European universities for entry that Fall, and never returned to Harvard to complete his doctoral thesis. Yet, given his stated objective of attending Harvard to become a statesman, "he had undoubtedly received a thorough intellectual grounding" in "the restructuring of the post-war world. ... He became familiar with many schools of thought, both in economics and politics" and "awoke to the dangers of political and philosophical principles he [once had] held dear." "Trudeau definitely emerged from his cave. A new man was gradually coming into being."[48]

After leaving Harvard, Pierre Trudeau took a summer job in hard, underground labour at the Sullivan gold mines in Quebec, alongside workers who likely didn't know and certainly didn't care that he and his family owned a significant number of shares in the operation. John English surmises that Trudeau's motivation in taking the remote and very physical job "was similar to the journeys to the wilds of earlier summers," that is, to test himself in a concretely physical way and escape the abstractions of his studies. However, English speculates further that such an undertaking was also fueled by Trudeau's "profound desire to know 'the other,' and in the postwar world where labour and socialist parties thrived, the 'worker' was an 'other' that Trudeau believed he must know." Despite his desire and best efforts, Pierre was keenly disappointed "when he discovered that he stood apart." "I am not assimilable. I don't speak like them. I don't think like them." English elaborates further: "their drinking habits bothered the young ascetic, but he was more troubled ... by the emotional distance between him and the other men."[49]

In the meantime, Trudeau's relationship with Thérèse had stalled. The young couple had talked about traveling to Paris together, even about marriage. However, there also had been periods during which Pierre was jealous of her associates in psychology and tried, without great success, to increase her interest in politics. Moreover, despite adoring "her daughter's brilliant and rich beau, Thérèse's mother found him "a strange young man,"[50] and did not encourage the relationship.

Trudeau left for France on his own, where he enrolled for the European fall term in the prestigious École Libre des Sciences Politques (Sciences Po), harbouring the intention of "having what he called a bloody good time."[51] Paris had returned to life and with public intellectuals like Sartre, Camus, Beauvoir, and Merleau-Ponty, was in the midst of reviving its unique blend of literary and philosophical discussion and debate. The presence of a few other Canadians, including his friends Roger Rolland and François Hertel, as well as several other former Brébeuf students, afforded Trudeau the kind of emotional support and camaraderie in adventure he sometimes craved. He was a loner in the sense of plotting his own course, but if his interests and inclinations received the support and enthusiasm of a few others whom he judged worthy, so much the better. Since Trudeau had given himself a relatively light course-load, designed to broaden his intellectual reach and perhaps prepare him for further studies, he was free to indulge his love of art, philosophical and political debate, and pranks (such as "dropping dead," one by one, with his friends in Parisian salons and cafés).

Nonetheless, Trudeau's stint in postwar Paris during the 1947-48 university year did provide what Clarkson and McCall describe as perhaps "the most exhilarating and important thing that ever happened to him ... In short, he ... embraced the precepts of personalism, a radical Catholic doctrine that had become a formidable post-war ideological rival to existentialism in France."[52] In his late twenties, Trudeau found himself stretched intellectually and personally between the demands of his strong Catholicism and his obsession with his own personal freedom and desire to explore and extend himself at every opportunity. Personalism suggested a way to reconcile his conflicting needs and resolve tensions between not only his faith and personal freedom and exploration, but also between the different political theories and perspectives he had studied.

According to Clarkson and McCall, it was through his immersion in personalism that:

> Trudeau found the rationale for a way of being that released him from many of the problems that had plagued him for years. By embracing the almost Protestant belief that he could incarnate the Divinity in his own person, he could channel his conflicting feelings—his difficulties with intimacy, his guilt about his wealth, his scorn for capitalists,

his hostility toward authority, his ambivalence about his French-Canadian identity—into practical action.[53]

In his memoirs, Trudeau describes the pivotal role that personalism played in his personal and political thought. In Paris and later at the London School of Economics:

> I completed a search that I had begun at Brébeuf in my adolescent years. On what values would I base my life? ... The issue of freedom had obsessed me since high school. ... Reconciling predestination, the infinite power of God, with human freedom intrigued me ... It was my consciousness I wanted to obey, taking precedence over even the commandments of the Church or the rules of the college.
>
> [In Paris] I deepened my knowledge ... of personalism, a philosophy that reconciles the individual and society. The person ... is the individual enriched with a social conscience, integrated into the life of the communities around him and the economic context of his time, both of which must in turn give persons the means to exercise their freedom of choice. It was thus that the fundamental notion of justice came to stand alongside that of freedom in my political thought.[54]

The centrality of Trudeau's interpretation of personalism to his future politics is elaborated further in an essay that appears in a volume edited by him and Thomas Axworthy.

> I have long believed that freedom is the most important value of a just society and the exercise of freedom its principal characteristic, [but] the value with the highest

priority in the pursuit of a Just Society had become equality. Not the procrustean kind of equality where everyone is raised or lowered to a kind of middle ground.

I mean equality of opportunity.[55]

The combination of intellectual enlightenment and mischievous frivolity in which Trudeau engulfed himself in Paris during the academic year of 1947-48 further eroded his romantic relationship with Thérèse Gouin, who began to notice that the emotional outpourings that characterized his Harvard letters were much less pronounced in his missives from Paris. Pierre's letters now contained more elements of disagreement, jealousy, and possessiveness, sometimes upbraiding her for her coolness and defiance, much of which focused on her independence as related to her passion for psychology and psychoanalysis, which Pierre seemed to assume also might extend to her male colleagues. Troubled by his own reactions, and acceding to Thérèse's wishes, Trudeau began a course of psychoanalysis with Georges Parcheminey, a Parisian analyst, with the expressed aim of seeing if he could understand better his role in their troubles and in his life more generally.

Parcheminey had a reputation as a "common sense" Freudian psychoanalyst who soft-pedaled psychoanalysis as a science and urged Trudeau not to take himself and his problems too seriously. In response, Trudeau gradually came to believe, despite the hesitations and occasional dismissiveness about psychoanalysis he expressed in his letters to Thérèse, that the process was helping him understand himself. In his therapy sessions, he recounted his past and explored his present by discussing his dreams and life experiences. Trudeau's father featured in many dreams, mostly with the affection of the dreamer. Occasional impatience with his mother and envy of his sister and brother, particularly with respect to their more settled, married lives, also were evident. Other themes included his strong sense of duty to his family, his possessiveness (financial and otherwise), and his sense of inferiority. In notes he recorded at the time, Trudeau discussed conflicts between his desire for independence, which often contained elements of aggression, mixed with caring about what others thought of him. At one point his notes read, "It is the combination of timidity and aggressiveness. I was not able to reveal myself openly in the genital phase because of restrictions."[56]

In response to these self-interpretations, Parcheminey advised Trudeau "not to make too much of his own analysis and to avoid so much self-criticism." Parcheminey did allow that the restrictiveness imposed by Trudeau's religious convictions was strengthened by the sense of duty instilled through his upbringing and that he "sublimated his strong sexual desires through his religious and intellectual activities as well as through sports and adventures, and reassured him that "his absence of sexual intercourse did not mean that he had homosexual tendencies" and that his sexuality "was normal." Parcheminey added that "one or two years after marriage, all should go well,"[57] apparently disregarding his own strictures against taking psychoanalysis too seriously as a predictive science. For his part, Trudeau noted that abstinence was much less evident in French than in Quebec Catholics.

Despite the psychoanalysis, in the early summer of 1947, Thérèse broke off her intensely emotional relationship with Pierre, leaving him apparently shattered. In a letter to her brother Lomer, dated July 10, 1947, Trudeau wrote, "It is exactly 24 hours ago that your sister removed all reason for me to live."[58] However, despite his apparently sincere mourning of the end of his romance with Thérèse, the end of their intimate relationship did not produce a prolonged sulk. Finished with his coursework at Sciences Po and back in Canada during the summer of 1947, his schedule was filled with meetings and social engagements with current and future friends and politicos, including Gérard Pelletier, Claude Ryan, and others, and included a motorbike trip in the Canadian north. Having secured his political connections in Quebec and enjoyed his northern excursion, Trudeau secured a first-class berth on the *Empress of Canada*, enroute to a doctoral program in political science at the London School of Economics, leaving his Harvard PhD dissertation unfinished.

In London, Trudeau was without the Montreal and Brébeuf friends he had in Paris, and he stayed alone and aloof—like "a young nobleman on a Grand Tour, very intelligent but quite disengaged."[59] In Paris, Trudeau had mostly ignored the atheist existentialism of Sartre and others, but under the sway of French personalism and French culture more generally, and aided by his foray into psychoanalysis, he became less constrained by the ecclesiastical authority of the Catholic Church. He also had been intrigued by how Emmanuel Mounier and other left-wing French personalists had turned to socialism and communism in their attempts to fashion a more relevant Christianity. In the autumn of 1947, the London School of Economics was considered by many to be a socialist institution—a very distinguished one with considerable academic prestige.

Harold Laski, whose writings Trudeau had studied at Harvard, was perhaps LSE's most renowned political scientist. As the Cold War began, Laski (who also was chairman of the British Labour Party) was highly controversial in his socialist beliefs and his encouragement of open debate at LSE and beyond. Under Laski's tutelage, Pierre Trudeau was able to integrate his political views: "everything I had learned until then of law, economics, political science, and political philosophy came together for me. ... I was to acquire more knowledge and to encounter countless options throughout my life. But my basic philosophy was established from that time on, and it was on those premises that I based all my future political decisions."[60]

Trudeau enjoyed many one-on-one and small group discussions in several courses he took with Laski. He recorded his reactions in notebooks he kept of his readings and educational experiences, reactions that display a sophisticated and ongoing understanding and exchange of different views and arguments. Laski was not a proselytizer, but a warm and humorous man who, despite considerable powers of persuasion, insisted on rigorous analysis, active debating, and intellectual autonomy. Although the Jesuits of Brébeuf also had appeared to applaud the autonomy and independence of their pupils, Laski actually practiced doing so. He even went so far as to invite well-known speakers to express and defend positions and perspectives antithetical to his own. He also encouraged students to follow and get involved in actual politics, believing that no one can truly understand or teach politics who does not know politics at first hand.

With Laski, Trudeau learned to focus on ideas and their possible coherence and utility, irrespective of their labels. Given Laski's encouragement and openness to a wide range of views, Trudeau was able to step outside of his previously held positions and experience directly, through debate and animated discussion, a much broader portfolio of political perspectives and possibilities. "Pluralism had become part and parcel of Trudeau's thinking."[61]

After Brébeuf, Trudeau gradually became much more suspicious of the invisible power wielded by authorities who never seemed to stray far from their self-interest. Under the influence of Parisian personalists like Mounier and Jacques Maritain, and through interactive exchanges of political and economic positions and ideas with the social democrat Laski, Trudeau began to formulate what would become his uniquely pragmatic, functionalist, and pluralist agenda for the Canadian federation. He was ready to enact Laski's dictum of practicing what he now preached, ready to test himself and his leadership potential in the cauldron of real political involvement. He abandoned his doctoral studies once and for all, and began to make plans to insert himself in the life-world of Canadian politics. However before doing so, he felt the need for one final, educational undertaking, this time a completely out-of-classroom and self-directed experience of world travel.

Recovered from a succession of colds and flu in the Spring of 1948, one of which put him in Charing Cross Hospital for a brief stint, Trudeau, now 28, embarked from London on yet another of the many physical and intellectual challenges he set for himself, with the purpose of acquiring the personal strengths and experiences to achieve his destiny as an influential political leader. What was to be a year long adventure began in Europe and included a "harsh initiation into the globetrotter's craft"[62] behind the Iron Curtain, which after World War II, separated Europe's western and eastern parts. During his travels, Trudeau was jailed, deported from some of the countries he visited, and at least once resorted to using false documents to cross from one country to another. Having arrived in Turkey from Communist Europe and without the security of a Canadian embassy, he obtained a British passport from the embassy of the United Kingdom that allowed him to continue his adventures throughout eastern Asia, where he traveled and lived among some of the most poverty stricken and downtrodden of the world's people.

Reflecting on his journey, Trudeau attributed the subjugation and degradation of the world's lower classes, and the contempt in which they were held by others (including some of the priests and professors with whom he found shelter during his travels), to their lack of "material well-being and education."[63] He began to see how his strong commitment to personalism, with its emphasis on the rights, freedoms, and dignity of each individual human being, could be combined with a kind of left-leaning liberalism that championed education and socio-political participation. In his mind, the ideal of such a liberal polity was to give all citizens, through education (and the capability it conferred), an equal opportunity to participate in all levels of social and political life.

Applying these ideas to Canada, he began to understand how "a party like the Liberals, slowly moving leftwards, could in theory be the best party to lead the nation as a whole towards the people's society of the future," despite the likelihood that "The Liberals' commendable desire to borrow the best aspects of socialism ... will inevitably clash, with the [Party's] financial interests." Equally important, "One should not associate one's destiny with a single social group, such as labour unions and agricultural cooperatives, one should instead develop a policy for the entire nation, not for this or that part of it."[64]

During his year of dangerous and instructive travel in 1948-49, Trudeau indulged both his curiosity about other ways of life and his love of adventure, with the aim of learning as much as he could about the world, its people, and himself. With his travels concluded, as he approached the age of 30 he had no detailed plan for how his destiny might unfold. Nonetheless, he felt he had every reason to believe that his carefully cultivated intellectual capability, now mixed with an understanding and appreciation of a diversity of cultures and ways of life, would serve him well as he anticipated a future as a political leader in his home province and nation. But first, he had to await, and help to create, the right opportunity for leaping into the fray of Canadian politics as an active and influential participant. This proved to be a process that was much more prolonged and tricky than he might have anticipated. In fact, he was about to enter into an unexpectedly protracted and frustrating period of political apprenticeship, which lasted for almost two decades following his return to Canada from his world travels.

Peter Lougheed's parents did not display the widely divergent characters of those of Pierre Trudeau, but they did represent both Western and Eastern Canada. Edgar, Peter's father, might best be described as lively, fun-loving, cheerful, and sociable, with a penchant for the good life. Educated at Western Canada College (a high school for boys, now renamed Western Canada High School) in Calgary, he later studied at McGill University in Montreal before enrolling in the Canadian army during World War I. Most of Edgar's wartime was spent in Britain organizing supplies for the allied troops and spending lavishly on the entertainment of friends and acquaintances. Nonetheless, Edgar did see action in France in 1916, and returned to Canada at war's end with the rank of Captain. Back home, he enrolled in the Faculty of Arts at the University of Alberta, before completing a degree in law at Nova Scotia's Dalhousie University. The University of Alberta's student newspaper, *The Gateway*, noted Edgar's decision to head east to continue his studies: "In order that the U of A may recuperate, Edgar Lougheed has decided not to take his master's degree, but to go on in the profession of law."[65]

At Dalhousie, Edgar met the attractive and popular Edna Alexandria Bauld, Their wedding in 1924 was reported as "one of the smartest social events of the season," with the bride described as "a petite, determined and vivacious woman with large eyes and an engaging smile."[66] Once married, Edgar and his new bride settled back in Calgary in a small, modest bungalow close to Sir James' and Belle's Beaulieu mansion, a testament to Victorian opulence. With the birth of their first son Donald in 1925, Edgar and Edna moved to a larger home at 1731-9A Street, where Edgar Peter Lougheed was born on July 26, 1928.

With the market crash of 1929, things started to go downhill for Edgar senior. Much of the extended family income was realized through rental revenues, which began to dry up as companies and offices closed their doors. The brokerage firm of Lougheed and Taylor also was losing money, and when Taylor died in 1930, followed by the deaths of two of Edgar's brothers (one by suicide), Edgar was left alone to handle the family's various enterprises. Unfortunately, his talent for organization did not extend to matters of commerce, and when he insisted on paying shareholders the full value of their investments to secure the family's good name, a number of relatives who depended on his success as an economic manager were not happy. Scapegoated for the sudden downturn in the family's fortunes, Edgar began to drink heavily. After his mother's death in 1936, Beaulieu was seized to pay back taxes on the mansion and property. Soon thereafter, Edgar and his family downsized from their 9A Street home into Calgary's Moxam Apartments. To add to his humiliation, Edgar was forced by the Metropolitan Life Insurance Company, which held most of the mortgages on the Lougheed family holdings, to allow the Royal Trust Company to take over management of the family's remaining properties. Edgar himself was reduced to the role of Estate Manager, at a salary far below the annual income he previously had been receiving. Poor Edgar never seemed able to outgrow the long shadow cast by his father, Sir James.

Despite his losses, his drinking, and his growing resentment about "being brought to heel by the callous money lenders from the east,"[67] Edgar retained his easy social persona and developed a sense of humility that allowed him to cope with his reduced circumstances.

After Edna, whose Nova Scotia family also had been hit hard by the Depression, suffered a nervous breakdown that saw her hospitalized briefly at the Provincial Mental Hospital in Ponoka, Alberta, Edgar moved the family to 121B Sifton Boulevard, on the outskirts of Calgary. That move, in 1939, had a salubrious effect on all the Lougheeds. In this, at the time, more rural setting with its large garden, Edgar and the boys grew their own vegetables, which Edna canned. The boys enjoyed their bedroom views of the Elbow River and spent much of their non-school time outdoors, even in the winter months, especially when the Chinook winds raised temperatures and spirits. Edna bought a bike and took up bridge, becoming a master player. When, in February 1940, Edna's third child died at birth, she and Edgar immediately adopted a baby girl, named Barbara.

With the new baby and home, the Lougheeds began to dig themselves out of their decade of distress. Peter later recalled this period of his life, despite his father's scattered bouts of drinking, with genuine fondness: "We were in the depression when everyone else was in it. … In spite of the crisis time they were to me days that I remember as happy, easy going and fun."[68] Eventually, after the Second World War, when rent controls were lifted, Edgar was able to regain clear title to most of the remaining Lougheed properties, allowing the family to move to a large and more centrally located home at the aptly titled address of 2215 Hope Street. Five years later, after a business trip to Victoria where he met with his brother Norman, Edgar stopped in Seattle to visit friends. On the evening of March 30, 1951 he passed away from a coronary occlusion at the age of 57, in the dining room of Seattle's Olympic Hotel.

Although Peter and his older brother had been born into the closest Alberta had to provincial royalty, their experiences during the 1930s had shown them other sides of life that undoubtedly helped to bolster their resilience. In the words of biographer Allan Hustak, "The proverbial silver spoon in [Peter's] mouth may have been a little tarnished by the depression but he … would learn to apply his own polish quickly."[69] Daughter of a prominent Nova Scotia family, Edna was the primary force behind her sons' desire and drive to excel. Her grace and polish hid an iron will. Refusing to accept what, for the Lougheeds, were reduced circumstances, she, with the help of a hired maid, kept an immaculate and comfortable home, replete with fine furniture, china, and silver ware. Her competitiveness was tied to a strong sense of correct behaviour. Winning was important, but to count as winning, it had to be dignified and without conceit. Her sons knew what was expected of them—a combination of achievement and decency.

Peter took full advantage of his position as second son. By carefully observing the reactions of his parents to his older brother Don's attempts to get what he wanted, Peter learned more subtle and diplomatic ways of advancing his own agenda, interactions that recognized others' needs and desires. According to Don, "If mother wanted the facts, she'd come to me. If she wanted tact, she'd ask Peter." "If she'd bought a new hat, for instance, it was always Peter she'd turn to for comment."[70]

Those who knew Peter well as a child and adolescent were convinced that he would do great things. As a boy, he had a loyal group of friends who regarded him as their social and athletic convener.

Given his mother's insistence on success with style and his own penchants for organization and leadership, he was well equipped for a future career in politics. Although it often has been said, it apparently is not true that Peter declared in high school that he someday would be Prime Minister of Canada. Nonetheless, to his friends at that time, like Bruce Redmond, "Peter was naturally a leader; he was president of the students' council. ... [He] was known as 'The Demander.' He had the ability to make people do things; it must have been born in him. He wanted to excel in whatever he did."[71]

One story from his youth that has been repeated many times attempts to explain his motivation for and interest in a political future that would see him championing causes that combined his own interests with those of Alberta. It concerns Peter's observation of his family's humiliation at the time they lost the family estate. As told by Allan Hustak, a 10-year-old Peter broke into the deteriorating Beaulieu on the afternoon of August 23, 1938, several years after it had been seized for tax arrears and his family evicted. As described by Hustak, Peter wandered the halls and rooms of the mansion that once had been visited by British royalty, which included Kings Edward VII and George VI as boys, before hiding to observe with indignation the auctioning of his family's possessions. These included an entire library of several hundred leather-bound volumes that went for a mere twenty-two dollars, hardly a princely sum even in those days.

According to a family acquaintance, "Peter Lougheed never forgot that auction."[72] Taking confidence from his distinguished background, he vowed to stand against economic insult and what he considered to be wrongful profiteering of the kind he had witnessed as a young boy on that mid-summer day at his once family home in Calgary. True to his mother's teachings, his sense of insult was not only deeply personal but made him want to assist and rescue others who might be devastated by similar experience and circumstances. Years later, many would refer to Lougheed as a Red Tory, in the manner of John A. Macdonald, R. B. Bennett, and John Diefenbaker. As Premier he kept a steady eye fixed on the prosperity of all Albertans, going so far as to enshrine the promise of such a future in his Alberta Bill of Rights of 1972, which acknowledged the right of every Albertan to liberty, security of the person, and enjoyment of property, including the right not to be deprived thereof except by due process of law. The auction at Beaulieu left its mark. Where Trudeau's commitments to human dignity and freedom were rooted in his philosophical inclinations and academic studies, Lougheed's similar inclinations derived mostly from his direct personal experiences, aided by his parents' concerns that their children be considerate of others, whatever their circumstances.

Peter began grade school at the prestigious private institution, the Strathcona School for Boys. However, soon thereafter, his family's fiscal misfortune necessitated a move to Earl Grey Public School, where he was a good, but not outstanding student, who excelled at athletics. At Earl Grey and subsequently at Rideau Park Public School, Peter became friends with several of those who were to maintain lifetime ties to him, loyally sticking with him through the ups and downs of later business and political pursuits. His athleticism, self-confidence, and good looks made him popular with classmates and teachers. When Peter moved on to Calgary's Central

High, which allowed high school fraternities, many of his closest friends moved with him. As the acknowledged leader of this group of friends, Peter excelled at recognizing and organizing opportunities for athletic and social gatherings and adventures. Another Calgary Central student, Ivan Head, who went on to become a foreign policy advisor to Pierre Trudeau, recalls that with his Kappa Kappa Tau pals, Peter was "like a king with his courtiers."[73]

Of course, being the centre of his social and athletic group brought with it both accolade and criticism. Although celebrated by insiders, more than a few outsiders responded to Peter less positively, some sensing an underlying insecurity, bordering on shyness, which required the constant boosting of his sense of worth and wellbeing. However, even those who expressed such reservations seemed to have nothing malicious to say about Peter's character or conduct. True to his parents' teachings, Peter carried himself with a style and manner that was respectful of those around him, both within and outside his close circle. In the classroom, he was not an intellectual but he managed to achieve good grades in most of his subjects, with more mediocre success in math and science. French was the one subject with which he struggled most, a struggle that continued when, in his later life, his occasional attempts to learn the language met with a similar fate. Indeed, Peter's apparent infelicity with languages effectively focused his political ambitions at the provincial rather than the federal stage on which his grandfather Sir James and his grandmother Belle's uncles had performed.

It was on the playing fields that Peter shone and solidified his growing band of admirers. In his own words: In high school, "I was an extrovert, always doing things, just so busy in sports that any serious reading was limited."[74] In addition to playing most school sports, Peter was offensive halfback for the West End Tornados football club, which defeated the Winnipeg Fort Rouge Rods 18-6 to win the 1945 Canadian Junior Football Championship. In the championship game, Peter was the hero, leading a Tornados' comeback with a 57-yard touchdown run and more than doubling the total number of rushing yards gained by the entire Winnipeg team. Peter's better than average but not stellar, academic standing probably also was not helped by the fact that he worked a variety of occasional jobs throughout his high school years. These included part-time work at the Hudson Bay Store, Purity Flour Mills, and caddying at golf courses in Calgary and nearby Banff.

Although sport, especially football, was central to his life throughout high school, Peter's reputation as a team player went beyond the playing field. In his final year of high school (1946-1947), he relied on his popularity as an athlete to be elected President of Central High's first Student Union, the establishment of which he had proposed. Combining his mother's drive and ambition with his father's easy-going sociability, he used sport as a vehicle to develop and hone his abilities and enthusiasm for leadership and organization. He delighted in motivating teammates and strategizing for games as much as in his on-field performances. At a time when school guidance workers used vocational interest inventories to assist students to make decisions about possible careers to pursue after high school graduation, Peter's scores were exceptionally high in "persuasiveness." It is easy to imagine him thinking about putting this supposedly natural talent, together with his organizational and leadership abilities, to good use in future careers in law and politics.

After high school, Peter and several of his Central High gang decided to leave Calgary and head north to study at the University of Alberta in Edmonton. Delighted, recreation director Maury Van Vliet welcomed them with open arms. A smaller athlete himself, Van Vliet appreciated Peter's feisty aggressiveness, tempered with his extreme coachability and strong commitment to cooperative team play. When the university football program folded after Peter's second year, due to a lack of competition from other schools and a significant operating deficit, Peter and a couple of his U of A teammates were picked up by the fledgling Edmonton Eskimos professional football club, coached by Annis Stukus. Like Van Vliet, Coach Stukus and his Eskimo teammates found the undersized Lougheed (at 160 pounds) to be something of a marvel. According to Stukus, Peter "had the guts of a burglar, he was no bigger than a minute, no one could stop him, he never seemed to get hurt" and "He was one hell of a team man."[75] Nonetheless, his size alone prevented much playing time and Peter was used mostly to run back kicks, where his grit, speed, and seeming indestructability served him well. All-star and hall of fame running back, Normie Kwong, who later served as Alberta's Lieutenant Governor, described Lougheed as "a trier, maybe a little small, but he took his punishment and never whimpered."[76]

In the university classroom, Peter was a good, but not exceptional, student in his law classes. Then Dean of the Law Faculty

Wilbur Bowker commented about Peter that "If he wasn't all that imaginative, he had a solid grasp of the essentials. In spite of his many extracurricular activities, he was responsive in class."[77] And, of course, Peter was well liked and established many bonds with his fellow students that were to prove useful in the future. The "extracurriculars" that Bowker referred to included Peter's stints as President of the U of A's Student Council, Sports Editor for *The Gateway*, and assistant coach of the junior varsity football team.

The story of Peter's ascendency to President of the U of A Student Council was in many ways a trial run in developing the strategies and practices that marked his subsequent political career. In his third year at the university, Peter stood for election as Chairman of the University Athletic Board, figuring that his reputation as an athlete would ensure an easy victory. When he lost, Ken Moore, his roommate at the time, claimed that "it taught him never to take anything for granted—and after that he didn't."[78] Later, with the Presidency of the Student Council in his sights, Peter adopted a carefully planned campaign by first using his athletic success as a basis for editing the sports section of *The Gateway*, the experience and notoriety from which propelled him into the position of Student Council Secretary. Thus positioned, Peter waged a hard fought campaign with three other candidates for the Council Presidency. One of the losing candidates, Peter's high school classmate Ivan Head, a fellow law student at the U of A, remarked that Peter "ran rings around us. It was another example of his first-rate organizing talents and an early demonstration of his ability to get votes."[79] Head added that Peter's victorious campaign for Council President, "pretty well decided that he wanted to devote part, if not all of his adult life, to the public sector. It was obvious that he had the ability to gather the confidence of an electorate."[80]

Violet Henry, who later would work for the United Nations in New York, was Council Vice-President during Lougheed's term as President of the U of A's Student Council. Violet would have preferred Ivan Head to be elected instead of Peter. She had the same concerns harboured by some of Peter's former high school peers about his reliance on the support of his jock friends to bolster his self-esteem. What might this bode for his willingness to represent the majority of students with other interests and backgrounds? Violet also suspected that Peter might resent the fact that she, unlike him, had been elected by acclamation. In time, however, she was pleased to discover that Peter did not treat her like "a token female" and she came to feel "very much a part of the student administration," although she also believed that "we certainly didn't accomplish anything memorable."[81]

Another extracurricular activity, one that came to preoccupy Peter during most of his days at the University of Alberta, was his courting of Jeanne Estelle Rogers, the vivacious and gregarious daughter of a Camrose physician. Once again, Peter launched a carefully planned campaign in which he arranged an introduction through a mutual friend. When that didn't work, he persisted until Jeanne eventually accepted an invitation to a football game. After that, Peter made sure to ward off other suitors by keeping her "booked up" well in advance for parties and other university events. A music student who was studying piano and voice, as well as German and Latin, Jeanne brought a style and polish to Peter's socializing, a finesse he previously had lacked, despite his many achievements and popularity. According to a sorority sister, "Peter could be as pugnacious as a bantam rooster, but I think because of Jeanne he became more studious. She was a moderating influence on his behaviour and you could detect him becoming more mature in his dealings with others around him."[82] Jeanne was quick to recognize Peter's political ambitions when he often left her feeling somewhat deserted as he worked the crowd at parties and gatherings, practicing what would become his "glad-handing style."

Peter's close friends also remarked a gradual quickening of his political interests, noting that it was not unusual for their after class discussions to stray from the playing field into matters relating to how things were being run on campus and beyond. To them and many others, it seemed obvious that Peter's future was in politics of some kind. He had developed a calm, polite, and decent style as President of the Student Council, one that did not try to conceal his views or intentions, but that built on his strengths of personality and temperament. Nonetheless, some who worked closely with him, remarked inklings of oversensitivity to personal criticism or criticism directed at his friends. But as to his political leanings, Peter gave little indication—focusing on particular issues and problems as they arose, without betraying any definite political affiliation or ideology. Such pragmatism suited his personal leadership style, one in which he excelled at considering and drawing together multiple and differing perspectives to fashion a consensus that could be linked to a feasible course of action. Where Trudeau's life and politics would be guided by his strong commitment to ideas, Peter Lougheed was a master of practical know-how.

When he graduated with his LLB in the spring of 1952, Lougheed received one of 12 gold rings known as "Executive A Awards" for outstanding service to the university community and life on campus, a ring that he often wore subsequently with great pride. However, on that same evening, Peter failed to receive the 'Block A' award for excellence in athletics, one which he had been counting on and was disappointed to forego—another reminder that he never should take anything for granted, a slogan that he adopted through his subsequent life and career.

During his time at the University of Alberta, Peter Lougheed had matured into a mostly decent man, somewhat humourless, but constant and sincere in his purposes and pursuits. He could be depended upon to take on difficult tasks and roles, not only for the prestige of doing so, but with a dedication and resolve to get things done. He had learned mostly to control his occasional outbursts of fierce temper and usually gave careful consideration to both those who shared his beliefs and those who did not. He was a tough competitor, but one who also knew how to negotiate and compromise. With Peter, you typically knew where you stood. There were few aspects of his character that left others scratching their heads and wondering what to make of him. He had the gift of persuasion and he backed it up with his best efforts to achieve what had been agreed upon.

Jeanne and Peter had put off marriage until Peter had completed law school. After a candlelight ceremony on June 21, 1952, followed by a honeymoon at Harrison Hot Springs in BC's lower

Fraser Valley, Peter began an articling internship at the Calgary legal firm of Fenerty, Fenerty, McGillivray, and Robertson. Then, toward the end of August, he interrupted his articling, so that the newlyweds could drive to Cambridge Massachusetts in time for the start of Harvard University's fall term. Peter had been accepted into the Harvard Business School's Master of Business Administration Program. As Jeanne explained, "Peter always had things pretty well mapped out, even before he met me. Harvard was always part of his planning."[83] The long drive to Cambridge in their blue Ford, a wedding gift from Peter's mother, took longer than expected, and they arrived just in time for the commencement of Peter's classes.

The Harvard Business School had been established in 1908, and modeled after the *École de Sciences Politiques* in Paris, with the express purpose of educating highly qualified public administrators for diplomacy and government service. Consistently ranked among the top business schools in the world, the School has produced many famous graduates (from Robert McNamara to George W. Bush), and become famous for its *case method* of teaching. At the time of Peter's studies at Harvard, the Business School was not only continuing to experiment with its case approach to instruction, but also was changing the mix of students enrolled through its highly competitive admissions system. The aim was to ensure, as Nelson Aldrich put it, that "sons of the lower middle class were admitted to mix with the careless sons of obnoxious wealth, the ambition of the one bound with the style of the other, creating a new Republican class of leader."[84] Although certainly not "careless" or "obnoxious" nor "lower middle class," Peter probably appealed to an Admissions Committee that always was on the lookout for interesting and talented international students to add to the student body of an institution considered one of the very best of its kind in the world.

Knowing that no matter how well he did, only 50% of students enrolled in the Harvard MBA program would graduate, Peter initially was bothered and intimidated by the unpredictability of his student situation at Harvard. "It was terribly competitive, nothing like the University of Alberta; the pressure was constant."[85] Those who have watched the 1970s movie and TV series *The Paper Chase*,[86] will be familiar with what Peter Lougheed experienced in class after class. Each class session was constituted as a hypothetical corporate boardroom. An internationally famous professor would enact the role of Chairman of the Board, demanding specific answers, actions, decisions, and justifications from particular students, based on their pre-class readings about various business scenarios, often modeled on real-world examples. When a student responded in a way that gave the professor an opportunity to demonstrate or make a particular point, often to the detriment of the brave student who had volunteered or been singled out to make a response, the professor might continue to bombard the student with additional follow-up questions and scenarios.

For the first six weeks, Peter Lougheed adopted what for him was a hitherto unheard of tactic of trying to "hide" as much as possible. However, about halfway through the fall term, his professor of marketing, Edward Brown, often credited with creating the "shopping mall" concept, zeroed in on Peter, who having prepared well for the class, acquitted himself with some distinction. From then on, any trace of self-conscious shyness vanished from Peter's in-class repertoire: "In fact, for the rest of the year, you couldn't shut me up."[87]

Peter's sense of belonging received another boost when he discovered that Charles Bliss, a distant relative of his mother, was a professor of accounting at Harvard who taught in the Master of Business Administration Program. The fact that Jeanne was on campus, having found employment in one of the University's secretarial pools, also helped the Lougheeds fit into Harvard campus life. Increasingly immersed in his studies, Peter was fortunate to have Jeanne with him. In addition to her campus job, she, who before their recent marriage still had plans for a career as a singer, also took on the jobs of home-maker and accountant, looking after their small apartment near the Harvard campus, preparing meals, and ensuring that all their expenses were duly recorded and did not exceed their spending limits.

Once accustomed to campus life and routines, Peter enjoyed comparing and testing his own ideas and thoughts about business and governance against those to which he was being exposed in his courses and readings. The approach taken in the Harvard Business School was to downplay theory that was not grounded in and connected to the actual work and problems facing private corporations and public, government agencies. It was an approach that suited Peter well.

In one of his courses, taught by future Nobel Prize winner in economics, Paul Samuelson, Peter grappled with the economic theories of John Maynard Keynes. Keynes advocated government use of fiscal and monetary policies to mitigate the impact of recessions and depressions by stimulating public and corporate spending during such hard times. Samuelson was a neo-Keynesian who developed complex mathematical models to test and support Keynes' general theories of employment, interest, and money. Nonetheless, Lougheed remained skeptical, agreeing that "government intervention is a major factor in the economy," but doubting that "government fiscal policy could ever be as decisive"[88] as Keynes and Samuelson believed.

While Trudeau occasionally showed considerable faith in, as well as a good deal of scepticism about, the theories and predictions of social scientists, like economists and psychologists, Lougheed generally preferred to refrain from drawing any conclusions in the absence of a carefully informed consideration of their likely utility in particular circumstances. Although Trudeau became more sympathetic to this kind of ground-level pragmatism over the course of his political career, Lougheed consistently placed a high value on the practical wisdom of keeping one's options open and adjusting to events as they unfolded. In the specific case of adopting or not adopting Keynesian economic policies, Lougheed's reservations flowed from his first-hand knowledge of the rapid adaptability of citizens and corporations to act in their own best interests in ways that were not easy to anticipate, no matter how elegantly formulated in mathematical terms. After all, he was the grandson of Sir James, and knew all the family's stories of business success and failure.

At the end of his first year at Harvard, Peter took a summer job through a training program offered by Gulf Oil, an experience that was to prove prophetic for one of his main initiatives during his future as Premier of Alberta—the protection and development of Alberta's non-renewable resources, especially oil and gas, for the benefit of all Albertans. The summer job took him and Jeanne to Tulsa, Oklahoma, centre of one of North America's major oil booms during the 1960s. At the time, Peter's primary motivation was to keep his options open. If an anticipated political career did not work out and the option of a conventional law practice did not appeal, a career in one of the head offices of the oil industry was an obvious possibility, one in which he could make ready use of the skills and knowledge gained through his legal and business studies.

Oklahoma's petroleum deposits lie within the US Mid-Continent Region that includes Louisiana, Texas, and New Mexico. From 1900 to 1944, Oklahoma ranked first or second amongst all the Mid-Continent states in oil production. During this time, Tulsa became known as the Oil Capital of the World, becoming famous for pioneering the first large-scale secondary recovery programs that allowed the state to continue high rates of production after initial finds were becoming exhausted by conventional drilling methods. Nonetheless, by the 1950s, both new discoveries and secondary recoveries had fallen behind depletion rates, and many oil companies began to relocate to greener pastures, mostly overseas, where their superior recovery technologies yielded high profits. This was the Oklahoma that Peter Lougheed visited in the summer of 1953.

What he witnessed that summer in Tulsa was the frustration, sudden joblessness, and depression in civic morale being experienced by Oklahomans as the oil companies departed and the state's economy withered in their wake. In some ways, life and work in Tulsa reminded

Peter of life in Calgary (which he linked to Tulsa), and in the state capital of Oklahoma City (which he linked to Edmonton). Since the discovery of oil in Leduc in 1947, the petroleum business and the lives of many of the citizens of Alberta had been "booming." The idea that Alberta might become an economic and cultural backwater once its natural resources had been extracted, bothered Peter greatly, and he began to think carefully about how the "bust" scenario he witnessed first hand in Tulsa might be avoided in his home province.

Back in Cambridge for the beginning of the second year of his two-year MBA program, Peter was able to add the real-life case study of Tulsa to those other case studies that populated his classes. He also added an optional course in International Finance to his remaining, required courses, in addition to researching and writing his MBA thesis. Ever supportive, Jeanne continued her work as a pool secretary during the day and helped Peter write class essays and his thesis in the evenings and on weekends. With her assistance, in the spring of 1954, Peter successfully completed his Harvard MBA. As they were almost ready to return to Calgary, Jeanne suddenly suggested they take advantage of their east coast location to tour Europe before heading home. A month in Europe also would give Peter a break after his demanding year of study, and a chance to consider a number of offers he was receiving from Central Canadian companies like the Bank of Commerce in Toronto, now that he was a fully accredited Harvard graduate.

In Europe, the Lougheeds visited eight countries, and celebrated their third wedding anniversary in Edinburgh. Peter fondly recalled their European adventures as the only time in his life that he was freed from all obligations, those imposed by others and especially those imposed by himself, with their demanding goals and schedules—"no mortgages, no responsibilities, no family, no job."[89] With ample time to relax and reflect, Peter considered his time at Harvard to have significantly broadened his horizons in ways that not only increased his understanding of complex organizations, but which also gave him a more solid and extensive knowledge, not only of the United States in particular, but much of the rest of the world as well. Jeanne agreed: "Being in Boston for two years … and taking the trip to Europe, … our eyes opened a lot wider."[90]

Nonetheless, after Europe, Peter was determined to get back to Alberta. Although his immediate tasks upon his return home were to complete his articling with what was now the law firm of Fernety, Fernety, McGillivray, Prowse and Brennan, and to pass exams that would admit him to the Alberta Bar and Law Society, Peter's political ambitions continued to simmer and grow. Importantly, he now had a specific problem that began to preoccupy him whenever his thoughts turned to his future in Alberta: "What happens when the oil runs out and nothing has been put in its place?"[91]

In many ways, Lougheed's childhood, adolescence, and early adulthood were less complicated than those of Trudeau—culturally, socially, and psychologically. Both men eventually developed coherent and powerful visions of themselves and of Canada, but Trudeau's would take longer to unfold and cohere, whereas Lougheed's were mostly in place by the time he graduated from the

University of Alberta with his law degree in 1952 at the age of 23. Early life differences in the sociocultural and linguistic contexts of Alberta during the 1930s and 1940s versus Quebec in the 1920s, 1930s, and 1940s probably contributed to the comparative stability of the overall context of Lougheed's early years compared to those of Trudeau. The fact that Trudeau's wealth always was available to shelter him from any turbulence in his early social life and education perhaps also entered into differences in their developing characters during their first decades of life. Nonetheless, it was clear to most who knew them in their early years that both were becoming forces to be reckoned with— physically and intellectually capable, forceful and competitive, and dedicated to making something of themselves and their lives.

Their graduate studies at Harvard moved both men beyond the horizons that had defined their lives and themselves in their home provinces while growing up and completing their schooling and law degrees. However, whereas Lougheed's Harvard experience, including his summer in Tulsa, provided a direct path to his future political plans, Trudeau's Harvard experience created considerable upheaval in his life plans and conception of himself, disruptions that would require further studies and life experiences to quell and direct. Through their graduate educations and into their pre-political careers, their life trajectories, already quite distinctive despite some similarities in their ambitions, diverged even further, partially explaining key differences in the pace and manner of their development as political figures of note. It is from here, as we shall see in the next chapter, that their life stories depart most significantly, with Trudeau taking almost 20 years to begin his political life after graduate studies, a feat Lougheed managed in approximately half that time and at a much younger age.

Chapter Three: Adult Lives Before,
and Initiations into, Politics

Despite being born nine years before Peter Lougheed, Pierre Trudeau began his political career as a duly elected federal MP in 1965, just two years before Lougheed was first elected as an Alberta MLA. In this sense at least, it seems that Trudeau, as some of his biographers have noted, did indeed take an unusually long time to find his footing as an adult able and willing to enter into the life he and others had anticipated for him during his childhood and schooling. Lougheed, on the other hand, followed a more conventional time-line for beginning his career as a provincial and nationally known political figure. However, once their hats were in the ring, both advanced with unprecedented rapidity to leadership positions in their federal and provincial political parties, and achieved almost immediate electoral success. What precipitated these rapid assents are stories about their adult years and careers before politics: as self-employed, and later, corporate lawyer (for Lougheed) and lawyer, writer/editor, and professor (for Trudeau).

A good way to think of this stage of pre-political adulthood in the lives of our protagonists is as an experiential and sociopolitical launching pad for their subsequent lives as public figures who made a lasting impact on Canadian politics and society. What happened between the completion of their graduate studies and their elections as Premier of Alberta and Prime Minister of Canada respectively are tales of extraordinarily propitious circumstances, good timing, and the unique combination of talent and personal determination required to capture moments of possibility that easily could have been missed if not for that special kind of star dust that seemed to wrap itself around them and guide their endeavours.

Upon his return to Canada following his year at LSE and his subsequent world travels, Trudeau found himself confronted with the problem of just exactly how he would use his education and life experiences to achieve his goal of securing a career in politics. He had a clear enough vision of how his personalism could mesh with his newly acquired Laskian federalism, but this only compounded the difficulties he faced in establishing a political career. Knowing his own political mind did not equate with finding a ready-made cadre of similarly minded provincial or federal politicos. Back living with his mother in her Outremount home, the most convenient thing to do might be to pursue a political career in Quebec. But how?

John English describes several changes in the Trudeau who had left Canada for study at the LSE, and the one who had come home after his post-LSE journeys. Well tanned from his travels and sporting a thin, yet full beard, the Trudeau who returned to Montreal in May 1949 now held "political views that had become more secular, liberal, and egalitarian, and that co-existed with a renewed yet different Roman Catholic faith."[1] More mature intellectually, he nonetheless retained an emotional unpredictability. The petulance and raw emotionality he had displayed in his earlier relationship with Thérèse Gouin, and in his misguided revolutionary flirtations while a law student at the University of Montreal, had been tempered by his experiences during his studies and travels abroad. What had not changed were Trudeau's desire to be "where the action is" and his penchant for the limelight. Both were amply provided by the Quebec Asbestos strike of 1949.

The Asbestos strike marked the beginnings of a sea change in Quebec society and politics. It began at Asbestos and Thetford Mines on Valentine's Day, almost two months before Trudeau's return from his world travels. The strike was over pay, working conditions, and union rights. It also symbolized a deeper conflict between two opposing views of the future of Quebec: as a somewhat mythical, traditional, rural, and agrarian society committed to the status quo authority of the Union Nationale Party and the Catholic Church, versus the reality of a rapidly changing and industrial society in which two-thirds of the population now lived in towns and cities. The strike was bitter and violent, with the strikers beaten and harassed by the Quebec Provincial Police, actions that turned much of the Quebec public and several leading clergymen against the Duplessis government, which was increasingly seen as anti-democratic. This was the state of affairs that awaited Trudeau, when, shortly after his return home, he accompanied his good friend Gérard Pelletier, now a reporter for *Le Devoir*, to Asbestos to join the union protests. When they arrived on site, they were strip searched by the police and ordered to leave town.

Never one to back down, Trudeau now threw himself fully into the fight on the side of the strikers. In this, he was joined by Pelletier, who introduced Trudeau to the secretary-general of the *Confédération des Travailleurs Catholiques du Canada (CTTC)*, Jean Marchand. At this time, Marchand was even more of a "gunslinger" than Trudeau. He also was a fiercely proud, passionate, and brilliant organizer and tactician. A gifted orator in his own right, Marchand asked Trudeau to address the miners about legal matters relevant to the strike. Still sporting his long and spotty traveling beard, Trudeau ridiculed the police and spoke powerfully about the miners' right to stand up and fight their oppressors in the name of justice, freedom, and democracy, all in language and manner that communicated immediately to the workers. Impressed, Marchand subsequently appointed Trudeau as a full-time, but unpaid, legal advisor for the *CTTC,* a commitment Trudeau maintained throughout the 1950s, involving himself in most of the major Canadian labour confrontations of the decade. The strike finally ended on June 13, 1949, and by July 1 everything was settled, with the strikers getting little of what they demanded. However, the confrontation marked a turning point in Quebec society and politics by alienating some of the more progressive Quebec clergy, who had supported the strike, from the traditional alliance between church and state in the province.

Trudeau's involvement in the strike, with his old friend Pelletier and his new friend Marchand, was to prove central to his political life for the next two decades, first as a champion of democracy in Quebec, using the vehicle of *Cité libre* (the political journal Trudeau helped to found, with Pelletier and others, in 1950), and later as a champion of a Canadian federation that included a progressive and democratic Quebec, during and after his rise to national prominence in the late 1960s. However, all of this was partially interrupted by a stint in Ottawa as a civil servant in the Privy Council Office in support of the Canadian Prime Minister and Cabinet.

Although he continued to work for the *CTTC* and to edit *Cité libre,* Trudeau also was anxious to seize an unexpected opportunity, through an academic acquaintance, to work in the Privy Council Office: "Because as the secretariat to the Cabinet, it was the key decision-making centre, and because I wanted to observe in practice what I had just finished studying in theory" at Harvard, Sciences Po, and LSE.[2] Taking the Ottawa job also may have been influenced by his failure to obtain a teaching position at the Université de Montréal, which would have allowed him to "share my newly acquired knowledge."[3] Unfortunately for Trudeau, the government and senior university administration "didn't want any professors 'who had studied in a communist environment, in London and Paris.'"[4] Despite rumblings of protest and change amongst some clergy, academics, and the public, Duplessis and most of the Church hierarchy remained firmly in power. Given his increasingly left-wing politics, his work for the *CTTC,* and friendship with democratic socialists like Frank Scott (an academic at McGill University's law school, poet, and national president of the Cooperative Commonwealth Federation, precursor to the New Democratic Party of Canada), there was little opportunity for Trudeau to apprentice as a political insider in Quebec.

Thus, Pierre commuted between Ottawa and Montreal on most weekends and breaks from July of 1949 until he left the Privy Council in 1951. The two years he spent there were invaluable as "an apprenticeship that was later to prove very useful."[5] Although it has seemed to some commentators that Trudeau was somewhat "lost" during the 1950s and spent much of the decade in a delayed adolescence marked by frivolous adventures and flings, there should be no doubting his persistent pursuit during this time of experiences he believed would position him for a future as a provincial or national political leader.

After Paris, London, and his subsequent world travels, Trudeau was "far from enchanted with Ottawa's dreary character, [however] there can be no doubt that [he] loved his job."[6] And why not, given his ambitions? As it turned out, "Trudeau was in the Privy Council office at a key moment in Canadian constitutional history."[7] In 1950 alone, there were two conferences that brought together federal and provincial officials specifically to discuss constitutional issues. Trudeau was given responsibility by his Privy Council boss, Gordon Robertson, for drafting reports and documents to assist the federal side in these negotiations, materials that "commanded the admiration and respect not just of his superior but also of members of Prime Minister St. Laurent's cabinet."[8] As a civil servant in St. Laurent's government, Trudeau had a front row seat and direct involvement in the constitutional issues and debates which were to form such an important part of his legacy as one of Canada's longest serving Prime Ministers. "Trudeau's time in Ottawa ... clinched his fascination with the various theories of federalism and its application in Canada. ... He became very interested in Canada, in how it worked and how it could fail. ... His Ottawa experience began to persuade him that the problems he observed in Quebec could be confronted through a more effective Canadian federalism."[9]

Yet, the doings of the Privy Council and federal government did not occupy all of Trudeau's time in Ottawa. Shortly after his arrival in

Canada's capital, his attention was drawn to a photograph in the Ottawa Citizen of a comely twenty-year old Swede, Helen Segerstråle, who had just joined the Swedish embassy, a five-minute taxi ride from the Privy Council Office. Trudeau, with his Jaguar, Harley-Davidson, Italian-tailored suits, and continental charm swept Helen off her feet. Within a year, they were planning to marry, with the consent of Grace Trudeau, who began to oversee Helen's conversion to Catholicism. At 31, Pierre was biddable. Unfortunately for Helen, he was also "an exacting lover, demanding in the attention he craved yet fiercely independent in his own allocation of time."[10] In the summer of 1951, Trudeau decided to leave the civil service and resume his world travels on a more luxurious budget before returning to a future in Montreal. By January 1952, Helen decided that marriage to Pierre was not a wise decision. Absence did not make her love blossom. When she refused to join him that spring in Europe, a suddenly repentant Trudeau wrote lovingly to her, apologizing for "the anguish beyond endurance that in the past year I have inflicted upon one who loved me more deeply than seems humanly possible."[11] But it was too late.

Upon his return to Montreal, Trudeau concentrated his energies on editing and writing for *Cité libre,* modeled somewhat after the French political and literary journal *Esprit,* edited by the personalist philosopher Emmanuel Mounier. Both journals aimed at linking progressive Catholicism with commentary on political and social issues. Although Trudeau had played a central role in the founding of *Cité libre* and was strongly supported by his co-editor, Gérard Pelletier, other founding members experienced Pierre's wealth and personality as sources of annoyance— neither the first nor the last to describe Trudeau as "a disturbing influence."[12] His combination of personal independence and mocking mischievousness was perceived as arrogant and unnecessarily aggressive. Yet despite such reservations, Trudeau and his ideas were prominent in early editions of the journal. Indeed, his many articles in *Cité libre* during the 1950s and 1960s chronicle his increasing political sophistication and maturity, helping him achieve recognition that allowed him to stand out amongst a generation of politically active Quebecers.

In these pieces, he argued against the Quebec nationalism he once had embraced as a law student. Such nationalism he now said was out of step with contemporary interests of Catholic and French citizens whose socioeconomic flourishing required a functional politics that promoted democracy and individual freedom. In an article in *Cité libre* in June 1950, he threw down the gauntlet to the alliance of Duplessis and the Catholic Church.

> We want to bear witness to the Christian and French fact in North America. Fine, so be it; but let's get rid of all the rest. We should subject to methodical doubt all the political categories relegated to us by the previous generation; the strategy of resistance is no longer conducive to the fulfillment of our society. The time has come to borrow the "functional" discipline from architecture, to throw to the winds those many prejudices with which the past has encumbered the present, and to build for the new man. Let's batter down

the totems, let's break down the taboos. Better yet, let's consider them null and void. Let us be coolly intelligent.[13]
This paragraph distills the main thrust of Trudeau's writings during the 1950s, both in *Cité libre* and elsewhere.

Quebec's political and religious leaders had developed a "devastatingly effective formula for maintaining their own power." They "preached that Quebec had a special destiny" that required it to remain "outside the mainstream of modernization," thus preserving its unique French Catholic society by adopting a "siege mentality toward Canada and the rest of the world." This was the "political authority … bestowed unchallengeably by God."[14] It was an authority that Quebec's church officials like Msgr. L.-A. Paquet had articulated throughout the twentieth century: "Our mission is not so much to light the fires of factories, as to maintain the luminous hearth of religion and of thought, making it radiate afar." What must be resisted is "The idea of authority born of the free will of man." "What must not be admitted is that the people itself is sovereign, and that, in choosing the members of a legislative assembly, it delegates to them the power to govern."[15] Such a conception of Quebec society was a red flag to Trudeau and his personalist philosophy of individual freedom, dignity, and reason. As his anger and frustration at this state of affairs grew, he felt he could no longer maintain the political neutrality required in the execution of his Privy Council duties as a civil servant.

Doing battle with the doctrines of Quebec nationalism and the authoritarian, anti-democratic views of the province's ruling elite, an elite to which he once had been apprenticed, now became his raison d'etre. In his articles for *Cité libre* and other Quebec magazines and newspapers, he honed his political ideas and communicative skills. As George Radwanski put it, "His writings of the period are striking for their distillation of sophisticated and diverse political theories into lean, pungent, and elegantly crafted sentences, and for their closely reasoned argument."[16] Although Trudeau had by this time discarded many of the political ideas of the Jesuits who had taught him as an adolescent, he retained and refined their Cartesian-styled argumentation from first premises, adding his own, well practiced shrugs and slight frowns (or their written equivalents). This was a style of presentation that served him well in his increasingly close contacts with, and appearances on, the Quebec media, especially television, where his friend Roger Rolland and others took careful note of his views, which were drawing the ire of Duplessis and the Church hierarchy. In a later interview cited by English, Trudeau described his strategy at this time: "I had searched for a way to put [intellectual change] in motion in Quebec in order to *renew* (italics added) ideas, old habits of thought, and old cultural customs. *Cité libre* was a path. Ottawa was not."[17]

Throughout the early years of his co-editorship of *Cité libre* and despite his successful stint as a Privy Council civil servant, Trudeau was not strongly committed to Canada's federal political system. However, as the 1950s progressed, he began gradually to see possibilities for how Canada might develop as a more successful state that also would work to the benefit of Quebec. Central to this emerging perspective was his own identity "as an author and an actor in the Quebec and the Canadian political process."[18] In his writings and interviews, Trudeau projected what many perceived as a brilliant, capricious intelligence. In his personal style, there often was an unpredictable bluntness, a hardness that could be unleashed in ways that savaged his foes, as he also tried to admonish and rally the people of Quebec to throw off their oppressors. In the December 1952 edition of *Cité libre,* he wrote about Quebecers: "In our relations with the state we are fairly immoral: we corrupt civil servants, we use blackmail on MPs, we look the other way when 'it concerns our interests'. And in electoral matters, our immorality becomes really scabrous."[19] In a later example, he begins by attacking the Liberal Party of Canada as an "overwhelmingly English-speaking party [that] should bear the blame for serious faults of omission with respect to the backwardness of democracy in Quebec" and continues with "The shameful incompetence of the average Liberal MP from Quebec was a welcome asset to a government that needed little more than a herd of *ânes savants* [learned donkeys] to file in when the division bell rang. The party strategists had but to find an acceptable stable master— Laurier, Lapointe, St. Laurent—and the trained donkeys sitting in the back benches could be trusted to behave."[20]

Given the aloof clinical precision of such commentary, it is hardly surprising that Trudeau was frequently accused of degrading and disliking his own people. But at the time, most readers took his reprimands as they were intended—as barbs to expose Quebecers to themselves and prods to change. Trudeau directed this same ferocity to both the Duplessis nationalists of the 1950s and to a later generation of Quebec separatists. In such diatribes, Radwanski sees "the visceral vehemence of a man confronting people he perceives as corruptors of something he holds dear."[21] In 1956, to rally against what he regarded as the oppressive force of Duplessis and his supporters, Trudeau helped to create and then acted as Vice-President and later President of Le Rassemblement (The Gathering), a diverse group of individuals from opposition parties, academic institutions, labour groups, and other forums and associations, who organized to oppose Duplessis and find ways to educate Quebecers about their plight. However, internal disputes over ideology and strategy eventually ensured the failure of the group as an active political coalition.

Then, suddenly in 1959, Duplessis died from a series of strokes and his successor Paul Sauvé suffered a fatal heart attack three months later. With some misgivings, Trudeau nonetheless threw his editorial weight behind Jean Lesage's Quebec Liberals who won the provincial election in June 1960. But Trudeau soon abandoned Lesage and his party when it seemed clear to him that they were culpable in not preventing a resurgence of another form of Quebec nationalism, as young Quebecers began a new separatist movement that quickly saw the birth of the terrorist FLQ (Front de Libération du Québec). In response, Trudeau, from the pages of *Cité libre,* attacked Quebec intellectuals as sitting around flapping their arms and "not realizing that French Canada is too culturally anemic, too economically destitute, too intellectually retarded, too spiritually paralyzed, to be able to survive more than a couple of decades of stagnation, emptying herself of all her vitality into nothing but a cesspit, the mirror of her nationalistic vanity and 'dignity.'"[22] As for the response of Quebec's youth to being rid of the Union Nationale, "freedom proved to be too heady a drink for the French Canadian youth of 1960. Almost at the first sip it went at top speed in search of some soothing milk, some new dogmatism," taking "refuge in the bosom of its mother the Holy Nation."[23]

Through all of this, Trudeau's sense of himself and his politics was being transformed, refined, and polished. Yet, he continued to befuddle both colleagues and adversaries with his peculiar combination of oscillating diligence and dilettantism. In his early thirties, Pierre Trudeau remained single and domiciled in his mother's home, with a personal wealth that allowed him to skip town for exotic places and experiences whenever he grew bored or felt the need of a break from his many roles as journal editor, labour advocate, and whatever else happened to interest him, but not claim his full attention. In the words of leading Quebec feminist and socialist, Thérèse Casgrain, most people grew tired of his habit of "launching ideas or movements, only to lose interest or turn to something else."[24] John English clarifies further: "It is hardly surprising that the blondes, the cars, the clothes, and the travel made even his friends wonder whether this extraordinarily gifted young man was truly 'serious.'"[25]

Trudeau himself devoted only five of his 368-page *Memoirs* to his life from 1951 to 1960 and maintained that he had no political ambitions during the 1950s.[26] What he says in these five pages is that, during the period that eventually saw Jean Lesage's Quebec Liberal Party take power from the Union Nationale, he had no interest whatsoever in belonging to the Union Nationale Party, the Quebec Liberal Party, or the CCF Party (precursor to the New Democratic Party of Canada), despite having many friends in the latter. He seems not to count his involvement in *Cité libre* and various advocacy groups for the promotion of democracy in Quebec, such as the Rassemblement and the Union des Forces Démocratiques (which he also helped found), as activities that reflected his political ambitions. The one significant personal consequence he notes that followed the death of Maurice Duplessis in 1959 was that he finally succeeded in securing a long-sought position as a professor of public law in the law faculty of the Université de Montréal.

Unlike Trudeau himself, recent biographers given free rein to peruse his personal papers and archives, like John English and Max and Monique Nemni, do not separate his political ambition and subsequent success from his activities and interests during the 1950s and early 1960s. English maintains that despite friends and detractors describing or worrying about the Trudeau of this period as "not serious ... he was. Trudeau's papers and writings indicate that the 1950s were fundamental in shaping the role he would later play so dramatically in both Quebec and Canada. That was the decade when he did become serious and consistent. Moreover, he began very ably to shape his adolescent thoughts of a public life into an adult reality."[27] What he actually did was to engage in a very purposeful project of creating a public presence by working extremely hard, despite his occasional dalliances and travels, on labour arbitration boards and journalistic writing dedicated to clarifying and presenting his political views.

When his book *The Asbestos Strike* appeared in 1956, it established him as a celebrity in Quebec, especially on radio, and eventually on the highly influential, relatively recent medium of television. After an initial struggle, he mastered television, learning to play to the camera for full effect and drawing praise from media guru Marshall McLuhan, who later described him as "The Man in the Mask." He advised Trudeau (soon a close friend) to "not worry about possible contradictions in his developing ideas … but [to] probe wherever his thoughts led him," contributing greatly to "Trudeau's warm relationship with the camera."[28] In a recently published collection of letters between Trudeau and McLuhan, Elaine Kahn includes a letter of January 24, 1969 from McLuhan to Trudeau, in which McLuhan elaborates the "Man in the Mask" theme: "The very cool corporate mask that is your major political asset goes naturally with processing of problems in dialogue rather than in the production of packaged answers. That is why I urge you to go on the air with small groups and to trade problems with them rather than seeking answers or stating mere points of view."[29] Interesting advice to a man prone to "going it on his own." As early as the summer of 1955, Trudeau had left behind any doubts he previously had entertained about the possibility of a successful career in the public eye. By this time he had developed confidence in his political views and in his ability to express them convincingly.

The late fifties saw the effects of Trudeau's attempts to market himself (although he would have hated this way of putting it) as something charmingly different on the political scene in Quebec and in Canada. In the words of Canadian historian John Saywell, who wrote a glowing introduction to Trudeau's later book *Federalism and the French Canadians*, Trudeau was "an experiment in Canadian public life, a refreshing combination of intellectual capacity and common sense …

a man [with] a quiet independence of mind with a strong socially oriented sense of purpose. ... The result will bear watching."[30]

Whenever and wherever he could, Trudeau voiced his arguments for more and better democracy in Quebec. When covering the provincial Liberal convention in 1958 for both the magazine *Vrai* and the CBC, Trudeau recognized the new Liberal premier Jean Lesage as an able leader but questioned his commitment to democracy and whether he was capable of building a strong resistance to Quebec's proneness to reactionary and authoritarian forces. What was to become his trademark "quick repartee" was in frequent circulation on Quebec media. New travels to China, the Middle East, Europe, and elsewhere, culminating in a very dangerous solo canoe trip from Key West to Cuba, furnished new fodder for interviews and articles. In these and many other ways, Trudeau was busy developing what many now would call, to his great chagrin, "his brand."

Nonetheless, the range of Trudeau's activities during the 1950s (labour lawyer, who also took on *pro bono* cases that interested him, Privy Council clerk, editor and essayist, human rights advocate, public intellectual and radio and television personality, university professor, world traveler, and playboy) conveyed a somewhat bewildering diversity that understandably occasioned wonderment about what he was really up to, if anything of consequence. Certainly he could not be accused of avoiding work and effort, as he became intensely involved in many of these activities. Nonetheless, the overall impression left on many observers was of a man approaching middle age, who was not yet committed to, and seemingly easily distracted from, a life course that would lead to the success and renown he seemed to be seeking. Radwanski describes Trudeau's psychological state at this time as one of reluctance to commit himself, stemming "from a fear of real responsibility and partly from a determination not to allow himself to be locked into any one option until he had completed his process of self-training," a process that appears to have extended right up to his election to Parliament in 1965.[31]

As we already have seen, Clarkson and McCall take a much more psychodynamic view of Trudeau's behaviour during his thirties, viewing him as still caught up in a delayed adolescence, typical of the "Jungian psychological archetype, the *puer aeternus* or eternal youth," with "too great a dependence on the mother"[32]—a devotion they connect to the early death of his father. Grace Trudeau's friends found the son's attachment to his mother touching; Pierre's contemporaries found it dismaying. The latter "saw the cosiness of McCullough Street as an imprisonment for Trudeau, no matter how much he protested that his mother always encouraged him to do what he wanted," remark Clarkson and McCall, who go on to suggest that someone with a "mother complex" suffers two typical disturbances: "homosexuality and Don Juanism."[33] They reject the possibility of homosexuality in light of the vigorous rejection of any such idea by Trudeau himself and the various women in his life.

Those who spoke about such matters generally agreed with Madeleine Gobeil, whom Clarkson and McCall quote as saying that Trudeau's "sentimental interests always lay with women even when he was young and shy. He was my first lover and in my experience beyond compare. No French Canadian who knew him well ever thought he was a homosexual—that was used by the English as a canard, and his separatist enemies picked it up." Clarkson and McCall conclude that Trudeau "was not a true Don Juan either. ... With most women he was very correct and gallant; certainly he was not a voracious seducer. Still, the guise of swashbuckling sexual adventurer obviously appealed sufficiently for him to try it on with increasing frequency as the 1950s wore on. Dating became another sport at which he could publicly excel."[34] Among Trudeau's female friends in the late 1950s, Carroll Guérin, who bore a striking resemblance to Grace Kelly, was a frequent companion, although she soon had competition from a young Ottawa student, Madeleine Gobeil, with whom Trudeau maintained a relationship that lasted until his marriage to Margaret Sinclair in 1971.

Interestingly, despite having raised the *puer aeternus* possibility, Clarkson and McCall do not return to it as a recurrent theme in Trudeau's life overall. Instead, they repeatedly refer to Pierre's youthful identification with Cyrano de Bergerac as providing a hero stereotype that fit many of Trudeau's actions and self-presentations. They claim that "It is revealing of Trudeau's contradictions that he, the ardent rationalist, carried with him into adult life the dream of emulating Cyrano, the arch-romantic"—"a brilliant wit and poet, a protector of the weak, enemy of the pompous and powerful, a fighter against tyranny ... who refused compromise, fripperies, and flattery." They go on to suggest that "with Cyrano, Trudeau was appropriating a mythic model for his life ... he would perform amazing feats and win special honours. He would ... climb alone to the heights."[35] Later in life, Trudeau himself was to comment:

"People said I was arrogant. I never was with nice people. Only with those who goaded me. But I was still spoiling for a fight. I still had something of the Cyrano temperament."[36]

Toward the end of their book, Clarkson and McCall maintain that Trudeau's "mythic hero was no hunk of a quarterback huddling with his padded teammates; it was Cyrano the swordsman fighting for his cause in open combat against incredible odds."[37] Into his final term as Prime Minister, Trudeau "had viewed the world as a Manichean universe where the forces of good were pitted eternally against the forces of evil. As the champion of liberty and democracy, his instinct was to define his enemies narrowly, challenge them relentlessly, and win by devastating them outright, with little thought given to conciliation or compromise."[38] That is, until, "In his maturity, Trudeau was able to set aside his Cyrano fantasy of climbing all alone to the mountain-top,"[39] and compromise with others in both his political and personal life.

But, as 1959 was coming to an end, despite his decade of preparing himself for great things, Trudeau "began to look even to his associates as though he would never settle down, never find a permanent job or a lasting relationship but would continue to fritter away his unusual intellectual gifts in aimless bohemianism and endless travel."[40] However, as already mentioned, his later biographers like John English and Max and Monique Nemni disagree with this assessment, maintaining that Trudeau, having purposefully gathered the real world political experience, knowledge, and many of the connections that would serve him well in his political future, was mostly biding his time until the right opportunity arose.

The first half of the 1960s would either make or break the political career that Trudeau had long anticipated and prepared for. Things did not begin well. Although Montreal had shed its provincial past and now afforded venues for ballet, opera, jazz, up-scale restaurants, and theatre, all of which Trudeau frequented with his several companions, he himself was ill at ease. Life as a university professor, editor and editorialist for *Cité libre,* and sometimes media personality brought with it piles of student papers to grade, challenging interactions with a new generation of writers and journalists, and attention that he needed, but loathed when things went badly. At this crucial time in his life and career (in his early to mid forties), he found himself sidelined from Quebec politics by events and his own choices, with uncertain prospects.

Neither he nor Gérard Pelletier received the kind of warm invitation to join Lesage's Quebec Liberals that had been extended to Jean Marchand, which Marchand declined, and which another friend and colleague, the Quebec journalist and television personality René Lévesque accepted and rode to a seat in the Legislative Assembly and a cabinet position as Minister of Hydroelectric Resources and Public Works. Trudeau later admitted feeling envious of Lévesque's good timing and feeling "a bit sorry for myself because I'd never been asked to get into politics ... I was against the party he had joined."[41] A wistful Trudeau elaborated that he probably "would always be on the outside writing articles about what the politicians should be doing and weren't." Yet, "for all his talk, he had never doubted that he should be on the inside."[42] The difficult part was to figure out how to get there, and to do so on his terms.

The problem with entering the political arena in Quebec was that despite agreeing with, even applauding, the Lesage Liberals' desire to modernize Quebec and several of their other initiatives, Trudeau was strongly against the left-wing neo-nationalism he observed in many of Lesage's ministers and members of caucus, including Lévesque, another friend and journalist Pierre Laporte, academic Léon Dion, and his old chum and co-conspirator André Laurendeau. At the same time, Trudeau's friendly relations with several members of what was soon to become the New Democratic Party of Canada also began to fray. He was especially upset when, in an attempt to gain ground in Quebec, the NDP promised to work out some kind of "two nations" arrangement to accommodate Quebec's historical position in the Canadian federation. With nothing going his way in the Quebec political scene, Trudeau and his friend Jacques Hébert, accompanied by three others, left Montreal and Quebec for a six-week tour of Mao's China, a visit recorded in their 1968 book, *Two Innocents in Red China.*

On October 1, 1960, approximately three months after the Lesage victory and the commencement of Quebec's Quiet Revolution, Trudeau found himself atop the main gate at Tiananmen Square in Beijing, celebrating the anniversary of the Communist victory in China. As the displays, dancing, and fireworks faded and the impromptu Canadian delegation was being herded back to its hotel, escorted by a party official, Trudeau suddenly ducked behind a pillar and fled into the huge crowd of celebrants. He returned to his hotel in the early dawn and later described "exotic orchestras, costumes of the moon people, strange friendships and new scents ... dark tresses, inquisitive children, laughing adolescents, brotherly and joyful men."[43] When the French edition of the book in which Trudeau and Hébert recounted their Chinese adventures was published on March 28, 1961, Trudeau urged the Canadian government to recognize and establish relations with China, which he predicted would become a major player in world trade. Little was said in the book or elsewhere by the authors that spoke to the hardships and atrocities that beset the Chinese people under Mao, including the starvation of more than twenty million in the great famine of 1960, the same year that the Canadian travellers were wined and dined and Pierre went walkabout in Beijing, although later the authors did admit to a degree of naïveté in their impressions and reports.

Trudeau's penchants for contrariness and being seen as youthfully "anti-establishment" during the 1960s perhaps explain his downplaying of the brutalities committed by Mao, but such "looking away" seems jarring given his otherwise strong commitments to democracy and individual rights and freedoms. Given that he found the automatized, McCarthy-style condemnation of everything communist that he perceived in many North Americans to be silly, his vaunted rationalism and personalism seemed strangely absent during his time in Beijing. A similar and equally peculiar tolerance was evident in his future interactions with Fidel Castro and other communist leaders who displayed strident and negative knee-jerk reactions to all things western. But then, Trudeau liked to think of himself as somewhat of a "leftist," despite the overall constancy of his liberal democratic political stance.[44]

Back home, Trudeau found that Lesage's Quiet Revolution was progressing rapidly. He greatly admired its secularization of education, improvements in social security, and adoption of a more international role, but continued to condemn its nationalism. As a staunch, if unconventional, Catholic and cultural pluralist, he also worried privately about the spiritual aridity that might attend an overly aggressive secularism. But his major concern remained Quebec nationalism and separatism, an antipathy that was stoked when he returned to the classrooms of the University of Montreal to discover students who were increasingly committed to these ideas and movements. In an article on nationalist alienation for *Cité libre,* he accused young separatists of being "unrealistic in not recognizing that they were aligning themselves with the most conservative" interests in Quebec society. "Separatism and neo-nationalism would close off [the French-Canadian community and] cut off the breadth of true freedom." Rather than looking only to themselves, separatists should instead open their intellectual and physical borders to prevent "our people from separating to death."[45]

In this, Trudeau disagreed even with his then most frequent female companion Carroll Guérin, who argued that it was absolutely necessary for young French-Canadians to establish their identity separate from English Canadians. Although he shared some aspects of this view (for example, a major reason for not associating himself with the CCF-NDP Party of Canada was his concern about the centralizing policies of their primarily English-Canadian leaders), Trudeau maintained strong rational and visceral objections to the possibilities for alienation, coercion, and intellectual and cultural stagnation he perceived in Quebec nationalism and the separatism it increasingly embraced.

So strong were Trudeau's convictions that nationalism and separatism would prevent Quebec from taking its place as a vibrant centre for progressive intellectual and social innovation that he began to feel misplaced in his life at the University of Montreal. Despite his professorial air, his writings, speeches, and ambitions were more immediately practical than academic. He began to worry that his plans for a life in politics were evaporating as he plodded along in political science and legal studies. He might disagree with the political positions and aims of his friends like Lévesque and Paul Gérin-Lajoie, but at least they were in the thick of it, making a real difference as political agents ushering in societal change. The classroom that had attracted him earlier, as a haven for reasoned reflection and insight, now seemed more like a trap. Some of this attitude is apparent, together with his antipathies to nationalism and separatism, in a highly influential article he penned in the summer of 1962 in *Cité libre*—"The New Treason of the Intellectuals."

In this article, Trudeau targeted Quebec intellectuals as aiding and abetting Quebec separatism and nationalism. He attacked their core idea that the Quebec nation must necessarily be sovereign. For Trudeau, in modern democracies sovereign power belonged to the people and is exercised on their behalf by duly elected and representative parliamentary bodies. To suggest otherwise was to court disaster. The worst atrocities in history should teach us "to insist that a particular nationality must have complete sovereign power is to pursue a self-destructive end." Modern states like Canada are polyethnic. "Every national minority will find, at the very moment of liberation, a new minority within its bosom which in turn must be allowed the right to demand its freedom." "French Canadians have all the powers they need to make Quebec a political society affording due respect for nationalist aspirations and at the same time giving unprecedented scope for human potential in the broadest sense."[46]

For Trudeau, nationalism threatened what his philosophy of personalism and his life experiences had convinced him were essentially necessary human experiences of dignity and freedom. What Quebec and Canada needed to focus on was not the collectivist, nationalist fantasies of academics. These were merely bourgeois postures that distracted from the more important business of social, political, legal, and economic reforms that could serve to ensure freedoms and opportunities for all citizens, not the bourgeois elite alone, and risked setting different nationalities against each other— wasting time and energy on the resultant and endless squabbling that would inevitably ensue. "Trudeau also believed that the highly emotional arguments of the Lesage government were increasingly diminishing both the social scientific and rational analysis of what was best for all citizens in Quebec."[47]

As the Lesage government embraced more nationalist policies, Marchand began to talk to Trudeau and Pelletier about the possibility of standing as Liberal candidates at the federal level. But, when Prime Minister Lester B. Pearson allowed 56 American Bomarc nuclear missiles to be stationed at RCAF bases in North Bay, Ontario and La Macaza, Quebec at the end of 1963, an outraged Trudeau openly mocked the Nobel Laureate Prime Minister as the defrocked prince of peace, borrowing a line from his friend and fellow essayist Pierre Vandeboncoeur. Any plans that Trudeau might have had to join Marchand and Pelletier as freshly minted federal Liberals were put aside.

Pierre Trudeau's total rejection of nationalist and separatist options for Quebec was increasingly separating him from old friends like Vandenboncoeur and François Hertel, and from Quebec political life more generally. In another of his *Cité libre* pieces, this one in May 1964, Trudeau lashed out at Hertel for irresponsible writings and comments that were serving to ignite acts of terrorism by separatist factions in the province. Seeking new associates, Trudeau began to meet with others, like Montreal lawyer Marc Lalonde, sociologist Maurice Pinard, and psychoanalyst Yvon Gauthier, who shared his concerns about separatism and wanted to understand it better so as to resist it, oftentimes using social scientific and legal analyses to frame their conclusions. Together, they published a manifesto in the May 1964 edition of *Cité libre*, expressing frustration at the lack of realism in Quebec politics and the absence of political leadership, especially in economic and cultural areas. As John English succinctly put it: by the mid-1960s, Trudeau had found "new friends [who] helped him find a different approach through 'functional politics ... as so many old friends marched off under a new nationalist banner."[48]

By the summer of 1965, Trudeau's political ambitions seemed blocked at both provincial and federal levels. His aversion to separatism and nationalism prevented him from joining with the Lesage liberals. At the same time, his inveighing against Pearson's nuclear flip-flop had not endeared him to federal liberals. However the latter desperately needed to find stronger Quebec candidates to ensure victory in an election they were anxious to hold in the autumn of 1965, while the beleaguered John Diefenbaker remained as leader of the federal Progressive Conservatives. Also mindful of his advance into middle age, at the urgings of young Quebec federalists aligned with Marc Lalonde and renewed entreaties from Jean Marchand, Trudeau finally dropped his reluctance and allowed Marchand to sponsor him and his friend Gérard Pelletier to Pearson and his caucus as potential federal liberal candidates. In their last article for *Cité libre* in October 1965, Trudeau and Pelletier described their decision to stand as federal liberals as one that was inspired by their desire to become associated with the pursuit of a more dynamic and progressive social policy for Canada and Quebec. Even then, Trudeau almost backed out of the deal when, despite Marchand securing the safe liberal riding of Quebec Mount Royal for him to begin his formal political career, he discovered that he would be running against his friend, political philosopher Charles Taylor, who would be representing the NDP in the same riding. Nonetheless, motivated by what he viewed as the only viable option open to him and with an awareness of his advancing age, Trudeau eventually made good on his belated jump into the political arena, and was duly elected as a federal member of the Canadian parliament. His political life had at last begun.

W. A. "Bill" McGillivray was a Lougheed family friend, and son of Alexander A. McGillivray who led the Alberta Conservative Party in the second half of the 1920s, without much success. Bill also was a full partner at the Calgary law firm to which Peter returned after his two-year stint at Harvard while completing his MBA. Bill had acted for Sir James Lougheed's estate, served as legal adviser and lawyer to Peter's mother after the death of his father Edgar, and now took grandson Peter under his wing. Although the firm of Fenerty, Fenerty, McGillivray, Prowse and Brennan did a good deal of business with the oil and gas sector, Peter worked mostly in civil litigation involving insurance companies and injured people, an arena in which he proved to be particularly competent. When Peter was completing his articling stint at Fenertys and associates, McGillivray, being careful not to show favouritism for his protégé, described him as a "decent and competent articling lawyer."[49] On October 10, 1955, Peter Lougheed was formally admitted to the Alberta bar, thereby becoming the first third-generation lawyer in the province of Alberta.

With his prospects looking up, and the recent arrival of a baby boy (Stephen), Peter and Jeanne purchased an older home at 2910 Montcalm Crescent in the Mount Royal neighbourhood of Calgary, moving out of a small bungalow they had rented in Lower Elboya after returning from Cambridge, Massachusetts. Jeanne designed and supervised renovations that included the construction of a sizable addition. The Lougheeds lived in their newly renovated Calgary home, welcoming two daughters (Andrea and Pamela) and another son (Joseph), until Peter's later political career necessitated greater proximity to Alberta's Legislative Building, and thus a move to Edmonton.

While Jeanne was reconstructing their newly purchased Mount Royal home and caring for Stephen, Peter worked 15 to 16 hour days, with results that began to attract the attention of other Calgary offices and companies. Lougheed knew that his expertise in both law and business administration gave him an edge over most other lawyers. However, his typical social awareness, coupled with his brief summer internship in the petroleum industry in Oklahoma, also had taught him not to broadcast his Harvard credentials, so as to fit in with the local business community and the oil sector in particular. What worked in Tulsa, obviously also worked in Calgary, for within six months of his admission to the bar, Peter was being courted by Everett Costello, general manager for Calgary's Mannix Construction Company, one of Fenertys' biggest clients.

McGillivray cautioned Peter not to be precipitous in accepting Mannix's offer, advising him to weigh carefully the advantages of the possible new position against the downsides of loosing the status of being in a prestigious private practice, hinting that as a house lawyer for a large corporation like Mannix, Peter would have much less authority and independence. The position offered by Mannix was assistant secretary and legal assistant to the general manager, Everett Costello, a long-time friend and confidant of company owner, Frederick Charles Mannix. At first, heeding McGillivray's advice, and somewhat concerned about his relative lack of experience and youth, Peter declined Costello's invitation. However, when Costello approached him again with an upgraded offer, Peter accepted it, and began to look forward to working with Costello and getting to know the highly successful and influential Fred Mannix. He officially joined the Mannix Corporation on June 1, 1956. Peter's dual knowledge of the law and business administration proved to be just what his new employer and his company required. Within a comparatively short period of time by company standards, he was advanced to the position of Vice-President, Administration. For the next six years, Peter Lougheed would work for Frederick Charles Mannix, to the benefit of both men and their aspirations. His experience at Mannix was to exert a profound effect on Peter's life and career.

Fred Mannix was an enigmatic, self-made man who shunned publicity and built an internationally powerful construction company through sound planning, energetic action, and a forceful personality. Like Peter's grandfather Sir James, Mannix was unsparingly devoted to establishing a strong western identity for business and commerce, one that would promote the emergence of political power that central Canada would need to acknowledge and reckon with. In the words of biographer Allan Hustak, "Peter Lougheed's family may have helped to build the city of Calgary, but the Mannix family helped to lay the foundations for the industrial development of Alberta."[50] In his life and political career, Peter was to represent and advance both legacies.

The Mannix Company was founded by a 17-year-old Frederick Stephen Mannix, Frederick Charles Mannix's father, in Manitoba in 1898. In 1903, Fred Stephen and his company followed opportunities for construction of railroads and municipal buildings to Alberta. Development of expertise in earth moving, led to future endeavours in the building of highways and irrigation projects, expanding into coal stripping in nearby Saskatchewan during the Depression years of the 1930s. Further expansion into heavy construction on a national level followed in the 1940s, with the building of airports and the dredging of harbours. Confined to a wheelchair with failing health shortly thereafter, Fred Stephen sold a major interest in his company to the large American international firm Morrison-Knudsen, on condition that his son, Frederick Charles, be retained as Mannix president within the new corporate structure. By the late 1940s, a series of company misfortunes convinced Fred Charles that he needed to regain majority control of his father's, and what he now regarded as his own, company.

Fred C. knew his family's company business from the ground up, having worked his way from field hand to upper management. He was fiercely loyal to his workers and they to him. Practicing a philosophy of "working your ass off" and keeping your mind on the job, just "the way I was raised in the camps and ... the way I've always lived,"[51] Fred bought out the Morrison-Knudsen interest and regained control of his company in 1950. From there, he built the company into an international construction firm that took on major projects all over the world, including railroads in Australia and Mexico and roadways in California. In Canada, there was hardly any major construction that did not involve Mannix. During Peter Lougheed's time at the corporation, his files included the Toronto Subway, the Great Canadian Oil Sands in Northern Alberta, the Bomarc Missile Sites in North Bay, Ontario and La Macaza, Quebec, the South Saskatchewan River Dam, and the Northern Alberta Resources

Railroad. Working with and learning from Fred Mannix involved countless hours spent in exhausting negotiations, contract disputes, and putting together complex deals. In doing so, "Lougheed gained the perfect training for his [future] political career."[52]

Some have described the relationship between Fred Mannix and Peter Lougheed as one of father and son, with Fred mentoring and grooming Peter in a way that his own father had not been able to do for him. If so, Peter did not see it that way: "The way we operated, I assure you, could not be [as] a father and son."[53] Nonetheless, the two men respected and admired each other, both benefitting greatly from their association. In many ways, Fred Charles Mannix represented and enacted free enterprise in its ideal form—hiring the best and brightest as management personnel, insisting that projects be undertaken with quality, timeliness, and integrity, being careful not to cut corners, and doing his best to ensure that projects were completed according to the intent of the contract, without resorting to contractual details and loopholes to maximize profits when unexpected obstacles were encountered. Obviously, Mannix's firm hand and insistence that others also honour arrangements as they had been negotiated sometimes created enemies, but Peter saw Fred as a man of his word and knew him to be a straight-shooter, who also made significant and anonymous contributions to charitable organizations, universities, and cultural agencies. In turn, Fred Mannix's mentorship mostly involved reciprocating Peter's faith and trust. Together, they negotiated, planned, and organized highly complex projects with their many powerful clients and partners.

Allan Hustak relates a story about the first time Peter was summoned by Mannix to appear at a board meeting of the Mannix Company, a few short weeks into his new job. The main purpose of the meeting was to determine whether or not to proceed with a legal claim against Westcoast Transmission concerning the construction of a pipeline in BC's Fraser Valley. When most of those around the table had agreed that Mannix had a strong case and should proceed with the claim, Fred turned to Peter. Lougheed disagreed, pointing to what he regarded as a few non-supportable items in the claim as prepared. Mannix, who greatly appreciated and admired his new hire's straightforwardness and careful preparation, had found his new lead, general counsel. "Lougheed was discerning enough to know what difficult contracts mean [and] he could boil it down so that an ordinary guy—and most of our people are ordinary—could understand it,"[54] opined Mannix.

Mannix was well aware of Peter's political ambitions when he hired and promoted him, and so long as Lougheed did not make use of his work at Mannix Corp. for any political purposes, encouraged the younger man to contribute time and energy to community groups and projects. The fact that Peter became involved in community endeavours that also involved future supporters of his political ambitions seemed not to matter to Mannix, provided that the future politician did not do so as a representative of Mannix Corporation. While at Mannix, but on his own time, Lougheed arranged half-time shows as a member of the Booster Club for the Calgary Stampeders CFL football team. As a member of the board of the Calgary Exhibition and Stampede, he promoted Canadian talent for the grandstand shows for that hugely popular annual event. His involvement in these endeavours yielded important advantages for his future political career in terms of contacts with powerful community and corporate leaders, and by making him familiar with the operations and effectiveness of television as a promotional vehicle. At the same time, Lougheed's social capital grew further as he was admitted to the Ranchman's Club and the Petroleum Club, both sanctuaries for members of the Calgary establishment.

In July 1958, Peter was promoted to vice-president of administration at Mannix Company Limited and made a director of the firm. With Fred Mannix as an influential role model, Peter was becoming widely recognized for his exceptional capabilities as a negotiator and administrator. Future Lougheed biographer David Wood worked for Mannix during Lougheed's tenure at the company. As director for public relations, Wood reported directly to Peter and spent a good deal of time with him, traveling to national and international meetings and conclaves, and making visits to construction sites. Wood's recollections of those days provide a first-hand account of Peter Lougheed's administrative style and character: Lougheed "was easily the best boss I had ever worked for— accessible, understanding, clear in his expectations, and prepared to back you up in your decisions and projects, especially if you had discussed matters with him first." Commenting on Peter's knowledge of contracts, owner negotiations, and handling of a bidding team, Peter Crawford, a Mannix administrative officer at the time, admired Peter's "ability to look at problems from all angles with a view to turning each stumbling block into a stepping stone."[55]

During their travels together, Wood and Lougheed mostly stayed focused on the negotiations at hand. However, especially over mealtimes, their conversations ranged more widely, and occasionally veered into politics. Before joining Mannix, Wood's Edmonton advertising agency had managed public relations for several political campaigns and candidates. During their conversations, Wood recognized Peter's political ambitions and encouraged him to focus his thoughts on federal rather than provincial politics, arguing that Ernest Manning's Social Credit Party of Alberta would be too tough a nut to crack. In response, Lougheed disagreed, maintaining that provincial politics might be "where the action is and where it should be and would likely remain." Wood adds that "If I made any contribution, it was to reinforce the knowledge that personal contact is the most effective method of communication, and that of all media, television, when used correctly, comes closest to simulating personal contact."[56]

As 1961 wound down, Peter Lougheed began to realize that his job with Mannix, especially the sustained, complex, and travel intensive negotiations it involved, was making it virtually impossible for him to pursue his burgeoning interests in politics and to spend time with his growing and expanding family. From the start to the end of his four-and-a-half year stint with Mannix, Peter had maintained a high level of respect for his boss, describing Fred Mannix as one who places "a high value on personal initiative, and respects and encourages those who display that. He has a strong feeling that the most significant thing that can happen in this country is for the individual to create and to control his own economic destiny. ... He has created an impact on the whole nation."[57] It was now time for Peter Lougheed to create an opportunity for himself to do the same, but in his personally chosen field of endeavour.

In December 1961, at the age of thirty-three, Lougheed resigned from the Mannix Corporation, although he continued to serve as a director on its board and as a legal advisor. On February 6, 1962, after a year of transition and preparation, Peter partnered with John Ballem and Marvin McDill to open a new law firm. Under his own roof, Lougheed was now free to devote more of his time and energy openly to his political ambitions, while ensuring that his growing family was an integral part of his life.

At the time Lougheed left Mannix, Conservative Party fortunes were falling at both federal and provincial levels. Subsequently, Prime Minister John Diefenbaker's majority Progressive Conservative government was reduced to a minority on June 18, 1962, and shortly thereafter lost the federal election of April 8, 1963 to Lester Pearson's Liberals. In Alberta, the provincial Conservatives, who never had held power in the province, hit a new low on June 17, 1963, when they failed to win a single seat in an election that once again saw Ernest Manning's Social Credit Party win an easy majority, claiming 60 of the 63 seats available.

Free from the restrictions Mannix had imposed on him, Lougheed was hoping to enhance his public persona, with an eye to pursuing a political career. However, he was not interested in serving on the backbenches of any federal or provincial parties as they currently were operating and, in his private view, mostly misfiring. For the time being, Peter was content with the steadily increasing profits of his law firm, projecting the image of a successful lawyer, and taking time to study and reflect on the lay of the political landscape. To these ends, he acquired and consumed a small library of volumes on the history and politics of western Canada and political biographies, including a work that would serve as a guide to his own political aspirations—John White's 1960 volume, *The Making of the President,* which recounted John F. Kennedy's successful pursuit of the American presidency. He also acquired some direct experience of political manoeuvring, while avoiding commitments to any provincial or federal party, by serving as a member of the Calgary Olympic Development Committee, with the goal of promoting Banff as a potential site for the 1968 winter Olympics. Although the Banff bid was ultimately unsuccessful, media coverage of the effort was extensive throughout Alberta, reaching a wider audience than that listening to Ernest Manning's Sunday radio broadcasts.

Shortly after Peter returned from the unsuccessful Olympic bid in Innsbruck, Austria, he ran into recently resigned, provincial Conservative leader Milton Harradence on the Easter weekend of 1964 in Banff. Harradence encouraged Lougheed, as a man of independent means, to consider running for his old job. Peter was initially skeptical, seeing no immediate reason why he should succeed where Harradence and others before him had failed. However, when apprised of Harradence's proposal to Lougheed, several party members and friends were considerably more enamoured of the idea than Peter was himself.

Edmonton stock broker Arthur Gregg was one of several Alberta conservatives who were imploring party president Gerard

Amerongen to call a leadership convention to replace Harradence. However, Amerongen was understandably reluctant to do so without the assurance that there were outstanding candidates ready to enter the ring. Gregg understood Amerongen's concern, but also worried that the Liberals, who had elected two MLAs in the recent election to the Tories' zero, were now in a position to replace the Conservatives as a "central right" party in the province. When Gregg expressed his concerns to one of his employees, Peter Turner, who had known Peter Lougheed when both were students at Calgary's Central High School and had caddied with him in Banff, Turner suggested he consider Lougheed. Gregg was immediately enamoured of the idea of Senator Sir James Lougheed's grandson as a possible Conservative leader and encouraged Amerongen to contact him to ascertain his possible interest.

At their first meeting in Calgary's Petroleum Club, Amerongen failed to penetrate Lougheed's cautious posture. "He gave me no assurance of anything. The most I could hope for was that he would give it some thought."[58] But at another level, Amerongen's gambit quickly began to pay dividends, as word spread rapidly about his Petroleum Club conversation with Peter. A small group of loyal Tories active in the Young Progressive Conservative Association of Alberta was particularly keen on Lougheed, considering him to be an ideal candidate with impeccable credentials and proven administrative understanding and ability. Sales executive Hayden Smith and lawyers Henry Beaumont and Garry Johnson invited Peter to attend their annual YPC Happy Valley barbeque. All three were impressed with him and pledged to work on his behalf. As Smith put it, "We recognized that

Peter was anxious to step into the limelight, but that he expected others to build the stage for him. He just wanted to wait until events fit into his program because he's a highly programmed guy." Elaborating further, Smith opined, "I honestly think that at *that time,* he felt it was beneath him to think in terms of doing the mundane things ... like knocking on doors."[59] Agreeing that Lougheed's personal achievements spoke for themselves, Smith and other young conservatives prevailed on Peter to recognize how committed they were to him and how committed he would need to be to his candidacy if he agreed to stand.

The mere fact that Lougheed had attended the YPC barbeque was enough to set chins wagging. Throughout the summer of 1964, rumours that Peter Lougheed was considering challenging Ernest Manning were the talk of the town in Calgary and beyond. As excitement surrounding his future grew, Peter himself remained cautious. It was not so much that he was reluctant to do the small things that would be necessary for electoral success, as Smith had suggested. His reluctance had more to do with his desire, and perhaps need, to feel that he was in control of his fate were he to enter the ring. In particular, he worried about the motivations of many of those who were supporting and encouraging him. Above all else, he did not want to be indebted to any special interests or "behind the scenes" power brokers. To clear the air, and his thoughts, during the third week of September, 1964, Peter and Jeanne Lougheed, together with his close, lifelong friend Harold Millican and Millican's wife Donna, drove to Jasper to relax and strategize with U of A friend Clare "Swede" Liden.

Both Millican and Liden were liberals. Millican's father was a prominent lawyer, after whom the Calgary provincial constituency of

Calgary-Millican was named. In fact, during their university days, Peter had agreed to attend a Liberal rally with Harold, but at the last minute decided against it. Unlike so many politicians, Lougheed was always keen to understand opponents and their points of view—perhaps a legacy of his experience of strategizing and enacting "game plans" during his football-playing days (think of football as a kind of "physical chess") and during his time with Fred Mannix. With the Millicans and Liden, Peter and Jeanne were able to consider his political possibilities in a reasonably balanced and objective way, During an intensive fire-side conversation, which Jeanne Lougheed viewed as "the most critical night" of Peter's fledgling political career,[60] the friends considered not only provincial possibilities for Peter, but federal ones as well.

In favour of the provincial option, Liden argued that "the opportunity to take over the Conservative party was clean and fresh. He could take it over and build it up as his own."[61] Millican also favoured a provincial focus, arguing that the Quiet Revolution taking place in Quebec under the Lesage Provincial Government would result in greater powers for the provinces—"Provincial rights will be the wave of the future. ... The action is going to be in the provinces—in Alberta."[62] Liden agreed, adding "Why play second fiddle to someone in Ottawa when you can be the boss in Alberta? You know you only like to be the boss!"[63] Although Jeanne and Donna retired around midnight, the conversation continued until dawn, with the other two men encouraging Lougheed to visit and talk to rural Albertans as well as those in Edmonton and Calgary, so as to broaden his understanding of the people of the province and to dispel any conceptions of him as a "city slicker." Although in many ways the trip to, and discussions in, Jasper would prove to be pivotal in Lougheed's eventual decision to run for the leadership of the provincial Progressive Conservatives, at the time the Lougheeds and the Millicans drove back to Calgary, Peter was still undecided.

However, shortly thereafter, Lougheed was forced to expedite his decision-making, when Gerald Baldwin, a prominent Alberta conservative from Peace River, announced his willingness to be nominated for the leadership of the Alberta Progressive Conservatives. Liden reacted by telling Peter that "You've got one chance, and it's now."[64] But others of Lougheed's inner circle were less certain. His law partners, Ballem and McDill, worried that the timing was not right, especially given the needs of their growing firm. Closer to home, his mother, father-in-law, and mentor Fred Mannix all considered such a move to be reaching too far and too soon. In his own mind, Peter worried that if he struck out at this early stage, any future attempts to get into politics inevitably would suffer. Moreover, even if he won the nomination, the provincial conservative party currently was in complete disarray and without any significant financial resources, points that were brought home to him when he attended the annual meeting of the Alberta Progressive Conservative Party in Red Deer on October 26, 1964, and later sought and accepted an invitation to sit in on a meeting of the party's executive. On both occasions, Peter was unimpressed, finding little in either gathering to encourage him.

However, Lougheed's time at the Red Deer PC meetings was not entirely without benefit, for it was there that he first met Lou

Hyndman, former aide-de-camp to Alberta's Lieutenant-Governor, J. Percy Page and, at the time, President of the Progressive Conservative Association of Alberta. At the executive committee meeting in Red Deer's Capri Hotel, the tall, Lincolnesque Hyndman emphasized the importance of long-term planning and organization, and of articulating what the party stood for, as opposed to what it stood against. Lougheed recognized Hyndman as a potential asset to the future development of the party. For his part, Lou later recalled that "Peter impressed me immediately."[65] Despite all the negatives and all the work that would need to be done, Lougheed came away from his Red Deer initiation into conservative party politics with one over-riding realization that both appalled and appealed greatly to him—he would have to build a new conservative party from scratch "without owing anything to anybody."[66] Also in his mind was the additional thought that, whatever their merits, Manning and his Social Credit colleagues were not doing enough to protect Alberta's natural resources—a legacy of his summer in Tulsa, Oklahoma. If he did decide to join the Alberta Tories, it was increasingly clear to him that Baldwin would not contest, but defer to him as a younger and more dynamic leader.

In typical Lougheed fashion, Peter began a systematic charting of challenges, obstacles, initiatives, and possibilities, as he simultaneously canvased friends, colleagues, and others whose capabilities he recognized and respected, about his chances and prospects. Could he count on their support, assistance, and above all else, their loyalty? At home, he and Jeanne discussed their mutual political leanings and inclinations extensively, as well as what they wanted most out of life. After their Mannix experience, both realized that a great advantage of Peter going into provincial politics would be that their home and family life would not be upended as completely as it would be if Peter decided to have a go at federal politics.

Once his mind was made up, Lougheed's general strategy was clear, if not easy to set in motion and maintain. He would need to win the support and leadership of the provincial PCs. He then would need to be elected as an MLA. Finally, he would need to lead his Progressive Conservatives to a victory over the long-incumbent Social Credit Party and the almost mythical Ernest Manning. But his first task, prior to the leadership convention of 1965 would be to meet and mix with as many Albertans as possible. With this in mind, Peter, with loyal friends and colleagues in tow, turned to Lou Hyndman, who offered his support and help. What followed was a typical Peter Lougheed whirlwind of activity.

At the first meeting of his leadership campaign committee on December 10, 1964, Lougheed stressed the importance of winning big, with at least 80 percent of the delegates voting for him on the first ballot. "The party is in such difficulty that we ... can't afford to emerge from the convention with a significant number of dissidents. I have to win in an overwhelming way."[67] For the next three months leading up to the Edmonton leadership convention on March 20, 1965, Lougheed led a life of constant meetings, travel, and appearances in an effort to make personal contact not only with all the leading conservatives in Alberta, but with as many voters as possible. Biographer David Wood, who worked with Peter at Mannix and was one of the architects of subsequent Lougheed campaigns, describes Lougheed's campaigning style as one replete with "charm and grace," admiring "his ability to go through a roomful of supporters, numbering in the hundreds, and remember not only most of their names, but in many cases the spouses' names and some of the areas of mutual interest," a feat that Lougheed "credits to his enjoyment of people."[68] In addition to Wood, other staunch supporters included Merv Leitch, Rod McDaniel, Ron Helmer, Roy Deyell, Ray Milner, Hoadley Mitchell, Peter Macdonnell, Allan "Chip" Collins, and of course, Lou Hyndman—a good mix of Calgarians and Edmontonians who would continue to serve Peter well throughout his political career.

When the leadership convention convened at Edmonton's Macdonald Hotel on March 18, 1965, there were three candidates, one of whom, John Scott, withdrew almost immediately, upon seeing the strength and organization of Lougheed's supporters, all of whom wore small, discrete gold and green buttons, featuring the words: "I'm for Peter." That left only Dunc McKillop, a 29-year-old Calgary lawyer with R. B. Bennett's old Calgary law firm, who was a godson of John Diefenbaker. McKillop apparently regarded his candidacy as a way of getting known, which might pay off in a future nomination convention, once Lougheed was soundly drubbed by Ernest Manning in the next provincial election, as McKillop assumed he would be. Chip Collins, who had worked with Peter at Mannix, "thought that the nominating convention bore all the marks of a well-orchestrated Lougheed meeting."[69]

Lou Hyndman officially nominated Peter, and was seconded by Charles Arthur Clark, editor of the *High River Times,* whose son Joe

Clark, then a Lougheed supporter, had persuaded him to do so to provide a rural balance to Hyndman's urban background. In his speech, Lougheed called on delegates to help him recruit candidates of "distinction, decency, and ability," who "would provide not an opposition, but an alternative"[70] to the incumbent Social Creditors. He also cautioned attendees that the journey they were starting would be "a long tough road."[71] When the votes were counted, Lougheed prevailed, receiving 300 of 330 ballots cast, which when announced caused the ballroom to erupt with celebratory applause and expressions of strong endorsement. Peter subsequently would often joke that, in consideration of what now would be required of him, he received as many condolences as congratulations that night in Edmonton. Nonetheless, the first hurdle in his attempt to establish a political career had been cleared. He was now officially the leader of the Progressive Conservative Party of Alberta. The next task would be to get himself, and hopefully a few others of his rejuvenated party, elected as members of the provincial Legislative Assembly.

To be successful in the next provincial election, Peter Lougheed had a lot of work and learning to do. In May of 1965, he spent time with conservative premiers in Nova Scotia and Manitoba, picking their brains and experience for tactics and strategies of party building. From his interactions with Robert Stanfield in Nova Scotia, Lougheed learned "that the leader of the party has to be the principal organizer and has to work harder than anyone else … the contributions of volunteers will be in direct proportion to the enthusiasm generated by the leader."[72] From Duff Roblin, Premier of Manitoba, Lougheed received excellent advice concerning selecting candidates—don't look for candidates who are "the best Conservatives; look for the best man regardless of his political affiliation. The trick is to identify the candidate who can win."[73] "Leading by doing" and "talent over partisanship" became guiding principles of Peter Lougheed's party building efforts. Both were dictums to which he adhered and both were to serve him well in rebuilding the Progressive Conservative Party of Alberta.

Lougheed's travels and search for ideas and talent during the spring of 1965 also took him to a conference at Mount Tremblant in Quebec, which was organized by the Power Corporation of Canada as a brain storming session for upwardly mobile young Canadians. It was here that he met Pierre Trudeau for the first time. According to biographer Allan Hustak, Lougheed was impressed by Trudeau's cool, objective assessment of the Quiet Revolution taking place in Quebec at that time and his willingness to openly challenge Quebec nationalists and separatists. Trudeau on the other hand recalled that Lougheed "did not leave a particularly memorable impression," a first assessment, or lack thereof, that Prime Minister Trudeau was to have ample reason to revise over the course of the next twenty years.

Throughout the summer of 1965, Lougheed put the finishing touches on his election strategy and got his support team in place. Calgary businessman Ted Mills would be his constituency organizer, Merv Leitch his policy advisor, and Rod McDaniel was to attend to issues of finance. While this was being accomplished, Lougheed also took time to travel to Ottawa to talk strategy with federal Conservative leader John Diefenbaker and several Alberta members of the federal parliament about assisting him to build a provincial organization and working out some guidelines for federal-provincial cooperation and non-interference.

Yet another priority was to establish a communications committee for organizing a media campaign that included advertising slogans and materials. Chairing this committee was Calgary public relations consultant John Francis, who had been at the University of Alberta when Peter was president of the Student Council. Other members included prominent Albertan broadcasters, personalities, and public relations consultants. The overall aim was to create an image of Lougheed as future Premier that would appeal to Albertans—a central component of which was portraying him as dedicated to a practical sense of mission and purpose for the province as a whole, urban and rural. The committee also discussed how to counter possible charges from Social Creditors and others that Lougheed was mostly ambitious for himself and that his "Ivy League" education might offend rural Albertans. Other decisions included under-selling direct mentions of his youth by creating impressions of maturity, which indirectly hinted at a youthful vitality. Similarly, direct appeals to Lougheed's illustrious ancestor Sir James were to be set aside because of worries about appearing too entitled. Instead, the promotional strategy was to present Peter Lougheed as the first Alberta-born Premier to be duly elected by his fellow Albertans, with whom he stood as one of them.

When Peter's first television appearance on CFRN's "Face the Newsmen" was judged less than satisfactory, a television subcommittee was charged with curbing undesirable hand gestures, controlling a slight lisp, and maximizing what nevertheless came across as an occasional, unusually attractive ability to relate to the cameras. Media trail blazer Gordon Love made his CFRN studios and camera crew available to the Lougheed team for grooming their boy—helping him learn to relax and move naturally from camera to camera, modulate his voice to convey sincerity and dedication, and time his comments to the airtime available. In all of this, Jeanne proved to be Peter's best and most trusted guide.

Yet another decision ensured that all the efforts of the Lougheed team and of Peter himself to build their party in Alberta would not be threatened by internal quarrels between provincial and federal conservative factions, as sometimes had happened in the past. Here, the strategy was deceptively simple, yet wonderfully effective. On September 9, in the middle of the federal election campaign of 1965, Peter's team issued the following brief press release: "As provincial leader, Mr. Lougheed does not intend to comment on federal matters except insofar as they affect the provincial administration."[74]

As 1965 turned to 1966, Lougheed's efforts and those of his team were beginning to show clear signs of impact and progress. Contributions to the Progressive Conservative Party of Alberta were up quite dramatically, and newspaper coverage was increasingly positive. At the Party's annual convention on January 28, in the Palliser Hotel ballroom in Calgary, almost a thousand people showed up despite temperatures of minus forty. On that same occasion, Peter Lougheed unveiled a party platform that stressed the importance of supporting local government at the municipal level through "guidance, advice and assistance" rather than "direction, control and restriction in their affairs." He also promised to "protect the individual citizen as much as improving the public good," and stated that his provincial government would "always have a long range plan for future development." Lougheed went on to stress the importance of free enterprise and sound financial management, promised to administer welfare in a way that accorded with human dignity, and pledged to develop Alberta's natural resources for the benefit of all Albertans.

A major challenge facing Lougheed, one that he did not mention explicitly during the January 1966 PC Convention, was how to position himself and his party in relation to a mostly unspoken alliance that had come to exist between Manning's provincial Social Credit Party and Alberta's Conservative members of the Canadian federal parliament. The fact was that most of these Albertan MPs were very happy to have the Socreds in power in Alberta. Things as they stood were working well for them, and they did not like the idea of Lougheed and the provincial Conservatives taking a run at Manning and his MLAs. Over the course of the many years in which Social Credit had ruled the province, Alberta's federal Conservative MPs had built up strong and reliable associations with the provincial Socreds and their voters, such that many Albertans, especially in the rural areas of the province, routinely cast their votes for Social Credit at home and for the Progressive Conservatives in Ottawa. As Lougheed was telling Albertans that the province needed a change, Alberta MPs like Marcel Lambert were reminding members of the Provincial Progressive Conservative Party that "We really depend on those Socred votes to get elected, you know."[75] In light of this reality, Lougheed realized he could not rely on existing understandings and relations between his provincial Conservatives and Alberta's federal Conservatives to build his party. In effect, he had to ignore these ties, establish his provincial organization without the help of Alberta's federal MPs, and recruit people as part of his team who were beholden to neither the provincial Socreds nor the province's federal MPs.

In his speech at the Alberta Progressive Conservative Convention early in 1966, Lougheed had a good deal to say about how he would work with Canada's federal government if he were to be elected as an MLA, especially if his party also was to win the next provincial election. What he said was that "We [the Lougheed Team] believe in a provincial government which gives strong support to the need in Canada for an effective central government. We believe in an Alberta government which recognizes the important role of leadership which can be performed by Alberta in federal-provincial relations."[76] This was a comment that often has been repeated by those who wish to maintain that Peter Lougheed's attitude to Canada's central government and the nature of Alberta's relations to it changed dramatically over the years in which he led the province as its Premier. However, Lougheed himself maintained that he always believed in the necessity of a federal system of governance for Canada, and that the key phrase in his 1966 Convention remarks was "an *effective* central government," which, as the future was to show, meant to him one that would recognize importantly unique needs and circumstances of individual provinces, how they differed one from another, and yet were all vital to a strong and progressive nation.

Newspaper coverage of Lougheed's Convention speech and the Convention overall converged on the opinion that it was an impressive beginning for him and his fledgling party as they prepared for the next provincial election. Yet, despite this promising start,

1966 proved to be an exceptionally difficult and challenging year for Peter Lougheed, both politically and personally.

In what should have been a time of celebration, Peter's election as leader of the Progressive Conservative Party of Alberta immediately created unforeseen problems. Peter's law partners John Ballem and Marvin McDill were unhappy with the new arrangements that saw Peter splitting his time between their law office and his extensive responsibilities in his new role in Alberta politics. Although all three partners had discussed their political ambitions when their firm was founded and agreed that it would be fine to use their law practice as a springboard into politics, the reality of Lougheed's having done so was not welcomed by Ballem and McDill, who now wanted Peter's law firm salary reduced, and the names on their firm's nameplate reordered, so as to reflect what they regarded as their altered degrees of commitment to their practice.

The impact of his partners' reactions on Peter, Jeanne, and their growing family, now including four children (Andrea, Pamela, and Joe had joined Stephen), was significant. Peter's job as leader of the provincial conservatives did not include a salary, family expenditures were rising, and Jeanne, who had been present when the three partners discussed their political ambitions during the formation of their firm, felt upset and betrayed. The partners' timing could not have been worse. Fortunately for all concerned, tensions were eventually resolved, if not forgotten, when Peter accepted a position in the law firm of his former college room mate, and now Alberta Chief Justice, Ken Moore. Ballem and McDill went on to distinguish themselves in the legal profession, with Ballem also becoming a successful novelist of crime fiction. Neither became politicians.

With all of this going on, Lougheed was continuing to organize the Progressive Conservative Party of Alberta in preparation for the next provincial election, including mounting his own campaign for a seat in the Alberta legislature. The week following his demotion at the law firm he had initiated, Peter declared his candidacy for MLA for Calgary West. Shortly thereafter, the Progressive Conservatives of Alberta solved their money problems by launching what become known as the "Lougheed Club," an exclusive invitation to 150 individuals willing to donate a hundred dollars annually to build "a responsible alternative in politics."[77] It took only three months for the Lougheed Club to meet its membership quota.

With travel expenses now defrayed, Lougheed was able to meet and strategize across the country with other conservatives like Premier John Robarts of Ontario and Dalton Camp, the national president of the Progressive Conservatives. From Robarts, Lougheed took to heart the solid advice not to make promises leading up to elections "that you are not prepared to keep if you should ever get elected."[78] In his meetings with Camp, Lougheed took great care to remain neutral in what then was a growing feud between Camp and backers of John Diefenbaker, one that would divide the national Conservative movement during the late 1960s.

Back in Alberta, Lougheed was finding it difficult to produce the wave of "new faces" he had promised in the field of progressive conservative candidates who would vie for all 65 of Alberta's MLA constituency seats in the forthcoming election. At the end of January 1967, only eight conservative candidates, including Peter, had been nominated, despite the best efforts of Lougheed and his supporters, whom Jeanne Lougheed described as "scratching around Alberta like chickens."[79] Even more worrying were the results of a poll undertaken by the Lougheed team to determine how well known Peter himself was among voters, which indicated an unexpected weakness in "name recognition."

Part of the problem seemed to be what also was a major strength of Peter's organizational strategy. Since his first excursions into school and university politics, he had relied on the active support of a number of loyal friends. As biographer and communications expert David Wood put it, "Peter Lougheed has an intense sense of loyalty and team support. ... The longer Peter has known you, tested your mettle, the more warmly you are likely to be regarded."[80] Long-time Lougheed friend, Jim Seymour (himself a former CFL player, with the Calgary Stampeders, who also was a trusted adviser to Peter) commented to Wood that "Lougheed's whole organization consisted of personal friends, people he had come to know either in his youth, or later in business, university, or social activities."[81] Unfortunately, such close ties and friendships sometimes could blind Peter and his core supporters to the views and perceptions of Alberta's voters more generally. Clearly, as the results of the recognition poll told them, they had a great deal of work to do to ready themselves for a future election.

The gravity of this situation hit home in an unexpectedly immediate way when Garth Turcotte, a young, inexperienced, but extraordinarily persistent NDP member of the provincial Legislative

Assembly, who had won a recent by-election only the year before, accused Alfred Hooke, Social Credit Minister of Municipal Affairs, and E. W. Hinman, former Provincial Treasurer, of pursuing personal gain in conflict with their public duties. Turcotte also chided Ernest Manning himself for insinuating wrongdoing on Turcotte's part by raising these matters in the Assembly. Things became so heated that Manning, proud of his impeccable ethics and quick to react to any accusation of impropriety, used the controversy to call a general provincial election for May 23, 1967. Anxious to steal the limelight from Turcotte and the NDP, Lougheed invited Manning to participate in a public, televised debate about how he and his party had handled Turcotte's allegations and related matters—an invitation that Manning immediately refused.

Still struggling to find suitable candidates and now faced with a shorter than anticipated timeline for doing so, the Lougheed team switched strategies. Although still attempting to field as many strong candidates as possible, they went into overdrive in those constituencies where they had secured what they considered to be candidates capable of winning seats as provincial MLAs. In doing so, they enacted several of the "press the flesh" tactics Turcotte and the NDP had employed in winning the Pincher Creek by-election in 1966: knocking on doors, holding local public meetings, and being careful not to appear too "slick." Losing that by-election to Turcotte, the first that he had faced as leader of the provincial Progressive Conservatives, had been a blow to Lougheed, who never took defeats lightly or failed to learn from them.

Lougheed's accelerated preparations for the forthcoming provincial election received a much welcome boost when the well-known and respected Dr. Hugh Horner announced he would be leaving national politics to stand for election as one of Lougheed's provincial conservative candidates. Horner's popularity in rural parts of Alberta was especially important in giving Lougheed's conservatives credibility in those areas. None of this worried Manning, who, confident of another landslide victory for his Social Creditors, spent time in Montreal, appearing at and celebrating Canada's Expo '67, a major centennial event that was receiving much greater public attention than the Alberta election.

With Horner joining his team, Lougheed was able to attract additional candidates of obvious quality, such as former CFL star and future Premier of Alberta, Don Getty, Calgary alderman and patron of the arts, Dave Russell, CRA tax assessor and reformed alcoholic, Len Werry, future Prime Minister of Canada, Joe Clark, and many others. Lougheed and his growing team of candidates received greater attention when Peter Herrndorf of CBC television in Edmonton produced an hour-long special that included footage shot by a five-person production crew who had joined Lougheed's campaign entourage. The program featured Lougheed's youthful vitality and solid career accomplishments in ways that generally enhanced his personal and political status as someone to be reckoned with. Peter received a further boost when Toronto's *Globe and Mail* predicted that his conservatives would elect a "corporal's guard" that would "assert the kind of pressure in the legislature that might be turned into a government next time 'round.'"[82] When Lougheed unveiled a

"Blueprint for the '70s," promising the provincial treasury's 600 million dollar surplus be used to increase and strengthen provincial services without raising taxes, the media again paid close attention.

In the build-up to the election, and still struggling to field a full slate of 65 candidates, Lougheed insisted that those candidates who were actively campaigning adopt his own version of the "touch the flesh" strategy that saw him and them jog or walk quickly from house to house in their constituencies, shaking hands in the wake of an advance guard who rang doorbells and announced the candidates and one or two highlights from their campaign slogans and promises. Here, Peter's habits of early morning exercise (jogging, walking, cross-country skiing) and moderation in general proved especially advantageous.

Yet another media-hyped spur to Lougheed's campaign was an all-party candidates debate at Edmonton's United Church on the evening of May 16, a week before the election. With Premier Manning fighting laryngitis, Lougheed stole the show, receiving loud and sustained applause when he remarked that "The difference between Conservatives and Liberals is that we believe that something that is needed to be done, needs to be done by the voluntary efforts of the citizens, not by the actions of a bureaucratic authority;" the difference between Conservatives and Social Credit is that "we believe the first responsibility of the MLA is to the constituent not to the party." Dave King, a party worker for Lougheed, summed the evening up rather nicely by saying: tonight saw "a marginal Anglican trouncing an evangelical Minister in a United Church."[83]

Lougheed's demeanour and strategy throughout the election campaign seldom varied. He worked hard with his team to ensure that as much of their planning as possible translated directly into the execution and results intended. He made sure to emphasize what he regarded as important differences between him and his candidates compared to those of the other party leaders and their slates of candidates. He continuously repeated the refrain that "Alberta Needs an Alternative," adding "Let's Start It in Calgary West." Such an approach was geared not to offend, and hopefully to attract, Albertans who had a strong admiration for Manning, but who also realized that he and his party had been in power for a long time and perhaps felt that a little competition from a stronger opposition party might lead to better governance over all. Throughout the campaign, Lougheed showed respect for Manning without deferring to him. As Ron Wood noted: "As far as a fresh new approach was concerned, Lougheed by nature did not like and never indulged in the old-style politics of verbally tearing down his opponents ... [in fact] he rarely mentions them by name."[84]

Of course, as expected, Manning and his Social Credit Party were reelected by a wide margin on May 23, 1967. However, with six Conservatives elected, including himself, Peter Lougheed was now not only the MLA for Calgary West, but also the official leader of the opposition in the Alberta Legislature. He had won Calgary West with 62% of the popular vote, one of the largest margins of victory in the province. The other Conservative victories by Hugh Horner, Don Getty, Lou Hyndman, Dave Russell, and Len Werry were also clear and solid wins. And the Conservatives had polled 26% of the overall votes cast in the province, surpassing any other party but the Socreds. Also important, "Peter Lougheed, starting from scratch, had shaped and built, his own provincial party without incurring any political debts to the federal PCs. ... He convinced a lot of skeptics that there could be and would be a viable alternative"[85] to the long reign of Social Credit in the province of Alberta. Lougheed's political career had been launched and he had every intention of making it count.

As they prepared for their future lives as officially elected representatives of their federal and provincial constituencies—the federal riding of Mount Royal for Trudeau and the provincial riding of Calgary West for Lougheed—both men had good reason to be confident about their futures. Importantly, given their characters and personal preferences, both had secured their political foot-holds more or less on their own terms, without significant debts owed to backers with whom they might have felt it necessary to make deals or compromise their principles. Yes, Trudeau was indebted personally to Jean Marchand and both men were indebted personally to those who had supported their campaigns and campaigned with them, but such ties are necessarily part of any campaign or major public undertaking. That neither Peter nor Pierre had compromised or camouflaged their essential personal and political views and styles was important. For two such highly competitive individuals with clear views about what they wanted to accomplish, any such compromises or constraints at this stage of the game would have been intolerable.

Trudeau's political mission was focused on his concerns for Quebec's wellbeing as an integral, vital, and progressive member of the Canadian federation of provinces. For him, such a status only could be achieved with the support of a strong central government capable of defending its legitimate rights and expectations without giving any ground to those who wished to destroy the very ideas of federal and provincial governance on which Quebec as part of Canada exists as a free, modern, and democratic society, recognized as such by the Government of Canada and the other provinces.

Lougheed's political mission was focused on his concerns for Alberta's wellbeing, as an integral, vital, and progressive member of the Canadian federation. For him, such a result could best be achieved by a loosening of controls by the Government of Canada on Alberta's rights to develop its natural and human resources in ways that best serve the people of Alberta now and into the future—a goal he understood as entirely compatible with the best interests of Canada's other provinces, who should have similar rights to develop their own resources for both themselves and the rest of the nation.

Trudeau's and Lougheed's visions of Canada and of relations between its federal government and the governments of its provinces proved to be exceptionally stable, persisting throughout the subsequent political careers of both men, and coming together in their vigorous exchanges and battles over natural resources and constitutional powers in the early 1980s. But before these memorable events, much happened during the final years of the 1960s and the decade of the 1970s as our protagonists took control of the Government of Canada and Government of Alberta. It is to these years in the political careers of Pierre Trudeau and Peter Lougheed that we now turn.

Chapter Four: Pierre Trudeau's Political Career
Before 1980

Beginning in 1968 and for seventeen years following his selection as leader of the Liberal Party and subsequent election as Prime Minister of Canada (with only a brief eight month interruption in 1979), Pierre Elliott Trudeau dominated Canadian politics. He became the third longest serving Prime Minister in Canadian history, behind William Lyon Mackenzie King and John A. Macdonald. During his time as PM, the tone and style of Trudeau's leadership changed subtly in ways that reflected his personal and public circumstances, his political manoeuvring, and his ambitions for the country. Nonetheless, during this entire time, his basic political philosophy and goals remained surprisingly consistent and focused.

Peter Lougheed's reign as Premier of Alberta from 1970 to 1985 was no less remarkable for the consistency with which Lougheed maintained and pursued his vision for Alberta within the Canadian federation, and even more remarkable for the success he had in transforming Alberta's politics, economics, and culture. Widely recognized as the best Canadian Premier of the second half of the twentieth century, Lougheed was mostly freed from the political ups and downs that marked Trudeau's Prime Ministership. In fact, the most challenging and vexing experiences that confronted Lougheed were courtesy of Pierre Trudeau's preoccupation with maintaining a strongly centralized federal government. Lougheed had his own vision for Canada, one that ceded more powers and control over their natural and human resources to the provinces.

Both men were deeply committed to Canada as a nation and federation, as understood within their respective visions of how it and its people might best be served. Peter Lougheed's vision for Canada was more pragmatic; Pierre Trudeau's was more intellectual; both visions were equally unshakeable. In this chapter and the next, the early and middle years of the political careers of Pierre Trudeau and Peter Lougheed are examined in ways intended to clarify their personalities, leadership styles, and political positions, especially those related to the division of federal and provincial powers and those regarding non-renewable natural resources—positions that would eventually lead to their epic clashes over oil and the constitution during the early 1980s.

Fuelling the perception of him as immaturely whimsical and dilettantish, even at the age of 46, once elected as a Liberal MP in 1965, Trudeau immediately headed off on a European ski trip "as though to affirm that his life had not changed much; he was as fancy-free as ever."[1] While he was still in Europe at the turn of the New Year, Prime Minister Lester Pearson telephoned him to ask if he would serve as his parliamentary secretary. When Trudeau "tried to duck the honour and the responsibility, Jean Marchand [insisted] that Pierre grow up and take the job," abruptly dismissing "Trudeau's explanation that he was going to Ottawa not in pursuit of power but because he wanted a platform for his ideas."[2] Fortunately for him and his supporters, this time Trudeau did not need to be told twice to mend his ways. He promptly returned to Canada and threw himself with gusto into his new position as Pearson's parliamentary secretary. Having done so, he discovered that he finally had made the right decision to enter an arena where he could excel and meet his own expectations. Madeleine Gobeil wrote to him that she was "quite glad that you are engrossed in politics now; and not ... returned to a way of life that you must admit was something of a dead end ... With hugs, even if you are in the Liberal Party."[3]

George Radwanski interprets the indecisiveness and unwillingness that Trudeau displayed in the first half of the 1960s to a "fear of real responsibility" and a "determination not to allow himself to be locked into any one option until he had completed his process of self-training," a process that "appears to have extended right up to his election to Parliament in 1965."[4] Radwanski, perhaps somewhat romantically, argues that "Trudeau is that rarity among politicians, a leader who did not crave power but rather tried consistently and genuinely to avoid it," going on to add that "His enjoyment of his office and its power is not the triumph of a man who has successfully captured a long-sought prize, but the surprised delight of one who finds himself revelling in something he hadn't really wanted."[5] To explain this view, Radwanski continues:

> Though his training and his general intellectual interests seemed to point him toward a political life, Trudeau's personal inclinations made him a most unlikely politician. From earliest youth, his preoccupation with his freedom made him shy away from any leadership role; to be a leader is to sacrifice some measure of solitude, and that, not surprisingly, held no appeal for someone who had identified, even in childhood with Cyrano's "to climb not

very high, perhaps, but all alone." ... Though he had many of the attributes of a natural leader—strength of will, force of personality, superior intellect, audacity, and the indefinable quality that commands the confidence of others—his disinclination was so obvious that none of his associates in the 1950s and early 1960s could envisage him in a leadership role.[6]

Contrary to later biographers like John English and Max and Monique Nemni, Radwanski concludes that "There was ... no stage of Trudeau's life before the 1960s when he seriously entertained the idea of going into active politics," quoting Trudeau himself as saying (in his typically evasive and noncommittal way), "I can't honestly say what I thought in my early teens or in my first ten years, because sometimes I will meet some very aged friend of my mother's or some distant aunt who will say, 'We said you'd be prime minister some day, and you said you would, too' ... but it certainly wasn't one of my motivating ideas in any relevant part of my formative years."[7] English and the Nemnis, with access to Trudeau's personal papers and archival materials unavailable to Radwanski, beg to differ.

That being as it may, once he accepted Pearson's invitation to be his parliamentary secretary, Trudeau was quite happy to use his new position as a platform from which he could announce his constitutional views and express his frustrations and concerns about what was happening in Quebec. In caucus, he lectured his colleagues on political and economic theory and their "application to the problems of the day ... quickly emerging as an intellectual leader of the caucus." At the same time, Marchand and Pelletier "concentrated on wresting complete control of the Quebec caucus from the party's Old Guard." Within half a year of their election as federal liberal MPs, "the three wise men" (or in Quebec, "the three doves") had control of "the Quebec wing of the federal Liberal Party, established in response to the Lesage administration's insistence that the federal and provincial Liberals split into distinct organizations." "With Trudeau leading the attack in the role of constitutional expert, they beat back all talk of special status for Quebec or massive constitutional change" and adopted positions that "Trudeau had been preaching in his writings for more than a decade."[8]

However, on June 5, 1966, the Lesage government in Quebec was defeated by a reinvigorated Union Nationale party led by Daniel Johnson, heightening the fears of Trudeau, Lalonde, Pearson advisor Michael Pitfield, and others of a much more severe and immediate nationalist and separatist threat. Johnson had campaigned on a promise to make Quebec a truly national state, with direct international ties to France and other French-speaking nations. In his acceptance speech, the new Premier pointedly remarked that his party had won 63 percent of the French vote in Quebec. The response of the federal government, spearheaded by Marchand and Trudeau, was a firm rejection of any special status for Quebec and any opting out of existing constitutional and intergovernmental arrangements by the Johnson provincial government.

Much impressed, Pearson appointed Trudeau federal Minister of Justice for Canada on April 4, 1967. To many, Trudeau seemed to jump on this opportunity with relish and dove into his new job with unfeigned delight, energy, and persistence. Even then, Radwanski maintained that "Trudeau had not leaped on [such] promotions as steps up the political ladder. On the contrary, he had resisted each time, still reluctant to accept direct responsibilities and the accompanying limitation on his freedom."[9] By December 1967, Trudeau had proposed criminal code amendments that decriminalized homosexuality, contraception, and abortion (under particular conditions), eased and modernized divorce proceedings, and had veered into constitutional matters by proposing, on his own initiative, the "entrenching of a bill of rights, binding on both the federal and the provincial governments, in the constitution," which "in turn would lead naturally to other changes, including the finding of a formula for amending and patriating of the British North America Act." It seemed as if Trudeau was "succeeding in bringing the whole Pearson government around to his own constitutional theories."[10] With Quebec and the Canadian Constitution once again dominating the political landscape in Canada and the New Democratic Party beginning to eat away at Liberal support in western Canada, Pearson's new Minister of Justice, recognized as an outstanding constitutional specialist and as a left-leaning liberal with growing appeal to English Canadians, found himself well positioned to be a pivotal force within the national government.

Trudeau also had become the darling of the Canadian parliamentary press corps, who jumped on every opportunity to recycle his deeds and words in ways that captured the imagination of many members of the Canadian public. With his uttering of "There's no place for the state in the bedrooms of the nation" and other "Trudeau-isms" (even if sometimes cribbed from other sources), he was branded by the media as a gifted phrasemaker and cool, charismatic customer with superb command of facts, eloquent arguments, and the best interests of the nation at heart. Praise from the English-language press intensified when Trudeau rallied the Pearson government to issue a strong rebuke (which he drafted) to Charles de Gaulle when, during a July 1967 visit, the French President called for a free Quebec ("Vive le Québec libre") before an enthusiastic crowd from the balcony of Montreal's Hôtel de Ville. Media gurus Peter Gzowski and Marshall McLuhan extolled Trudeau's brilliance, toughness, good looks, and athleticism, and other journalists and pundits like Peter Newman, Pierre Berton, and Norman DePoe joined in. With a federal election called for 1968 and Canada's centennial year of 1967 running out, Lester Pearson resigned as Prime Minister due to the sad fact of his failing health. It seemed like the gods themselves had finally succumbed to the preternatural charms of Pierre Elliott Trudeau. As Nino Ricci wrote, it began to look like Trudeau was ordained to lead both the "'backward' province [Quebec] and the rest of Canada out of the Dark Ages."[11]

If Trudeau's ascendency needed any further boosting, Pearson announced that his successor as leader of the Liberal party should be a French Canadian, thereby respecting a long-standing tradition of alternating English and French leaders of the Liberal Party of Canada. Marchand was the obvious candidate, but his English was not good and his close ties to unionized labour were seen as a weakness by many of his colleagues in the party. Trudeau, on the other hand, clearly was a man who fit the social and political times, which seemed to call for someone favouring a strong central government, who could function and communicate fluently in both official languages, and was just enough left of the political centre to contrast well with the Tories and to steal support from the NDP. With Expo 67 having given the country a new "cool" image, Trudeau's carefully constructed self-presentation fit the bill nicely. As John English put it:

> Trudeau ... was attracting increasing attention, which he shrewdly did not exploit. The plan he had developed in the late 1930s, when he first determined he wanted a public and political life, remained in place. He would cloak himself in mystery and be the friend of all and the intimate of none. ... the extraordinary discipline he revealed in bringing the Criminal Code legislation forward while simultaneously acting as the federal leader on constitutional matters dispelled most of the criticism about the swinging playboy who had never worked.[12]

Nonetheless, the swinging playboy image was far from anathema to many younger Canadians during the 1960s, and the now more politically serious Trudeau seemed more than capable of maintaining his reputation as a ladies' man. Madeleine Gobeil, teaching at Carlton University was a frequent Ottawa companion, introducing him to Sartre and de Beauvoir, and to his first glimpse of the James Bond movies he came to love. When in Europe, Trudeau spent a great deal of time with Carroll Guérin, domiciled primarily in Britain. Carroll, who shared a penchant for psychology with several other Trudeau paramours, had made unlocking Trudeau's emotionality a project. She retained a deep affection for him even after he had stood her up in Corsica in the summer of 1967 by failing to appear for a prearranged meeting at the Bonaparte Hotel, without any forewarning or explanatory message. So there probably was no need for him to feel too badly about being stood up in turn by the young Margaret Sinclair, who on a Christmas vacation to Tahiti with her family that same year, had agreed to meet Trudeau to go deep-sea fishing, but in the end had preferred to spend the time instead with a young waterskiing instructor.

As it unfolded, the new year of 1968 saw the Liberals gaining in Gallup Poll numbers on the Conservatives, who earlier had received a boost from their new Nova Scotian leader Robert Stanfield. Even though he knew that Marc Lalonde had spent his Christmas vacation organizing a potential Trudeau candidacy, Trudeau himself remained coy about his prospects. Marchand repeatedly told Trudeau that he had no wish to contest the Party leadership, and that Trudeau had a very good chance of winning it. Still Trudeau hesitated. He wanted to continue as Justice Minister on a planned tour to meet the provincial premiers and discuss constitutional matters, a tour that would need to be cancelled if he declared himself as a candidate for leading the Liberal party. As it turned out, a throng of reporters who suspected a possible candidacy bid from Trudeau followed and reported his every move on that tour—a tour that was full of highlights and was unexpectedly successful. With Trudeau introducing himself in person to the country's premiers, Marc Lalonde revved up his committee to elect Trudeau. But Trudeau still did not want to "go public" with his candidacy, at least until he had the opportunity of challenging Daniel Johnson at the constitutional conference of February 5-7, 1968 in Ottawa.

This conference turned out to be another bonanza for Trudeau's popularity in English Canada. Initially worried about the intensity of the exchanges between Johnson and Trudeau, members of Lalonde's candidacy team were galvanized into action when it became clear that the effects of their champion's words on English Canadians, tired of what they worried were tepid and ineffective federal responses to Quebec's threats to separate, were electric. Throughout the run-up to declaring his candidacy for the Liberal leadership, Trudeau entered into "the kind of cat-and-mouse game he was so good at, growing more deferential and coy the more people insisted."[13] By this time, Marchand had convinced Pearson to back Trudeau as his successor. It probably also helped that Pearson's wife Maryon was initially smitten by Trudeau. Nonetheless, Pierre continued to play the part of the reluctant bride, a strategy of deferral that potentially would allow him to "walk away at any moment with no loss of face" and yet ensured that he would be "plied with inducements"[14] and further assistance. Much of Trudeau's seemingly instant charm and quickness with "sound bites" also was carefully planned, something he had been rehearsing for years, as he honed his identity, style, and presentation. "The self-consciousness, the presumed audience was always there." The spontaneous flair, quick wit, and performance art were well practiced during a life in which "self-revelation and self-concealment were so interwoven."[15] And the practice paid off. With Marchand's and Lalonde's assistance and the influence of Pearson himself, Trudeaumania had been launched.

In his memoir, Trudeau recalls that throughout his candidacy for leader of the federal Liberal Party of Canada, he was beset by concerns about "protecting my sacrosanct personal freedom," seeking this "highest office after barely two years in Parliament and nine months in Cabinet," and without long and "deep roots in the Liberal Party."[16] Nonetheless, on February 16, 1968, Trudeau finally declared himself (the last to do so) as a candidate for the liberal leadership at the National Press Club in Ottawa, joking with the press that they "had a lot to do with it" and that if there was anyone to blame or thank "it's you collectively," so "now you're stuck with me."[17]. And stick with him they did, not only for the Liberal leadership race, but for the duration of Trudeaumania, until his election as Prime Minister of Canada on June 25, 1968.

But first, there was the leadership election at the Liberal convention of April 6, 1968. At Ottawa's Civic Centre, it took four ballots, with Trudeau leading the pack on all of them, before he acquired the number of votes necessary to ensure his election as Liberal Party leader. After the leadership convention and a Florida break with Marchand and others, Trudeau met with members of Pearson's cabinet on April 17, two days before Pearson formally resigned as Prime Minister and three days before Trudeau, as the new Prime Minister, announced his own cabinet. Another three days after that, on April 23, Trudeau declared in the House of Commons that a federal election would be held on June 25, 1968, and then dissolved the current session of the House.

On the election trail, Trudeau's love-in with much of the Canadian public continued, although the constantly repetitive grind of airports, motorcades, events, and rallies began to bore Pierre. Nonetheless, he mostly maintained his quick retorts, calmly cool presence, and occasionally mixed in an expert jackknife dive into a hotel pool or a few kisses with his adoring female fans, causing Globe and Mail columnist George Bain to comment, "If it puckers, he's there."[18] But despite such caustic comments by those not amused with his electioneering antics, Trudeau's popularity with much of the public peaked during the election campaign, causing his previously skeptical sister Suzette to exclaim to a friend, "My goodness, Pierre is like a Beatle."[19] Marshall McLuhan, renowned Canadian media and communication theorist, declared Trudeau a perfect fit for TV and instant news.

In the end, Pierre Trudeau was able to keep himself in the spotlight and much of the Canadian public in an anticipatory frenzy during the leadership race and throughout the federal election campaign of 1968. Finally, in his late forties, Pierre Elliott Trudeau found himself in the position he had imagined and was now ready to embrace—that of duly elected Prime Minister of Canada. Under their new leader, the Liberals had won a majority government, electing 154 MPs, compared to 72 Conservative MPs (who with their leader Robert Stanfield formed the official opposition), 22 NDP MPs, and 16 others.

Exactly how Trudeau managed his sudden rise to the pinnacle of Canadian political life, has struck many as difficult to determine. Nino Ricci nicely sums up such uncertainty:

[I]t is hard to sort out what was cunning on Trudeau's part
and what was luck, what was people imagining in Trudeau

what they wanted to see and what was really there. Given all the behind-the-scenes machinations that went into placing Trudeau just so in the spotlight, the idea that he simply burst on the scene out of nowhere through the sheer force of his charisma doesn't hold up. But neither does the argument that he had been calculating his rise from the start. … Whatever strategy there may have been in his oft-repeated habit of playing the reluctant bride, what made it effective was that Trudeau was clearly bloody-minded enough to walk away from the prize without regrets if he couldn't get it on his own terms. He had to be cajoled; he had to be convinced; he had to be kept on the path. Without a Marchand next to him, goading him on or a Pearson or a Norman DePoe, he might simply have strapped on his skis and hit the slopes."[20]

Perhaps so, but now that he had been elected, Trudeau would demonstrate a resilience that belied whatever masking of his true intentions might have been at play during his rise to power.

Trudeau's first term as PM (1968-1972) might be considered as one of the most experimental periods in the history of Canadian politics. Once elected, he strove to modernize the office of the Prime Minister, and the Canadian Government more generally, by adopting more rationally systematic standards of decision-making, policy determination, and implementation. He also attempted to apply a methodical strategy to his own term of office—one in which he would come to grips with the job, refine his plans, and overhaul the machinery of governance in his first year, prepare and introduce legislation consistent with his political and personal theories and plans during years two and three, and evaluate and use the hoped-for success of his and his government's efforts as a basis for re-election in the last year. At least this was the plan, but like many a professor's lecture, things don't always go as they are supposed to go.

Trudeau began by creating a large number of task forces to review and improve almost all facets of the government's operations. The assumption was that one needed to know what was going on and what was going well and poorly before attempting to introduce and legislate changes and prospective policies discussed during the election. Unfortunately, this careful, slow way of proceeding struck many voters as deeply at odds with the excitement and promise of Trudeau's campaign. The first throne speech of the new Liberal government was far from the call to action expected by progressive Canadians who had thrilled to the excitement of the chase. What they now were given seemed like a dull, bureaucratic primer that conveyed the overall message that they must temper their expectations in recognition of fiscal, procedural, and political realities that necessitated a tepid pace of prudent deliberation and implementation. Unlike the Trudeau of the campaign trail, Prime Minister Trudeau made it clear that he regarded his actual job as not one of looking and sounding good, but one of getting down to the business of governing with solid, well-calibrated legislation and forward-looking policies that must be carefully and critically considered and vetted. Bye-bye rock-star, hello professor! Inevitably, the rational, academic, and deliberate side of Trudeau ran afoul of the public's low tolerance for rationality alone. Where he had campaigned in an entertaining, charismatic way to which many voters responded emotionally, he now seemed to insist on governing in a seriously, straight-laced manner, with an emotionless *sang froid* that surprised and disturbed these same voters.

It quickly became apparent that Trudeau had overestimated the public's tolerance for what it regarded as tedious grunt work. At the rate public disaffection was mounting, it was going to require some pretty impressive accomplishments and nimble campaign footwork to regain anything resembling Trudeaumania by the time the next election drew near. The truth was that Trudeau had miscalculated not only because of his penchant for intellectual rationalism, but also because he found the federal fiscal cupboards surprisingly bare. Pearson's social programs were proving to be much more costly than imagined, making it extremely difficult for Trudeau to keep them going, let alone to take on the additional expenditures his anticipated reforms would require. In the meantime, inflation was running away with funds required for existing health and education spending. Although Trudeau had warned, on the campaign trail, that he would not govern as Santa Claus, many of his more enthusiastic supporters did not expect Scrooge to appear in Santa's stead.

The fact that his first round of reforms, once his task forces had reported, was devoted to such behind-the-scenes activities as strengthening committee systems to permit more efficient and informed deliberation, did not make for good headlines or television. All in all, by the end of 1968, Mr. Charisma had become Mr.

Disappointment—unexciting, business-like, and plodding. His occasional offhanded bluntness, mixed with bursts of jovial impishness, suddenly seemed more likely to give offense and betray arrogance than to attract admiration and affection. Many Canadians felt that they had been had.

Worse still, Stanfield's conservatives, previously thought to be a comparatively stodgy bunch, were proving adept at poking the Trudeau bear. When Trudeau accused them of being stupid and hypocritical by engaging in time-wasting filibusters, they immediately countered with chants of "Heil Hitler." In truth, Trudeau had been guilty of romanticizing parliament as a high-minded forum of reflection and deeply probative debate—serious legislators working together to consider the merits and demerits of possible ways of proceeding. When his ideal was nowhere in sight, he often displayed the worst of his unique combination of professorial and pugilistic personas. The results were not constructive. His opposition "victims," for whom the sometimes juvenilia of parliamentary exchange was merely a kind of game, "sensing that his contempt is more genuine and deeply felt than theirs, are outraged, but he cannot understand the distinction."[21]

Despite eventually bringing in a number of major policy initiatives (opening negotiations with China, passing the Official Languages Act, establishing a Department of Regional Economic Expansion, and attempting to engage directly with the Canadian public by holding numerous town hall meetings and issuing a variety of white papers as invitations to open discussion prior to introducing legislation), Trudeau continued to be perceived as coldly arrogant and was increasingly cast as anti-democratic. The "just society" he had promised on the campaign trail had created expectations of a noteworthy attack on poverty and related social justice initiatives that might spread the national wealth more equally across the citizens of the nation. However, having little fiscal room to manoeuvre, Trudeau's compromised measures, such as increasing Family Allowance payments to the poor at the expense of the middle class, did little to appease the growing public disappointment. His attempts to combat inflation and unemployment seemed only to make these matters worse.

Eventually, Trudeau decided to allow high unemployment as a means of fighting inflation. As the election of 1972 approached, the Liberal government found itself facing whopping cost overruns for unemployment insurance that created even more widespread fiscal pain. Both the Conservative opposition and the New Democrats trumpeted the government's fiscal incompetence. Focused on his efforts at rationalizing political procedures and comportment, and stunned by the ways things were turning out, Trudeau seemed to do little to position the Liberal team for the 1972 federal election, the results of which proved quite predictable. In fact, things might well have turned out far worse for Trudeau and his party than they actually did.

The fact that the Liberals suffered a loss of their majority rather than an outright defeat in 1972 perhaps reflected considerable pubic support for what he and his government eventually did manage to accomplish during their first term. Despite Trudeau's miscalculations and unexpected style of governing, his first term as Prime Minister saw raises to the old age pension and guaranteed income supplement, the launching of a much needed Law Reform Commission to keep the country's legal system and practices abreast of societal change, and a well-executed and effective response to American President Richard Nixon's protectionist economic measures of 1971. Moreover, Trudeau had managed to take firm control of his own party and the reins of national governance. He also was gradually learning to absorb and reshape public perceptions to accord with his own sentiments and scenarios. Love him or hate him, Trudeau was not a prime minister who could be ignored. Perhaps the most positive thing that could be said about his first term in office is that he had begun to make government and its practices matter to a greater number of Canadians.

In his analysis of Trudeau's first term as PM, George Radwanski concluded that Trudeau's biggest error was to surround himself "with advisors who were intellectually formidable but politically inept and naïve" and whose advice "isolated" him "from an adequate understanding of what was happening to [the public's] view of him." "The dark side of Trudeau's view of himself as a political teacher was that he too often came across as the sort of teacher almost everyone remembers having had and hated at some point."[22] His Platonic attitudes and values were proving a hard sell to his Canadian contemporaries.

And then of course, there was the October Crisis of 1970 that saw Trudeau invoke the War Measures Act that temporarily turned Canada and especially Quebec into a police state, replete with thousands of troops and tanks patrolling the streets of Montreal. Within a year of John Lennon rhapsodizing that "If all politicians were like Pierre Trudeau, there would be world peace,"[23] this was Trudeau's response to the kidnappings of British diplomat James Cross and Pierre Laporte, his former schoolmate and Quebec's Minister of Labour, and the subsequent murder of Laporte by the radical separatist Front de liberation du Québec (FLQ). To make things even more personal for Trudeau, one of the FLQ leaders was Pierre Vallières, who had worked with Trudeau at *Cité libre* in the early 1960s. By this time, the FLQ had figured in six deaths and hundreds of bombings in Quebec.

If there ever was any doubt about Pierre Trudeau's strong belief in the rule of law as a foundation for a democratic society, it was dispelled by the famous exchange between him and CBC journalist Tim Ralfe, eight days into the crisis. In response to Ralfe asking him about the military presence on Ottawa's Parliamentary Hill, Trudeau, in his characteristically sardonic and shrugging way, replied: "There's a lot of bleeding hearts around who just don't like to see people with helmets and guns. All I can say is go on and bleed. It's more important to keep law and order in this society than to be worried about weak-kneed people who don't like the looks of a soldier's helmet." When Ralfe continued with "At any cost? How far would you go with that? How far would you extend that"? Trudeau declaimed "Well, just watch me,"[24] and as usual the country did.

At the time, Trudeau's handling of the FLQ crisis restored some of the public's confidence in him and his government. It was only later that reports of police abuses and excesses caused many to reassess their views, and Trudeau's star began to wane once more, especially in Quebec, and especially amongst its intellectuals, journalists, and political leaders. It also became clear that Trudeau initially had "been against the act, not trusting that the information coming from police and from the provincial government was reliable"[25] and that "he anguished in private as a democrat about suppressing civil liberties in favour of military action."[26] Nonetheless, after doing so and when talking to reporters, he acted "as though he were playing yet another 'I'm superior to you guys' game."[27] Still, public reaction to Trudeau in the immediate aftermath of the Quebec Crisis of October 1970 was overwhelmingly positive, especially in English Canada. However, his government's continuing financial woes, his frustration with the fickleness of the Canadian electorate, and his recent marriage and the birth of his first son on December 25, 1971, kept Trudeau from building on the bump of popularity that his handling of the FLQ temporarily created. Just when things looked like they might take a sharp turn in his favour, life intervened.

As Trudeau prepared to seek a second term in office at the beginning of 1972, it was clear, whatever his successes and missteps of the past four years, that his preoccupation with his Prime Ministerial and personal responsibilities had caused him to neglect the nurturing of the grass roots of the Liberal Party itself. He had gained control of his government but had failed to harness the morale and political power of ordinary liberals and party members across the country. The fact that some of his closest advisors and members of Cabinet realized this lapse when Trudeau himself did not was clear when he read out a campaign statement, which was immediately denounced by leading members of his government. Both Finance Minister John Turner and Trudeau's mentor Jean Marchand decried the campaign plan as being "too much of a 'you never had it so good' declaration"[28]

Without agreement about how they would present themselves to the public in the 1972 election, the Liberal Cabinet decided to compromise. "The campaign theme 'The Land is Strong' would not be announced as such but would simply be allowed to develop in the course of speeches. And develop it did, quickly but disastrously. For the Liberals in 1972, the land was weak."[29] In the end, and only after a recount in one constituency that saw the Liberals prevail by a mere four votes, a slim Liberal minority government was elected. Just two seats now separated the Liberals from Robert Stanfield's Progressive Conservatives.

Trudeau always hated to lose, but at no point did he consider stepping down as party leader and Prime Minister. He immediately told his party he would not resign, a decision applauded by the majority of Liberal MPs and Cabinet ministers. And, sure enough, when the first Liberal government caucus meeting following the election was held on November 8, 1972, Trudeau was once again in full control. "His eyes coldly penetrating, his focus clear, his determination striking, he rallied his forces for the future war."[30]

Trudeau now realized that his approach to governing during his first term in office had been "too cerebral. Politics can't be conducted at such a rational level, devoid of all emotion. The voters wanted a leader to guide them, and I was giving them a professor."[31] Having realized his basic mistake, Pierre Trudeau was anxious to make amends and prove his mettle. As his pride and combativeness kicked into high gear, he found himself "mentally rolling up my sleeves; I felt charged with the spirit of combat that had eluded me throughout the election campaign."[32] "I was entitled to form the government, and I drove up to the Governor General's residence full of confidence, dressed in a Native buckskin jacket and driving a sports car, to show that we were treating the results, not as a defeat but as a challenge, and there was no question in my mind of giving up."[33]

Trudeau's push for redemption and self-rescue was carefully planned on several fronts. He would not change his basic policies and goals but would alter his tactics and priorities in recognition of the realization that politics was more irrational and a rougher sport than he had assumed. He vowed to be more impassioned and less subtle. He also realized he had to change his approach to and dealings with the Liberal Party itself, especially its rank and file membership. To this end, he asked for the help of veteran Liberal strategist Keith Davey, which itself signalled to the Party's establishment that he was willing to play ball with them.

Together, Trudeau and Davey moved to schedule small group meetings with active Liberals across the country. Trudeau's solitary lunches were replaced by lunch-hour meetings with individual and groups of Liberal MPs, which allowed him to listen and better understand local circumstances and concerns at the constituency level. Another purpose of such meetings was to encourage Liberals to respond to criticism of the government "by saying: 'That isn't true. I talked to the PM and he told me."[34] Trudeau also initiated and followed up on correspondence with Liberal MPs and party members, asking for regular updates and comments. He insisted that all his ministers consult with every riding in their area of responsibility every two months, and do so in person every six months. Detailed reports of such meetings were to be sent directly to, and discussed at subsequent one-on-one meetings with, Trudeau himself. Apparently Pierre learned to relish these meetings and was soon playing a hardball game of internal accountability politics that was balanced by a more upbeat, team-building persona in public venues.

Other changes were targeted at handling opposition parties on both the right and the left, so as to protect his minority government and rebuild his popularity with the general public. Trudeau also made it known that he would not regard any House of Commons defeat as a loss of confidence. Instead he proposed that members of the House must declare any motion advanced as a matter of confidence, thus placing the burden of initiating any non-confidence procedure directly on the opposition parties. Should any such motions be forthcoming and successfully passed, rather than turning control over to any other party or combination of parties, he would dissolve Parliament and call another election. He further boxed in the other parties by reserving the right for the Liberals unilaterally to declare, as a matter of principle, any motion made in the House a vote of non-confidence, but only after it had been made.

With these booby-traps in place, Trudeau could devote more time to convincing Canadians that he was genuinely repentant for mistakes he had made during his first term, and demonstrating his renewed commitment to his job as Canada's Prime Minister. His altered public tone was well illustrated in a debate on the Liberal's Throne speech early into their minority government. In this speech, Trudeau promised "to try and correct those areas in our administration where we had been incompetent … without in any way turning back on our Liberal principles and without in any way withdrawing from the faith we … have in the land. … We, as Liberals, always tend to err on the side of liberty rather than on the side of gain."[35] This example also illustrates what was becoming a characteristic oscillation between self-flagellation and self-justification—any humble pie was joined with an assurance that any errors were errors of unintentionally clumsy implementation, not flaws in Liberal policy or principles. Trudeau would strive to do a better job of adequately explaining and defending his initiatives and plans for the country but his core principles and policies would remain essentially unchanged.

Within six months of what would be an 18-month stint as a minority Prime Minister, Trudeau's Liberals clawed their way back up the polls to a level that indicated the strong possibility of a majority if a new election were to be called. Trudeau interpreted these indicators as proof that his reformed manner and stratagems were working as intended, freeing him to add a bit more combativeness to his dealings with opposition leaders and MPs. Alternating between humility and toughness, he stopped presenting long-term, complicated plans in favour of shorter-term targets that could be stated and argued crisply and succinctly—a timely and decisive response to immediate difficulties and concerns. Old age pensions, family allowances, and veterans payments were increased and/or tied to inflation, federal subsidies reduced costs of milk and bread, electronic surveillance was restricted, and tax cuts introduced to the benefit of low and middle income earners.

The more Trudeau showed his passion for the country and his policies, even as he over-simplified them, the more the public responded with warmth and enthusiasm. In Radwanski's view, Trudeau "transformed himself into a more effective politician and a less open and unique leader."[36] Surprising even himself, Pierre found this new way of doing politics "more interesting and stimulating than I would have thought possible. Ever since my youth I had been a loner, very jealous of my freedom ... In politics, a healthy dose of gregariousness is not a fault. I learned this lesson the hard way. ... I [now] jumped into action feet-first ... I entered more energetically and completely into the fulfillment of the mandate that had been given me, and I accepted fully all the responsibilities that went with it."[37] He now realized that he could not govern without political strategy in combination with his principles and ideals. "You know, if I wanted to be right rather than prime minister, I'd have stayed in university."[38]

Riding high in the polls, when the Tories and NDP combined to defeat his 1974 budget, Trudeau picked up the gauntlet in fighting mode: "eyes blazing, face contorted with anger, gesticulating wildly, the prime minister" accused them of defeating his budget "because they were more interested in an election than in all his important anti-inflation measures." He looked with scorn on Stanfield's freeze-and-controls proposals ("Zap! You're frozen!").[39] Throughout the campaign that followed what Trudeau insisted was the opposition parties' unnecessary election, he stayed on his new course, never reverting to the self-assured and playful manner of the 1968 campaign or the professorial detachment of that of 1972. His speeches were straightforward and simple, laced with wisecracks, razor-sharp repartee, and memorable phrasings. He avoided as much as possible press conferences and open-line programs, wary of being ambushed. Where he previously had kept his personal life separate from his political life, for many appearances on the campaign hustings, he now was accompanied by Margaret.

In retrospect, Trudeau admitted, that as much as he claimed to find minority governance invigorating and focusing, he "had been ready to go to the people to solicit a new mandate, on whatever day the Opposition parties might commit the mistake of uniting against us. In fact, I had even been asking myself whether it wouldn't be necessary to incite our opponents into making that fatal error."[40] Given how much Trudeau apparently enjoyed his 18 to 20 months as a minority Prime Minister, and given what transpired after the Canadian electorate gave him a new majority government on July 8, 1974, he might well have wished for much more of the comparatively uninterrupted focus and resolve that marked his minority years.

For Trudeau, the next four years of his majority mandate were the most challenging of his political career. He began his new majority term with greater political understanding and experience, and had regained his popularity with the Canadian public, who now embraced a national mood of confidence in what promised to be his dynamic leadership. Despite all this promise, within two years of the 1974 election, Trudeau had dived to his lowest level of popularity as

Prime Minister. The Liberals found themselves trailing novice party leader Joe Clark's Tories by almost 20 percentage points in the national polls. What was even more surprising was that Trudeau, buoyed by significant political and personal strength and support at the end of 1974, proceeded to make what was essentially the exact same mistake he had made during the first year of his rookie term as Prime Minister.

Once again, he decided to devote the first year of his new majority mandate to taking stock, gathering as much input as possible, and planning the rest of his term, through to the end of 1978. The only difference was that this time around he decided to adopt a more invitational and open approach in his information gathering and planning, asking his newly appointed ministers to join with him in conducting an elaborate year-long "priorities exercise." Once the views of his ministers had been gathered in meticulous detail and synthesized into an overall program of priorities, directions, and initiatives, the synthesis was returned to the ministers and their department officials for further vetting and implementation. In the end, much of the material proved to be overly general, philosophical, and difficult to fit into practical agendas and actions.

Although Trudeau defended all of this internal governmental activity as essential to ensuring eventual efficiency in achieving specific policy targets, the sad truth was that it was perceived by the public as doing nothing, and in fact seemed to induce many government officials, who were often wary of making tough decisions, into a state of general paralysis. Despite their resounding 1974 victory and all the campaign slogans that had launched it, none of these amounted to a workable plan of action. The priorities exercise that was intended to mend this state of affairs succeeded mostly in giving leading liberals, who had endured two hectic and bruising years of minority government, a recess in which to catch their breath. The net result was a lethargic start from which Trudeau and his government never seemed to recover—a squandering of what should have been a time of significant accomplishment and national renewal for the governing Liberals and the Canadian public.

To seal their fate, by the Fall of 1975, the Liberals were forced to impose price and income controls to combat runaway inflation in the Canadian economy, the very action that Trudeau had openly scorned and ridiculed when proposed by former Conservative leader Robert Stanfield during the previous election campaign. In words that would come back to bite him savagely, Trudeau had described Stanfield's proposed controls as "an approach that had failed everywhere it had been attempted, 'a proven disaster looking for a new place to happen.'"[41] By the time that Trudeau's Minister of Finance, John Turner resigned his post in 1975 and was replaced by Donald Macdonald, the country's suddenly dire financial situation dominated the Government's agenda, forcing the cancellation and scrapping of what remained from the ill-fated planning and priorities exercise.

In the midst of this tailspin, Trudeau himself seemed to become indecisive, unnerved, and overly cautious, exactly the opposite of the bold leadership Canadians had expected from him. Commenting on his decision to accept the advice of his new Finance Minister when Macdonald told him "There's no choice" but to introduce controls, Trudeau, in his memoir, recalled that:

"As I had feared, for imposing wage and price controls my government and I paid a heavy price in lost credibility." He goes on to bemoan the damage to his reputation as "a straight-shooting guy who told the truth as he saw it and who wasn't just a devious politician." "The extent of the damage became clear from the uproar that erupted over some rather innocuous remarks I made [in December 1975] in a year-end television interview"[42] In that interview, Trudeau opined that "we have been unable to make it work—the free market system" and suggested that "a new society of the future might require more, not less, government intervention ... I found myself accused of everything from communism to fascism."[43] Realizing the gravity of the situation he had created, Trudeau told his cabinet that he would step down as leader if his cabinet was unanimous that he should do so.

To compound Pierre's difficulties, his close professional relationships with and support from the other two of the "three doves," Gérard Pelletier and Jean Marchand, had begun to unravel as he became increasingly reliant on Keith Davey and other English Canadian advisors. Pelletier had grown weary of the incessant partisan bickering that seemed to him to dominate federal politics. Still on warm personal terms with Trudeau, he saw less of him after Pierre's marriage and increasing reliance on his new "inner circle" in the PMO. Aware of his friend's unhappiness, Trudeau appointed Pelletier as ambassador to France, a post the latter relished, but which removed him almost entirely from Trudeau's Ottawa circle.

Marchand, however, was a different matter. Unhappy with being replaced by Davey and with what he regarded (correctly) as a ministerial demotion to the Department of Transport, Marchand became increasingly upset at no longer being consulted regularly by the Prime Minister. He and Davey did not get along and Marchand's heavy drinking became heavier, resulting in a string of unfortunate incidents, including two car accidents. Refusing to accept Marchand's resignation, but moving him to an even more fringe position as a minister without portfolio, Trudeau then asked Marc Lalonde to replace Marchand as Trudeau's Quebec leader. "The three wise men were now part of history, and Pierre Trudeau, who had initially seemed the most unlikely politician of them all, was the only survivor."[44]

Late in 1976, Trudeau wrote in a policy document entitled *The Way Ahead*:

> Rather than relent in the pursuit of social goals, it is both possible and desirable to seek a substantial reduction in the rate of government expenditure and direct government intervention, and to search for alternative strategies—less expenditure-oriented—to serve the legitimate social concerns of government, and in fact to better serve society ... If we truly want governments to do less—for us, and to us—we as individuals and in our private institutions will have to do more—for each other.[45]

Ironically, this clear statement of the basic choice he thought faced Canadians (or any citizens at any time), one that so clearly reflected his own view of individual rights and responsibilities to one's self and one's society, was mostly ignored when it was delivered on the same day that wide-spread protests against governmental controls erupted across the country.

Trudeau's second full term as a majority Prime Minister did include some arguably notable accomplishments, such as the creation of a national petroleum corporation (Petro-Canada), the abolishment of capital punishment, the establishment of closer links with the European Economic Community and with much of Latin America, and indeed the eventual easing of the nation's inflationary spiral. However, in the end, there was surprisingly little to show for what could, and perhaps should, have been a golden period for Canadians, especially for those committed to the social justice and improvements they had understood Trudeau's 1974 campaign to promise. To comprehend more fully the fate of Trudeau's second majority government, it is helpful to consider three matters that increasingly occupied his time, energies, and attention from his re-election in 1974 to his defeat by Clark's progressive conservatives in 1979: Trudeau's ongoing preoccupation with what colloquially has become known as "the Quebec question," his increasingly ineffectual dealings with the oil-rich province of Alberta, and the emotional demands of his marriage and family life.

During this time in his career, Pierre Trudeau was undoubtedly preoccupied with events in his personal life. Despite his continuous and sincere attempts to separate the public from the private, his life with Margaret and their three sons (Justin, born in 1971, Alexandre in 1973, and Michel in 1975) could not easily be compartmentalized to fit his typically precise daily schedule. Married life with children is tricky to balance with work requirements at the best of times, and neither Pierre nor Margaret, despite their obvious love for their children and the assistance of domestic staff, seemed prepared for the inevitable realities. The daily demands and responsibilities of familial domesticity began to erode what many Canadians had viewed as their fairy-tale romance.

After the focused and concerted energy he expended during his two years as a minority Prime Minister and the onerous election campaign that followed, it was perhaps natural for Trudeau to "at least subconsciously … reward himself with a calmer more reflective year," which the "priorities exercise" made possible.[46] Pierre also had to help Margaret adjust to being relegated to the roles of housewife and mother after sharing centre stage with him during the successful 1972 campaign. Her role in that contest had given her greater confidence and self-esteem, which now came crashing down. Two months after the election, she was admitted to the Montreal General Hospital suffering from severe emotional stress, the sources of which she papered over in a subsequent interview aired on the CTV television network a few weeks later.

Clarkson and McCall described the Trudeaus' unraveling marriage in the following terms:

> Two wilful people, emotionally arrested in adolescence,
> had contrived to meet and greet and were about to part
> again in an agonizing marital conflict that would sap
> Trudeau's political energy for the next five years. For
> reasons that had to do with their individual needs, they
> had each gone into marriage harbouring delusions about
> the other that were to have horrendous consequences,
> both private and public.[47]

Margaret herself, in her first memoir, *Beyond Reason*, described her emotional state the morning after the 1974 electoral victory as she sat alone at breakfast. Anticipating a phone call from Pierre that never came, she wanted his thanks for her assistance during the campaign, traveling thousands of miles to keep pace with an unrelenting and almost impossible schedule of attending, hosting, and speaking at event after event. "I waited; and I waited. It was absurd of me—everyone was exhausted, why should they have thought of me? But something in me broke that day. I had been used."[48] Stating that it was then that her "rebellion started," Margaret continues with "From then, until the day I walked out of 24 Sussex three years later, it built up momentum in fits and starts. It took many different forms: a sad ending of my love for Pierre; a return to the inner turmoils and confusions; ... a sense of mounting claustrophobia that had, like some enormous bubble, to burst soon." And burst it did. "As a woman in her early twenties who had led a largely feckless existence, she was ill prepared to live with a man whose official role put demands on her that she found constraining in the extreme."[49]

"After July 1974, she entered into open combat with her husband to get the attention she craved, [including] a solitary holiday in Europe where she searched fruitlessly for a former lover," [and] fell "in love with an American senator (later revealed to be Edward Kennedy)."[50] "She became more and more outrageous, acting up wildly in public in Canada and abroad," culminating in "impulsively flying to Toronto for a Rolling Stones concert and ... some impromptu partying with the rock stars that caused a minor crisis in Trudeau's office."[51] Margaret increasingly spent her time "jetting back and forth across the Atlantic ... trying out men, jobs, and hallucinogens in a rampage of publicity that seemed mainly aimed at wreaking revenge on her husband for having kept her well-shod and pregnant in his prime ministerial fortress."[52]

For Pierre, the constant gossip surrounding their marriage and their ongoing quarrels over money, their children, and other matters were disorienting. Used to being able to distance himself from emotional upsets, he grew increasingly frustrated. When an attempted reconciliation failed after Margaret backed out of a tentative agreement, Trudeau realized they never would be able to coexist harmoniously. Supervising and caring for their three boys now fell to Trudeau, who with the support of his domestic staff proved to be a devoted and capable father. Indeed, Margaret's absences from their lives allowed him to plan, arrange, and manage daily family times after work and during special trips and getaways, in a way that would have been impossible with her present. Nonetheless, there can be no doubt that Margaret's "capering ... damaged Trudeau's reputation as a political leader as well as his dignity."[53]

Throughout the 1970s, Trudeau's biggest political problem, other than the Canadian economy and the ever-present threat of Quebec separation, was an ongoing fight with the oil-rich province of Alberta over that province's un-renewable natural resources. In the 1968 federal election, Trudeau's liberals won 4 of 19 constituency seats in the Province of Alberta. In 1972 and 1974, all Alberta seats went to the federal progressive conservatives. "After the 1974 election,

Trudeau's major difficulty in federal-provincial relations appeared to be with the western provinces, especially Alberta."[54] During his 1974 election night speech, in an attempt to placate Albertans and their Premier Peter Lougheed, Trudeau offered an olive branch by way of an apology for the Liberals' poor showing in the West and a promise to govern for all Canadians. Trudeau knew he had to improve relations with Alberta, and privately he respected Lougheed.

In 1975, Trudeau replaced Donald Macdonald, who had been highly critical of Lougheed (once calling him "vicious") with Alastair Gillespie as Minister of Energy, Mines, and Resources. One of Gillespie's first acts was to raise oil prices, a move that Lougheed welcomed as creating a "sense of stability" in the oil patch.[55] However, the looming peace never did more than loom. Shortly thereafter, the creation of Petro-Canada as a federal crown corporation that would act to implement and regulate Canada's oil policies and practices outraged American and Canadian petroleum corporations in Calgary. The Petro-Canada announcement seemed even more ominous in the context of Trudeau's end-of-year musings—in which he speculated about the possible need for the federal government to "take a larger role in running institutions, as we're doing now with our anti-inflation controls" ... to make sure that "the strong and powerful don't abuse their strength and power in order to take freedoms away from the little man."[56] For many in the oil patch, such rhetoric confirmed their view of Trudeau as a power-hungry socialist. Although Premier Lougheed did not share this particular view, he was, by background and inclination, not inclined to take such musings without a fight.

Peter Lougheed was the son of a proud Alberta family and a former professional footballer and lawyer, with a keen understanding of the Canadian and international corporate world. Elected in 1971 as Alberta Premier, replacing a long string of Social Credit governments in the province, Lougheed soon displayed a flare for the media and a strong determination to represent the interests of his province, including those of a number of newly formed Alberta oil companies which were now thriving in a sector still dominated by larger and more established American petroleum giants. Like many Albertans, Lougheed was concerned about the way "our destiny was formed by outside forces—the railways, the pipelines, the banks, and, above all, the federal government—acting on matters of direct importance to us but without consultation." "I didn't go into politics to oppose Pierre Trudeau. I went into politics because I thought we could get things done provincially in Alberta that would right old wrongs."[57]

On taking the reins as Premier in 1971, Lougheed moved quickly to modernize the bureaucracy of the provincial government, with the aid of some of Alberta's most talented professional and business people, whom he convinced to join his cabinet. By the mid-1970s, he had attracted Peter Meekison, distinguished University of Alberta political scientist and expert on Canadian federalism, to work within a new ministry he had created upon his election as Premier—the Ministry of Federal and Intergovernmental Relations (MFIR). As Deputy Minister of MFIR, Meekison proved to be especially important to Lougheed's efforts to develop strategies for dealing with Ottawa in general, and with respect to the sharing of oil and gas revenues in particular. Lougheed and Meekison worked through the Alberta

Petroleum Marketing Commission and the Energy Resources Conservation Board to increase the costs of Alberta oil and gas to out-of-province consumers. They also placed new royalties on leases of provincial crown land to the province's oil companies. Lougheed and his government then used portions of the revenues generated to grow and enhance an Alberta-based, local petrochemical industry and to establish an Alberta Heritage Savings Fund that channelled some provincial resource revenues into a development bank that would fund the diversification of Alberta's economy for a future in which oil reserves eventually would be exhausted.

By the end of the 1970s, the Lougheed government had found another use for their increased petroleum revenues—loans to poorer provinces at highly attractive rates. With these loans, Lougheed escalated his efforts to enlist other provinces in his ongoing fights with Ottawa over resource pricing and revenue. When Trudeau was anxious to reopen the country's constitutional arrangements to combat Quebec separatism, Lougheed encouraged other premiers to join him in demanding any concessions on the constitutional front be linked to greater control of their own resources and economies. High on Lougheed's list of targets was the "Victoria amending formula" that gave only Ontario and Quebec veto powers in negotiations between the provinces and the central government.

By this time Lougheed had established himself as a leading advocate for the western provinces. He now began to reach out to the Atlantic provinces, where anti-Ottawa resentment was on the rise, encouraging maritime premiers to think hard about whether they too might not be on the receiving end of resource rip-offs from

Ottawa in their fisheries and off-shore petroleum ventures. If so, Alberta would be there to lend a hand. In effect, he began to squeeze central Canada from both the west and the east. The upshot of this remarkable change in the Canadian political landscape was much in evidence during constitutional conferences between the provinces and Trudeau's federal government in 1978 and 1979. Now, whenever "Quebec made its demands, the Anglophone premiers from the hinterland were no longer willing to watch from the sidelines. They acted as an alliance in which each supported the others in asking for extended powers."[58]

The cumulative effects of Trudeau's domestic woes, long-standing and ongoing battles with Quebec over its provincial sovereignty, more recent but growing confrontations with Alberta, and his struggles to manage the federal economy were obvious when the Liberals won only two of fifteen by-elections for parliamentary vacancies in October, 1978. By this time, it seemed like Trudeau had fallen well short of what Canadians had expected of him during his second full term as Prime Minister of a Liberal majority government. The outcome of the next federal election, which Trudeau and his Liberals had delayed as long as possible, seemed a foregone conclusion. Observers, both within and outside government circles began to look anxiously or with relish at the toll the past four and a half years had taken on Trudeau himself.

According to his biographers Stephen Clarkson and Christina McCall, as the federal election of May 22, 1979 loomed, Trudeau began to appear distant and removed from his work and the issues facing him and his government. His old pattern of intense periods of detailed, rigorous attention to his prime ministerial tasks, interrupted by brief getaways to places of solitude, play, and relaxation, was no longer in evidence. It had been replaced by a moody, unfocussed, and brooding half-presence in which he often seemed bothered and preoccupied. Matters that could no longer be ignored prompted hurried, precipitous reactions and decisions. Trudeau's apparent indifference screened much of the emotional turmoil, humiliation, and shame he was experiencing in his home and office, to the point where "Things fell apart for Trudeau ... in all the major areas of his prime ministerial concerns."[59] The only surprise was that despite Trudeau's preoccupations and the missed opportunities of his majority government over the past almost five years, the Liberals somehow managed to limit the Tories to a minority government in the 1979 election.

As Joe Clark's newly elected Conservative minority took control of Canada's government after the May 22nd federal election, Pierre Trudeau had a lot to think about. The day after his election loss, he awoke to newspaper photographs of Margaret dancing at New York's infamous Club 54, taken in the early hours of that same morning. Several days later, Margaret returned to Ottawa to pack up her belongings and spend time with her three sons, but also improvised a farewell party for her previous household staff, during which she encouraged RCMP security officers to toss Pierre into the swimming pool at 24 Sussex Drive. Little wonder that the proud, and sometimes haughty, former Prime Minister was looking forward to a summer and early autumn away from Ottawa and the public eye. But, first he had to cut his losses.

Not surprisingly many liberals were now openly questioning his leadership. John Turner and Donald Macdonald both had considerable support to replace Trudeau as leader. Pierre himself thought Macdonald would be an acceptable replacement. Many of Trudeau's most loyal cabinet ministers had lost their seats in the election. He also had to make tough decisions to reduce his political staff. Gone were the perks of the prime ministerial office he had come to enjoy and Trudeau took such losses as daily reminders of his failure. Yet, he also found an attractive freedom in being less encumbered by the daily routines of government, a freedom that got him thinking about more time with his three sons and life beyond politics.

Nonetheless, on July 19, he called a press conference to announce his intention to remain as leader of the Liberal Party of Canada. "I'm staying on. In my judgement, I'm the best man,"[60] thereby countering reports of his loss of interest and giving himself time to reflect on his future. But, even then, he seemed uninspired to show that he really was the best man, at least with any consistency. "Bored and unhappy with his situation, bored also with himself, Trudeau went through the motions of being Opposition Leader."[61] The conventional wisdom was that he would stay on for a year or so and then leave.

After his July 19 press conference, Pierre Trudeau effectively went into hiding to lick his wounds and regain his balance. He took a long canoe trip in the Northwest Territories, during which he paddled day after day with men half his age, enjoyed a backpacking adventure with architect friend Arthur Erickson in Tibet, grew a beard, dated classical guitarist Liona Boyd, and took a train trip with his three boys to tour the national parks in the Rockies. In the meantime, Margaret gave an interview for *Playgirl* in which she described her participation in the sport of celebrity love-making and talked about how enjoyable she found describing intimate details of her life with her notoriously private husband who remained steadfast in protecting his personal privacy.

Little wonder then that Pierre, in his unfamiliar new positions as leader of the official opposition and the country's most famous cuckold, was deeply ambivalent about the opening of parliament on October 9, 1979. Nonetheless, his mood had improved over the summer. "When Trudeau left Ottawa, he had been grumpy, blaming his aids for the bad election result. ... In the fall, after his holiday, his mood was better."[62] When Trudeau asked Prime Minister Clark his first question in the House of Commons as leader of the opposition, he started slowly and then came out swinging. In mockingly soft tones, he asked Clark about his failure to reach agreement with the provinces on energy pricing, something the Conservatives had flayed Trudeau for being unable to do. He then chided Clark for not being able to handle Premier Lougheed of Alberta and went on to ridicule Clark's proposed sale of Petro-Canada and the Conservative's plan to relocate the Canadian Embassy in Israel to Jerusalem, as being ill advised and demonstrating his shortcomings as Prime Minister. In perhaps his most fiery flurry, he made the Liberal benches rise by savagely skewering Clark's idea that Canada was best understood as a "community of communities," a view that flew in the face of Trudeau's long-standing belief that the rights and freedoms of individual citizens as persons were best guaranteed by a strong federal government dedicated to the common good of all Canadians, not just those in particular regions of the country. Would the country really be better off as a "confederation of shopping centres," with the Prime Minister as "head waiter to the provinces?"[63]

Throughout October, Trudeau delighted in the public spat between fellow Conservatives Clark and Lougheed. However, with more time on the hill, his performance was increasingly uninspiring. For the most part, the only animation he achieved in the Commons was in defense of his own past policies and most cherished views. Liberals began to plan for a future without Trudeau—debates about which often pitted English and French Canadian members of the party against each other. "In private, he was telling confidants, I just don't want to be Prime Minister again."[64] As civil war seemed about to break out in the Liberal Party, an increasingly insular and small group of loyal supporters in the Prime Minister's Office (PMO) struggled to keep up some semblance of a party platform and the flagging spirits of their leader. Prominent in this tiny group were Jim Coutts, Trudeau's long-serving principal secretary, Tom Axworthy, Trudeau's chief policy adviser, Allan MacEachen, Liberal house leader, and Marc Lalonde, long-time friend and now the Liberal's energy critic. Nonetheless, on the morning of Wednesday, November 21, Trudeau told the Liberal caucus that "it's all over," and at a later press conference he explained that he was leaving "to have more time with my family," but that he would still work to defeat the separatists in the forthcoming Quebec referendum. He ended by telling reporters: "to turn an old phrase around, I'm sorry I won't have you to kick around any more."[65] Through all of this, one person Pierre did not confide in was Margaret.

More than anyone else, it was Coutts who held off the growing "ditch Trudeau" factions after the Liberal defeat in the spring of 1979, adroitly turning them against each other, while simultaneously doing everything he could to confuse and undermine the new Conservative Prime Minister Joe Clark. One of an increasingly small number of Albertans who would admit openly to being a Liberal, Coutts had a personal antipathy for Clark that dated to their debates in a mock parliament during their student days at the University of Alberta. Coutts distained Clark's abilities and regarded his election as a mere fluke. It was Coutts who was behind the infamous "Joe Who?" jokes that began to do the rounds amongst Canadian movers and shakers. "What are you doing with that turkey?" Clark supposedly replies, "It's not a turkey; it's a duck," only to be told "I wasn't talking to you, I was talking to the duck."[66] Coutts was confident that the Tories would fall on their own swords, given the notorious infighting that had plagued Canadian Conservatives in the past—conflicts between fiscal and social conservatives and over what to do about their inability to establish a foothold in Québec. Coutts did his best to convince Liberals that Clark's inexperience and ineptitude inevitably would run him aground on such shores.

Even with Trudeau apparently gone, Coutts continued to compare Clark to his predecessor. As it turned out, and very unfairly to Clark, Coutts' and others' personal attacks ensured that Clark's careful and earnest approach to the job of leading the nation was interpreted as fearful rather than careful, in direct contrast to the supposedly combative and intellectually elevated certainty that had marked Trudeau's leadership style in the past. Following Coutts' lead, the Liberal rhetoric turned up the heat on Clark as a comparatively insignificant "wimp" on a national, and especially international, stage—the very stage on which Trudeau had paraded confidently. Under this kind of attack, by the end of 1979 the Tories were widely perceived as weakly led, bungling the economy through blind adherence to the planks of fiscal conservatism, and failing to achieve the co-operative federal-provincial relationships they had promised. These and other expectations had taken a back seat to conflicts over national energy policies that pitted Premier Peter Lougheed of Alberta against his Ontario counterpart, Bill Davis, with Clark on the outside, looking on in apparent wonderment and confusion.

As Conservatives battled Conservatives, Coutts and his small band of co-plotters continued to turn up the heat. Following Conservative Finance Minister John Crosbie's "face the facts" budget, presented on December 11, 1979, Coutts, MacEachen, and Lalonde were privately gleeful. They immediately portrayed the Tory budget as sticking it to the working people, and as revealing the Bay Street lackey hiding behind Clark's progressive façade—the budget of a party and a leader without a heart. Perhaps even more importantly, Coutts and his group finally were succeeding in restoring a sense of entitlement and purpose to the liberal rank and file, many of whom considered themselves to be genuinely concerned with social justice and equity, which according to Coutts et al. were being eroded by Clark and his band of red Tory hypocrites.

Thus had the mood of many liberals, if not of their leader, been transformed as the night of Thursday, December 13 approached, a night that would see the Conservative minority government face an expected vote of confidence on their budget. Having refused to conduct polls of their own, even when urged to do so by their pollster Allan Gregg, the Conservatives also refused to delay the vote until the following Monday when they would have a fuller compliment of members in the House. The Liberals, on the other hand, following Allan MacEachen's canny advice had quietly arranged to have all but one of their MPs present for the vote, including a Liberal member who was brought by ambulance to participate. After the vote, when a reporter commented that the Tories displayed courage and principle in proceeding with the vote that brought down their minority government, a prominent Liberal happily remarked, "That wasn't bravery. It was stupidity. Those klutzes can't even count."[67]

As the soap opera of the Conservatives self-inflicted defeat approached and unfolded, Trudeau often had seemed distanced from the goings on. He sometimes refused to ask questions in the House, at one point telling his parliamentary assistant Joyce Fairbairn, "I'm finished. I'm out of it."[68] He even appeared to be unaffected by the astonishing events that had so quickly turned the tables in favour of the Liberals. He had cast his vote against the Tory budget with an air of resignation, apparently unmoved by the historical moment in which he was participating.

And yet, even during his summer getaways, there were signs that the cornered lion had not entirely lost his political will and was following events closely. In discussing their eight man, summer canoe trip in 1979 down the Hanbury—Thelon rivers in the Northwest Territories, Canadian news executive Tim Kotcheff described how, on arrival for the adventure, Trudeau "seemed distant, aloof, and contemplative—perhaps still feeling the sting of rejection at the hands of the fickle electorate."[69] Given that Trudeau was 60 years old and dispirited, Kotcheff and the others "harboured nagging doubts about Pierre" and how he (and they) would fare on the difficult rapids, dangerous rocks, and three-mile portage that dotted the almost 1,000 kilometer course they had set for themselves. But not only did Trudeau hold his own, he proved to be a "hard, steady paddler and often kept his canoe ahead of the pack, ... where born leaders want to be."[70] As the trip continued, Pierre, increasingly relaxed and happy, easily managed the gruelling Dickson Canyon portage and began to open up, becoming "the best companion you'd ever want on a hazardous trip like this," even if "we sensed he could never be our 'buddy.'"[71] One day, when a small plane appeared, Trudeau quipped "it was probably someone coming to tell us that the Joe Clark government had overthrown itself"[72]—an uncannily accurate forecast of what was to come and seemingly an indication that Trudeau himself was well aware of this possibility.

Of course, by the time the Conservatives actually shot themselves in their collective feet on December 13, 1979, Trudeau already had resigned as leader of the Liberal opposition. Nonetheless, when asked following the vote of non-confidence, about the possibility of his return, Pierre turned Delphic, saying "I have had enough of it: I will come back only if the Emperor asks me three times on bended knees"[73] and requested "the caucus hold a secret ballot on the question."[74] In his own account of events, Trudeau explained: "Caucus is made up of the people I am with all the time in the House of Commons. If they're not enthusiastic about me, I'm not coming back."[75]

When Trudeau opened the Liberal caucus meeting the following morning (his resignation not yet having been made formal), "his reluctance [to stay on] was evident as, in a low monotone, he insisted on near unanimous support,"[76] even knowing that many of those present opposed him. Trudeau then left the caucus meeting to drive to Montreal, where he was negotiating the purchase of a home for himself and his three boys to occupy during his retirement, another indication that he did not expect to be reconfirmed as leader of the party.

Remaining to ponder the matter of leadership were some caucus members who were vehemently opposed to Trudeau's return. These included the tiny western Canadian contingent, but consisted mostly of Ontarians who favoured Don Macdonald or who hoped that John Turner might reconsider his decision not to pursue the party leadership. Of course, there also were some who preferred, for a variety of reasons, to run the next election under Trudeau's leadership, including a large majority of MPs from the Maritimes and Québec, as well as the rest of the Ontarians. It was Allan MacEachen who, in what several of his caucus colleagues "would later recall as the most brilliant speech of his career,"[77] convinced the caucus to act decisively. MacEachen's main argument was that the only thing that possibly could prevent the Liberals from carrying the next election, given the most recent data by party pollster Martin Goldfarb, was a divisive leadership race. Such a possibility was easily avoidable, given that they had a proven, veteran leader in Trudeau. After this, the caucus eventually voted unanimously, but not on a secret ballot as Trudeau had requested, to support his return as leader.

MacEachen's next audience, the national executive of the Liberal Party, which now was required to support the decision of the caucus, was much less biddable. During an emergency meeting held on the morning of Saturday, December 15, there was ample evidence that many members of the executive were angry that Coutts and MacEachen had not informed them of the plan to bring down the Clark government. More generally, they were miffed at "the unelected influence of Jim Coutts and Keith Davey."[78] Fortunately for Trudeau, if indeed he did want to return as leader, much of this animosity did not extend to Allan MacEachen because of his long and distinguished service to the Liberal cause, dating back to the years of Louis St. Laurent.

Against demands of executive dissenters that the PMO in-group led by Coutts should not be allowed to control access to the leader and act without involving the executive, MacEachen argued that the Liberal MPs had little choice about rejecting a budget as reactionary (and opposed to everything the Liberals stood for) as the one proposed by the Clark Tories. Adding that the polls promised a Liberal majority in the now forthcoming election in February of the coming year and that a divisive leadership race at this point would be disastrous, MacEachen managed to assuage anxieties of twenty of the thirty-one attendees at the emergency meeting, who eventually voted in favour of Trudeau as leader. With the caucus and executive onside, two of the genuflections requested by Trudeau had been exercised.

What remained was for Trudeau's closest friends and allies to convince him that they were behind him and would stand with and actively support him if he accepted the nomination of the caucus and executive. In his memoir, Trudeau makes it clear that "if I was to stay on, the third effort of persuasion would have to come from my friends and close colleagues. I wanted to make sure they were prepared to stay on as well, because if I was not surrounded by friends and associates who were prepared to fight their way back with me, I was not going to return."[79]

This final knee-bend was accomplished through a succession of various and hurried events that occurred on the Sunday afternoon and evening of December 16, after Trudeau returned to Ottawa from Montreal, and throughout the day that followed. Worried about how Don Macdonald might be reacting to events of the past two days, given that Trudeau himself previously had supported Macdonald as his successor, one of Trudeau's first actions upon his return was to talk with Macdonald by telephone. As Pierre still had not fully decided his course of action, Macdonald assured him that he was ready to take over as leader. When he was asked by Trudeau if he would run as an MP, were Pierre to remain, Macdonald said "No."[80] Later Sunday evening, Trudeau met with the Liberal Party's official agent, Torrance Wylie, Senators Alasdair Graham and Gil Molgat, representing the national executive, and Allan MacEachen and Jacques Guilbault, representing the English and French members of the caucus. Together, they poured over "hot off the press" polls, conducted that very weekend by Martin Goldfarb, showing the Liberals with solid and increasing numbers if Trudeau were to lead them. However, it also became clear at this meeting that Trudeau faced significant opposition in Ontario, where Macdonald and one or two others had strong pockets of support. Trudeau also made it clear that he would not accept conditions that the party executive might wish to impose on him. After additional views and arguments were vetted, Pierre agreed to reconsider his resignation and deliberate carefully about a return to lead the party in the election that was fast approaching on February 18, 1980.

The day after (on Monday, December 17, 1979), Pierre Trudeau moved quickly to consult further with some of his conversationalists of the previous day and with additional close friends and political allies about his "hypothetical" return as leader. These included Gérard Pelletier, Jacques Hébert, Coutts, Axworthy, Davey, and MacEachen. He also met with about-to-retire clerk of the Privy Council, Gordon Robertson, and with Michael Pitfield, previous Privy Council clerk, asking the latter if he would consider doing the job again if Trudeau were to contest and win the election. That same day, Judd Buchanan, Bob Andras, and John Reid, representing the Macdonald or Turner Ontario liberals, urged Trudeau to resign. The three Ontarians had consulted with other leading Liberals in their province and claimed that Ontario favoured moving to a convention and a new leader. For different reasons, Trudeau's close and long-term friends and supporters Jean Marchand and Marc Lalonde from Quebec also advised him not to return as leader, mostly because they (being unaware of the party's polling results) thought he could not win and they wanted to protect him from further humiliation. "However, Gérard Pelletier, whom Trudeau trusted most, strongly urged him to stay to fight the forthcoming referendum battle, while Coutts and MacEachen warned that Turner might now return to politics and defeat Macdonald in a convention. All the while, Davey and MacEachen appealed to Trudeau's sense of duty and his distrust of Turner."[81]

After he had lunched at the Château Laurier Grill with Gordon Robertson, Trudeau joined Coutts, MacEachen, and Davey, who also had lunched at the grand old hotel, to vet and clarify his remaining concerns. These included his discomfort about being unfair to Macdonald, what would happen to his new home in Montreal (and, by implication, his plans to retire and raise his boys), and wondering whether or not he would exhaust his welcome and the good will that many Canadians still seemed happy to extend to him.

Confounded by Trudeau's seeming unwillingness to take the plunge, Coutts encouraged Ed Lumley, an Anglophone and ardent supporter of John Turner, who now agreed with Coutts that it was too late for a change in leadership, to talk directly to Trudeau. Later on the 17th, Lumley arrived at Stornoway with Don Johnston, another member of the Party's right wing, to convince Trudeau that his support went well beyond his staff and members of the Party's left wing. Trudeau listened carefully to what they had to say and later, after another call to Macdonald (who confirmed his own desire to stand for the party leadership, but also stopped short of advising Trudeau), left Stornaway for a walk around the Rockcliffe Park neighbourhood of Ottawa.

Still uncertain about which way Trudeau would jump, Coutts, who might have been encouraged by Trudeau to do so, asked Tom

Axworthy to help prepare two speeches for a press conference scheduled for Tuesday, December 18 at 11 a.m.—one for Trudeau to deliver if he was coming back as leader; the other if he was not.[82] What exactly happened on the morning of December 18 is the subject of differing accounts from Trudeau, as recorded in his memoirs,[83] and Coutts, as reported by Trudeau biographers Clarkson and McCall.[84] All agree that Trudeau was undecided until the last moment, but appear to disagree on exactly what and when that last moment was. For Trudeau, it was immediately upon waking on the morning of the 18th that he suddenly realized with alarm that the private decision he had made not to return as leader before falling asleep the night before was the wrong one. According to Coutts, it was only after a morning telephone call he made to Trudeau that same morning, that Trudeau finally relented to his and the Party's desire that he return.

In fact, by Coutt's account, as reported by Clarkson and McCall, Trudeau still was saying "no," when he first answered the telephone, a response that had the frustrated and increasingly worried Coutts rushing to Stornoway to argue his case in person. "What are you afraid of?" he asked Trudeau and went on to say that "You have nothing to lose other than a couple of months for the campaign. ... But if we win decisively—and the numbers indicate that we can ... you will be able to achieve your political goals."[85] These goals included battling Lévesque on the referendum about Québec sovereignty and moving on to pursue the constitutional agenda Trudeau had long sought. Coutts also made an existential plea concerning Trudeau's legacy—"*Then* you can retire and the obituaries ... will be very different from the ones you saw in November."[86] The pair then left for the downtown Ottawa press conference, where an anxious Tom Axworthy breathed a sigh of relief when he recognized that Trudeau pulled from his pocket the longer of the two documents that had been prepared the day before.

What went on in Trudeau's mind during the December 17 walk and in the early to middle hours of Tuesday, December 18, 1979? John English speculates that "Surely, he reflected deeply on the implications for his boys. ... Trudeau's mind must also have dwelt on the warnings of Marchand and Lalonde, friends with whom he had shared so many battles in the past. Then there was Macdonald, who had been loyal when others had not and whom he had assured of his support only a few weeks earlier." But, it was likely that more strategic thoughts and images that stirred his deepest political yearnings also intruded: "a scowling René Lévesque and the separatist banners and hecklers who confronted him regularly on Montreal streets. He could hear Pelletier's voice telling him that he could not walk away from the challenge."[87]

Stephen Clarkson and Christina McCall, after reviewing a number of comments made at the time and subsequently by Trudeau himself, also conclude that Trudeau was "still fixated on the federalist-separatist struggle. For him, the possibility of plunging into it once more from a position of renewed strength overrode all other considerations. ... At the age of sixty, he knew what he wanted from life, and when the moment came, he called on the courage he painstakingly developed as a puny boy and shy young man and seized this last best chance that history was offering him."[88]

It would be surprising if either English or Clarkson and McCall were far off the mark in their speculations. How could Trudeau, given the circumstances in which he found himself, possibly not have wrestled with the thoughts, concerns, and possibilities they imagine? There is clearly a desire conveyed in their speculations for a more comprehensive explanation of Trudeau's decision to "stay on"—one linked to his prior life experience "as a puny boy and shy young man," to his life ambitions and causes "at the age of sixty," and to his own evolving sense of himself, his destiny, and his legacy, so as to seize "this last best chance that history was offering him."

As Pierre Trudeau contemplated whether to stay or go as leader of the Liberal Party of Canada on the evening of December 17 and the early morning of December 18, 1979, it certainly was not Joe Clark and his conservatives who occupied most of his thoughts. Trudeau had repeatedly made it clear that his reasons for entering politics and for pursuing the prime ministership were two-fold: "One, to make sure that Quebec wouldn't leave Canada through separatism, and the other was to make sure that Canada wouldn't shove Quebec out through narrow-mindedness."[89] As the new year of 1980 beckoned, it was clear to Trudeau that there were numerous factors that had contributed to the existing state of Quebec-Canada relations, many of which were lodged in the complex niches of Canada's French and English histories, and a few of which he himself had added to the mix. He must have focused particularly on how his handling of the October Crisis of 1970 and how his subsequent actions as Prime Minister had contributed to or forestalled what he most wanted to achieve—a Canada that welcomed a "grown-up" Quebec and a Quebec that earned and received the respect and belonging it craved.

Radwanski makes a strong case that Trudeau was "convinced that the problem resided not in any serious deficiency in the structures of federalism, but in the failure of English and French Canadians to make proper use of those structures."[90] This failure, he attributed to a second failure—the inability of French and English citizens to "regard every part of the country as their own. To the extent that the French withdraw into Quebec and the Anglophones into the other nine provinces, the results must inevitably be the rise of rival nationalisms which will tear the country apart."[91] If Quebec defines itself only in terms of the French population within its borders, it inevitably comes to regard itself as a nation-state, a nation apart. Further, in Trudeau's view both Quebec and the rest of Canada were at fault—English Canada for disregarding the cultural, linguistic, and socioeconomic rights and aspirations of Quebec; Quebec for falling back into "a sterile, negative provincial autonomy," an autonomy that further encouraged "paternalistic centralization."[92] To combat Quebec's tendency to turn inward, Trudeau planned to encourage and promote "a sense of equality in, and proprietary right to, Canada as a whole."[93] His hope was that Quebecers would come to see all of Canada as their rightful home—thus, his rejection of "two nations" and "community" solutions, such as those proposed by Joe Clark, and to some extent by Peter Lougheed.

To make Quebecers at home in Canada, Trudeau's efforts as Prime Minister had focused primarily on language policy. Within months of becoming Prime Minister in 1968, he introduced the

Official Languages Act that provided every Canadian citizen with the right to interact with the federal government, its agencies, and corporations in either English or French. Unfortunately, many English Canadians mistakenly interpreted the OLA as somehow forcing French on them, misunderstandings that neither Trudeau nor the Canadian media worked sufficiently hard to dispel. Nonetheless, when asked or challenged, Trudeau was clear that the OLA "is not an imposition on the citizens. … The citizens can go on speaking one language or six languages or no languages if they so choose. Bilingualism is an imposition on the state [to provide services in both official languages] and not on the citizens."[94] Of course, Trudeau's initial efforts to accommodate Quebec's linguistic concerns with the Official Languages Act were later overtaken by more dramatic events such as the establishment of the Parti Québécois, the October Crisis of 1970, and the eventual election of the PQ under the leadership of Réne Lévesque in 1976.

While all of this was going on, Trudeau continued to plug away at the language issue on the constitutional front. Specifically he advocated adding to the British North America Act (the first Canadian constitutional document) a charter of human rights that would ensure that Francophone Canadians could use their language in public institutions, like schools and courts, anywhere in Canada, just as Anglophones had long been able to do in Quebec. This was a powerful tool to ensure the language rights of French Canadians throughout the country, but, as a constitutional amendment, it required the approval of provincial premiers. Unfortunately, Trudeau's many attempts to secure such constitutional rights had not succeeded by the time the

Parti Québécois had won the 1976 Quebec election. For the most part, formally declared reasons for delay were primarily economic, as many provincial premiers objected to the costs associated with implementing the guarantees Trudeau proposed.

Nonetheless, throughout his extended run as Prime Minister of Canada from 1968 to 1979, Trudeau succeeded in giving French Canadians a more genuinely influential role in the Canadian government. In less dramatic and public ways than his attempts to safeguard use of the French language across the nation in matters of state and federal governance, he undoubtedly succeeded in breaking long standing traditions of refusing important cabinet and other federal leadership portfolios to French Canadians. He personally appointed French Canadians to many prominent positions in his cabinets, and in Canadian life more generally, including Commissioner of the RCMP, Governor-General, Chair of the National Film Board of Canada, and many others. In doing so, despite all of his personal and political problems during the mid to late 1970s, Trudeau convinced most Quebecers that progress toward language equality was being made and that the federal government was not an alien body from which Quebecers were excluded. Nonetheless, much remained to be done.

It is highly likely that the central question confronting Pierre Trudeau during his walk on the evening of December 17, 1979 was whether he would, and could, be the one to succeed in the difficult task of ensuring a respectful, progressive, and lasting place for Quebec within the Canadian federation. Given Trudeau's strong intellectual and personal commitments to both Canada and Quebec, at the very centre of his ruminations likely was his legacy with respect to the question of how a vibrant, modern Quebec might best fit into the new constitutional framework he had been contemplating since his decision to enter federal politics in 1965—a vision of Canada as a progressive, pluralist, person-centered, and multicultural nation overseen by a strong central government. With his decision to stay on as leader of the Liberal Party of Canada on the morning of December 18, 1979, Trudeau renewed his commitment to enacting such a vision as the great challenge of his life. By securing the support of his cabinet, his party, and his closest friends and colleagues, he emerged from his *annus horribilis* at the end of 1979. The circumstances of the past year had forced him to confront his past failings and to seek the support of his friends and advisors to overcome them. In what was left of his political life, he was ready to commit himself fully to achieving his vision of Canada. With the three genuflections he had requested in place, he had readied the dice for one last throw. Now all he had to do was to convince the provincial premiers to allow him to proceed.

Chapter Five: Peter Lougheed's Political Career
Before 1980

When first elected as a Member of Parliament representing the federal constituency of Quebec Mount Royal in 1965, Pierre Trudeau joined a Liberal Government in power. In contrast, Peter Lougheed, upon his election to his first political position as Member of the Legislative Assembly of Alberta for Calgary West in 1967, joined a fledgling opposition of six Progressive Conservative MLAs that included himself as their inexperienced leader. Trudeau, who was familiar with federal government procedures from his work in the Privy Council Office in the early 1950s, was immediately appointed as parliamentary secretary to Prime Minister Lester Pearson, giving him ready access to current happenings and plans of the government in power. Peter Lougheed had to start from scratch with none of these advantages. Where Trudeau had been courted and prepared by the political establishment in Ottawa, Lougheed was a raw outsider, without access to what was going on and being planned in the halls of Ernest Manning's Social Credit empire.

About the only similarity between their very different entries into the chambers of power in Ottawa and Edmonton respectively, was their personal ambition to succeed and to do so on their own terms—terms dictated, in no small part, by their visions of Canada and what they wanted to accomplish for their country and their home provinces. In having such ambitions and goals, they were alike; in terms of the specific nature and content of their ambitions and goals, they were about as far apart as two committed federalists could be.

When Peter Lougheed began his new jobs as MLA and Leader of the Opposition in May 1967, he discovered that the Socreds had provided neither office space nor budget for his party, which had never governed in Alberta. To make matters worse, it was not possible for him to gain any immediately clear picture of how the provincial government operated because the Socreds had been in power for so long that they effectively had stopped following most parliamentary rules and conventions, relying mostly on improvised systems of their own that proved quite opaque to the uninitiated. Manning himself presided over his court with an iron will, founded as much or more on his Baptist beliefs as on the now dusty documents of legislative and government procedures, protocols, and requirements. As Peter Lougheed quickly discovered, dealing with Manning was like "starting your coaching career against Casey Stengel."[1]

Needless to say, all of this was more than a tad bewildering and potentially troublesome to Peter Lougheed, whose major goal for his first term in the Alberta legislature was to present himself and his party as a credible alternative to Manning's Social Credit Party. It would be challenging to develop a party platform of policies, plans, and operations that would work smoothly and efficiently in the absence of knowing how things were being done. Nonetheless, Lougheed was nothing if not committed, and he had his own goals and people in place. Moreover, it turned out that he would not immediately be required to navigate an actual sitting of the Legislative Assembly of Alberta. After years in power, the Social Credit government had fallen into the practice of holding only one legislative session each year. Since the first sitting of the legislature after the May 1967 election would not take place until February of 1968, Manning had inadvertently given his talented rookie adversary plenty of time to get his ducks in a row.

Taking advantage of what he had learned from his meetings with conservative provincial leaders like Robert Stanfield, John Robarts, Duff Roblin, and Ross Thatcher, Lougheed began by negotiating carefully with Ernest Manning. He used a combination of polite assertion and insistence when requesting government funds so that he could execute his responsibilities as opposition leader. "All we are asking is to bring the provisions for the opposition into line with other provinces. Anything less is completely unsatisfactory and ignores the popular vote."[2] Throughout these negotiations and the subsequent implementation of their results, Lougheed donned the mantle of "premier in waiting." He seldom appeared on government business without a few members of his conservative team surrounding him, adopted a notable air of authority, and maintained a thoroughly businesslike demeanour. He wanted to set an example for his MLAs and appear responsible and serious to the Alberta public. Of course, this was easier for Lougheed than for some of his entourage. He was only an occasional drinker, a non-smoker since his days at Mannix, and already practiced considerable public and private self-discipline and constraint consistent with his ambitions and goals. Once, when reporters and cameras arrived at a meeting between Lougheed and Trudeau, on one of the latter's infrequent trips to Alberta, Lougheed discreetly slipped the screwdriver he had been sipping beneath his chair.

Lougheed put the year of grace provided by the Socred practice of one annual meeting of the provincial legislature to good use. After a summer vacation with his family to attend Expo '67, which included an unproductive attempt at French immersion, Lougheed got down to business. Despite his French language struggles, Peter's summer vacation was to prove useful for his political ambitions. It provided him with a genuine respect for Quebec and its struggles and grievances, an understanding that would come in handy during his later battles with Trudeau over resources and constitutional powers. Back home, Lougheed continued to consolidate and grow his party organization, prepared detailed plans for the next provincial election, whenever that might be, and tweaked policy platforms and directions. He engaged Ted Mills as executive director of the Progressive Conservative Party of Alberta, and together they made plans to ensure a consistent party presence in all areas of the province. Through a rigorous schedule of visits, meetings, discussions, announcements, and social gatherings, they put Peter, his MLAs, and party officials and organizers in direct contact with the Alberta public.

In September of 1967, Lougheed was invited to be a keynote speaker at the national convention of the federal conservatives in Toronto. After the first speaker had gone on far too long in the hot, humid conditions in Maple Leaf Gardens, Lougheed, to the delight of the suffering delegates, trimmed his remarks. He maintained his neutrality with respect to federal politics by refusing to endorse any particular candidate in what was a fractious leadership contest, eventually won by Robert Stanfield. He urged the delegates to look to the future, not to the past. He asserted that the people of Canada wanted a whole new political approach, one that was in tune with the changes going on in the rest of our contemporary society. He went on to discuss briefly changes such as the transition from a rural to an urban society, more hours of leisure for many Canadians, and "like it or not, [transitioning] from federally oriented legislation to provincially oriented legislation."[3]

Although an admirer of John Diefenbaker, Lougheed had gotten to know Robert Stanfield personally, and probably was not displeased when Stanfield was declared the new leader of the federal Conservatives. He now had a direct link to Ottawa. Stanfield was a featured speaker at the next convention of the Progressive Conservatives of Alberta. But perhaps an even better result of his Toronto Convention speech was that "a coast to coast television audience was made aware of Lougheed and his deep sense of caring for his province and for his country."[4]

Back in Edmonton, Premier Manning finally had agreed to Lougheed's request for funds and offices, and provided a somewhat meagre, but much needed, $10,000 and some very basic office space on the second floor of the Legislative Building. Cognizant of his own deficiencies, Lougheed asked former federal House Speaker and current MP Marcel Lambert to instruct him and his new MLAs on legislative rules and procedures. He also began to forge an opposition strategy through a series of meetings to which he invited not only his own Conservative MLAs, but also the three Liberals and one Independent who had been elected in the 1967 provincial election. His intent in doing so reflected both his personal inclination as a team builder and his growing sophistication as a political strategist.

The opposition strategy that emerged was crafted to appeal to both his own and the other four MLAs who were not Conservatives. By the time the legislative assembly was once again in session, Manning and his ministers were forced to answer questions and field criticisms from 10 opposition MLAs who often worked cooperatively to make discussions and debates more challenging to Socred ministers who were not used to having to defend their views and actions. And, even better, Albertans were starting to take notice of the new political dynamic that was settling into the legislative grounds on the northern shore of the North Saskatchewan River.

At the provincial Conservative Convention in 1969, an unprecedented 1,800 attendees appeared, after Ted Mills organized a phone blitz of Albertans who had shown interest in Lougheed and his MLAs. When Lougheed suggested that face-to-face contact always worked best, Mills crisscrossed the province in his own car, braving freezing weather and tricky driving conditions, concentrating on reaching folks he and others had not been able to contact by telephone. Lougheed wanted those who might be thinking of attending the convention to know that they would be welcome. At the convention, it was decided that Lougheed and his opposition members of the Legislature would tour the province to hold mini policy conferences and meetings outside of Edmonton and Calgary. Small discussions and meetings with individuals mostly replaced larger rallies, which Lougheed believed appealed mostly to the already committed. What he was after were conversations with the undecided. Above all else, Lougheed was determined to demonstrate that his Progressive Conservatives were hard working, responsible, and committed to establishing themselves as a credible alternative to the ruling Socreds, an alternative that was wide open to input from the citizens of the province.

Another important feature of Lougheed's strategy, between 1967 and 1971, was to prepare and present substantive opposition bills when the Legislature was in session. No longer would the role of the opposition be limited to reacting critically and negatively to what the Socreds were doing. Lougheed believed that most people wanted to be involved in doing something positive rather than tearing things down. Gradually, the positive spirit that pervaded the Alberta Tories undersized second-floor office space, with its open-spaced and patch-work quarters, began to catch on across the province. It was beginning to feel like something new and exciting was happening in the world of Alberta politics. Those in the know thought they could see that Ernest Manning himself was beginning to get a glimpse of what might lie in store for him and his Social Credit establishment.

Even when given opportunities that would have left many politicians salivating, Lougheed stopped short of savaging the incumbent Socreds. One such instance occurred when Frank Calder, a U of A student who was active in PC campus politics and who had been asked by Lougheed to check all "orders in council" on a weekly basis, discovered that one such order was missing. When Frank asked Attorney-General Edgar Gerhart about the missing file, Gerhart eventually produced it. When revealed, the contents of the file confirmed that at the same time as Gerhart had recently reassured Albertans that existing legislation was adequate to protect shareholders of the province's trust companies, a major Alberta life insurance firm was in severe financial difficulty. Even though Lougheed had previously raised his own concerns about better controlling the operations of trust companies to protect shareholders, he refrained from making public Calder's discovery. His rationale? "Because the company was owned by a lot of small farmers and people like that, he was concerned about the impact on the depositors and shareholders and how they would be affected."[5] The matter was dealt with and any punitive effects that might have occurred for Gerhart, the company, and its investors were averted.

Nonetheless, such reluctance to muckrake did not stop Lougheed or his MLAs from continuously keeping the pressure on Manning and his troops by seeking detailed explanations from the Socreds about government actions and expenditures—explanations that the incumbents had become inexpert at fielding from lack of recent practice. Like most things in the Lougheed political strategy, question periods (whenever the Legislature was sitting) were carefully planned and scripted. Lougheed's legal training of rehearsing possibilities and planning cross-examinations brought a new level of "know how" to the Conservatives' challenges. Arranging his MLAs as a "shadow cabinet," Lougheed held a daily caucus to determine which minister of the government to focus on, leaving the others for another day. Members of Manning's cabinet were beginning to feel the heat. Things were definitely changing in the province of Alberta's political landscape, but few Albertans anticipated what happened on September 27, 1968 when Ernest Manning resigned as Premier of the province.

◆◆◆

Manning's decision to resign probably involved several factors, but there can be little doubt that the timing of his resignation was directly related to his desire to leave the Premier's office while he and his party were still in power and more or less at the top of their game. If he were to do so, he could not afford to linger for long, now that Lougheed and his reborn Tories were showing real signs of life, gathering increasing support from Alberta voters, and beginning to nip at his heels. It might have been difficult for Manning to believe that the young Peter Lougheed had come so far in a mere three years. He may well have reflected on the symbolic irony of the handwritten note he had sent to Lougheed, upon spotting him in the legislature gallery three years previously in March 1965, just after Lougheed had been elected for the first time as an MLA, but before he had taken up his new position: "I hope your visit to the assembly doesn't dim your enthusiasm to enter actively into provincial public life. The first twenty-five years are the worst."[6]

What Lougheed saw at the time he decided to throw his hat into the ring of the Conservative leadership contest was that the ruling Social Credit Party was really an extension of the popular, brilliant, and unique Ernest Manning himself, and Manning was getting older. Moreover, his premiership was beginning to be taken for granted, with several Socred-held constituencies now populated by fewer than 200 party members. Lougheed sensed opportunity almost before it knocked, realizing that his modern outlook and connections, organizational abilities, and youthful energy and enthusiasm would play well against an aging Manning and his *ancien régime.* When his grandfather, Sir James, had died in 1925, Manning was already 17 years old. Surely the time had come for Sir James' grandson to take the reins and restore his family's good name.

Peter Lougheed was always eager to learn from his experiences, good or bad, successful or not. To him, Manning's resignation signalled an unexpected quickening of the possibilities he envisioned for himself and his party. If Manning was hearing footsteps, Lougheed was breathing in and running with the winds of change. The fact that Manning had not endorsed anyone to take his place as leader of the Socreds, not even his own son Preston, also was not lost on Lougheed, perhaps indicating that the Social Credit icon was uncertain about who among his troops might be able to take on Lougheed and his rejuvenated Tories.

Peter both liked and admired Ernest Manning, but he knew that Alberta needed a change of leadership and course. Above all, if the province was to flourish in a new age of unprecedented change, it required a government that could help its citizens meet the challenges being brought about by major growth and shifts in its population, in its resource development and management, and in its relationship with the federal government of Canada. In a November 1968 letter to the "Lougheed Club," Peter praised Ernest Manning for his many years of service and accomplishment as Premier of Alberta. Looking ahead to the Social Credit Party's leadership convention in December of that year, he predicted that Harry Strom would replace Manning as Premier. Lougheed's prediction proved accurate when Strom, with the support of enough old guards and the few young Turks of his party, did indeed prevail, becoming the first Premier actually born in Alberta, a short-lived distinction that was soon to be eclipsed by Lougheed himself when he became the first Alberta-born and duly elected Premier of Alberta, a mere three years later.

In the meantime, Lougheed kept up the pressure on the Socreds with a unique mixture of centre-right proposals for shifting more tax burden to those with the ability to pay, setting a goal of university education for 50 percent of Alberta's youth, and increasing funding for day care, universities, and mental health facilities, all without providing much detail about how such initiatives would be reconciled with his promise of fiscal restraint. However, voters nonetheless rewarded the youthful Tory leader and his party with a surprise and highly symbolic by-election win. On February 10, 1969, just three days before the provincial legislature reconvened, Conservative candidate Bill Yurko was elected in the Edmonton riding of Strathcona East, the constituency held by Manning himself from its creation in 1948 to his retirement four and a half months earlier. Yurko's astonishing victory was then followed by Conservative Bob Dowling's victory over Social Credit candidate Arthur Jorgensen on October 28, 1969. Rookie provincial NDP leader Grant Notley also finished behind Dowling.

The Conservative team of MLAs continued to grow in November 1969 when William Dickie, the sole liberal MLA remaining in the legislature, joined Lougheed's conservatives. PC prospects received yet another boost when a commission to redraw the province's obsolete electoral map, established by Strom's Socreds, did so in a way that gave greater representation to urban over rural areas of Alberta. Lougheed was well aware that much Socred strength resided outside the cities of Edmonton and Calgary, and although doing his best to appeal to rural Albertans, most of his own support at the time was in the cities.

1970 saw another wave of Tory proposals and promises in anticipation of a likely 1971 provincial election. Some, like allowing less party discipline over the voting of MLAs, were almost certainly intended to annoy the Socreds, rather than reflect Lougheed's own views, in which loyalty figured large. In the Legislature, Peter became more aggressively *ad hominem*, attacking Strom as "timid, weak and cautious in his dealings with Ottawa," and demanding outright changes to federal tax laws that he believed hurt Alberta's resource development and management, while maintaining that efforts by Strom and his government with respect to such matters were "puny."[7] With the 1970 legislature session concluded, Lougheed went into full campaign mode, holding luncheon meetings, giving speeches, shaking hands, and riding horseback in parades and local celebrations.

Peter was off and running in all the province's cities and many of its towns, meeting as many Albertans as possible. Lougheed was a formidable campaigner. Not only was he well versed about campaign issues and the Socreds' vulnerabilities, but the campaign trail offered many venues for him to display his phenomenal memory for those he had met, even if only briefly. Every year since he had become leader of the Alberta PCs, Lougheed had been the star attraction at a number of annual meetings spread throughout the province that served as fund-raisers and information exchanges between party members, supporters, and MLAs. On these occasions, Peter would astonish those in attendance by his ability to recall them by name, often making reference to their conversation at last year's or some other gathering.

On these and many other occasions, Lougheed also delivered speeches that arose extemporaneously from his discussions as he circulated and bantered amongst the various groups and tables of attendees who were enjoying their lunches or dinners. "Although his grammar was frequently incorrect, the effect of his memory for names and faces and concern for local issues made a huge impact"[8] on those in attendance. Lougheed's memory, either for faces on such occasions or for facts in cabinet and caucus documents, was a significant part of his political arsenal, and one that he practiced with intention to attract voters and to keep his ministers on their toes.

Throughout the 1971 campaign, Peter continued to insist on the necessity for change and renewal as the only options available to the province and its citizens. To this end, he and his team worked hard to create an impressive slate of highly qualified and attractive candidates. The Conservatives' organization was even better than in Lougheed's first campaign in 1967. When Edmonton lawyer Pete Savaryn suggested "NOW" as the Tories' campaign slogan, it caught on immediately. Soon thereafter, 2,000 people gathered beneath the Conservative Party's orange and blue colours at Calgary's Palliser Hotel for a convention, billed as the largest Alberta political gathering since the Socreds took power in 1935. Lawyer and strong conservative Ron Ghitter caught the mood of the gathering and the excitement it generated, and turned prophetic—"When history looks on this night, it will be remembered as the night the Alberta Conservative Party turned the corner and grasped the momentum to win the 1971 election."[9]

◆◆◆

The session of the Alberta legislature that opened on February 11, 1971 was a showcase of pre-election sparring. Lougheed's reaction to the governing Social Credit Party's Throne Speech was mostly to ignore it in favour of announcing his own plans for Alberta's future. These included a social action program to assist Albertans suffering from unemployment and mired in poverty, new opportunities for Indigenous Peoples, greater attention to education and health care, and an Alberta Bill of Rights to protect the civil liberties of all Albertans. In the legislature itself, Premier Strom did a decent job of jousting with Lougheed, reminding him that the entire Social Credit movement, from 1935 to the present, was based on the alleviation of social and economic difficulties and struggles of Alberta's citizens, and that in this he and his cabinet needed no help from an inexperienced leader of a small opposition party. However, Strom could not compete with the Lougheed juggernaut when it came to television.

Television commercials, interviews, and news clips played a huge role in determining the outcome of the 1971 provincial election in Alberta. On television, Strom was a non-performer, appearing stiff, awkward, and ill at ease. He was no match for Lougheed, who had spent long hours practicing and vetting his TV persona, with the aid of his communications team and the use of studio facilities owned and made available by well-heeled and well-connected supporters, who wanted to see Alberta's entrepreneurial environment modernized. Having seen how effectively Trudeau and his federal team had used television to defeat Robert Stanfield and his Tories in 1968, Lougheed's communications and media people were anxious to press home their advantage. They convinced Lougheed to hire Perry Rosemond, a Canadian living in Los Angeles with a flair for television, to spearhead their campaign advertising.

When Rosemond saw Lougheed in front of the cameras, he knew what to do. "What we did was kind of unique at the time. [Our] promotional announcements were based on transcriptions of our conversations ... on Peter's own ideas, in his own words. We shot the appropriate film, and distilled the essential Peter Lougheed."[10] In a surprisingly short period of time, the Tories private polling conducted by a California firm showed Peter and his party with a 22-point lead (46% to 24%) in voter support over Premier Strom and his governing Socreds.

With the Legislature recessed, Lougheed knew he had to do something to erode the strongly Socred leanings of Alberta's petroleum industry. Aware that several large multinational companies had begun to shift much of their exploration and production operations to the Arctic, leaving more than 300 smaller independents, many owned by Canadians, to fight over secondary recovery operations and reduced field exploration in Alberta, Lougheed decided it was a good time to advertise his long-held belief that "Government policy should recognize the best interest of the people by developing tax measures, financial assistance, and government policies to expand ownership by Canadians and assure greater involvement of our people."[11] To this end, he promised to provide appropriate incentives and rewards. He also suggested that it was time for Alberta to offset its heavy dependency on oil export revenues by actively promoting more secondary processing and industry in the province, with a view to employing and developing more home-grown talent. Of course, both the Alberta owned companies and the newly groomed talent consisted of people who actually voted in Alberta.

On another matter that was to figure large in Lougheed's subsequent political career, he had a good deal to say about Strom's June 1971 participation in a federal-provincial conference that Trudeau and his federal Grits had convened to approve a new Canadian constitution. Suspecting that Strom would be convinced to support Ottawa's proposal, Lougheed publically warned him against accepting any constitutional deal that would include the so-called Victoria Charter that would give Ontario and Quebec vetoes over any future agreements or amendments to the constitution without extending the same veto privileges to any of the other eight provinces. Lougheed received strongly supportive responses from most Alberta media outlets when he declared that if elected, he would not be bound by the drafting of any charter that included the Victoria formula.

When issued, Lougheed's warning was actually irrelevant because Liberal Premier Robert Bourassa of Quebec already had declared his opposition to the charter draft that the Feds had prepared. In the wake of Trudeau's 1970 invocation of the War Measures Act, Bourassa was demanding complete provincial control over social security, which the governing Liberals never would grant. In the end, a new constitutional agreement was once again deferred.

When Strom finally announced that the provincial election would be held on August 30, 1971, Lougheed's PCs ran a final two-month campaign "with the precision of those ramrodding a football squad on a road trip ... no detail was left to chance." The campaign "is almost Kennedy-esque in how the PC chief is met and led off at a run to blitz the streets and stores."[12] The tempo kept increasing during the last weeks of the election. As it did, the youthful vigour of many of the Tory candidates began to pay dividends, especially in Edmonton and Calgary. Without knowing the results of the PCs' private polling, most analysts still thought the Socreds would prevail. Those fearing more of the same from the "aging gang" began to encourage Lougheed to take off the gloves. But for the most part, Lougheed kept to the course he had set, staying fixed on his positive proposals and citing the advantages and strengths of his own candidates in comparison with their opponents. In doing so, he generally stayed clear of assaulting the integrity and competence of individual Socred candidates, although he was always ready to help voters read between the lines of the comparative descriptions he used to contrast himself and his candidates with Strom and his group.

To explain and justify his consistent attempts to straddle the centre of the political spectrum, Lougheed labeled himself a "pragmatist," who "always will be a free enterprise Conservative on economic matters." "On social matters, such as the rights of the individual, mental health reform, privacy, and social issues, we emphasize the progressive and reform character of the Progressive Conservative Party. For this reason some people have referred to me on occasion as a 'liberal Conservative.' But, frankly I do not believe the terms 'right' or 'left' are meaningful in modern politics. We stand for free enterprise—not socialism. We also stand for social reform and individual rights—not big government control."[13]

In the end, Lougheed's pragmatic blend of economic conservativism and social progressivism carried the day. Only 17 of 37 Socred incumbents were re-elected (including Strom), together with 8 new Socred candidates. Against this total of 25 elected Socred MLAs stood 49 Conservative MLAs. Grant Notley, leader of the NDP, secured the only other seat. Not a single Liberal was elected, leaving lots of room for Lougheed to practice his political pragmatism in the years to come.

As the newly minted Premier of Alberta, Lougheed had a pretty clear idea of what he wanted to do. Given his penchant for organization and strategizing, an obvious priority was to grease the wheels of governance by getting both the Legislature and the Alberta civil service to work together under his control. To do so, he had to be very careful in choosing his cabinet. In this, as in many matters, Lougheed was happy to canvas his wife Jeanne's opinion, having a high respect for her ability to size people up and fit them to particular jobs. In the end, the 22 members of his cabinet (the biggest in Alberta history) included almost all those who, along with Lougheed himself, had been Conservative MLAs before the 1971 election. Key appointments were Lou Hyndman as Minister of Education and Government House Leader, Bill Dickie as Minister of Energy, and Don Getty to head up the newly created Department of Intergovernmental Affairs, assisted by Lougheed's old friend Harold Millican (a card-carrying Liberal) as the non-elected Deputy Minister of that Department. Newcomer Conservative MLA Mervin Leitch was given the post of Provincial Attorney General, young Red Deer lawyer Jim

Foster was put in charge of Advanced Education, and Neil Crawford was appointed as Minister of Health, all positions closely associated with Lougheed's announced and intended priority initiatives.

Merv Leitch, a close friend, was one of Lougheed's most trusted colleagues and one of the first who Peter had approached to join his team when he first had decided to enter Alberta provincial politics. Like Lougheed, Leitch, who had won the gold medal for being at the top of his University of Alberta law class, was a tireless, meticulous worker. "When Merv spoke in the caucus room there was usually absolute silence, because his thoughts were always marshalled with great care and presented with impeccable logic."[14] Leitch, who was raised on a struggling Saskatchewan farm during the Great Depression, also was known to be a deeply compassionate and loyal man. He served as the Lougheed government's Attorney General (1971-1975), Provincial Treasurer (1975-1979), and Minister of Energy and Natural Resources (1979-1982), until his retirement from politics in 1982.

Merv was to play a huge role in Lougheed's battles with Trudeau's federal Liberals on both energy and constitutional matters. Jim Foster, who succeeded Leitch as Alberta's Attorney General in 1975, describes the working relationship between Lougheed and Leitch as vital to the Lougheed years in Alberta. "They both were extremely well organized and prepared. They read everything that crossed their desks and those of other ministers. There was a real bond of loyalty between them."[15]

Indeed, loyalty was extremely important to Lougheed. Not only did he practice it himself, sometimes to his detriment, but he expected and demanded it of others, perhaps a legacy of his background in competitive sport. Nonetheless, Peter did not view loyalty as inconsistent with criticism. In fact, one of the things he valued most in his close associates was an honest appraisal of their joint undertakings and his part in them. "What many did not realize about Peter, was that when all was said and done, he was willing to take advice, and when convinced was often willing to back down."[16] Of course, this did not mean that he was inconsistent in attending to what he regarded as his most central political goals, such as gaining greater control over and controlling the development of Alberta's natural resources for the benefit of its citizens. Although even here, he always sought council from his "team" when plotting, and sometimes changing, strategies.

After the 1971 Alberta election, the Provincial Civil Service was given a huge overhaul, with almost three quarters of previous deputy ministers relieved of their duties. Those who replaced them were a mix of Lougheed loyalists drawn from his old Calgary friends and Mannix colleagues, and a group of highly regarded and well educated authorities. These included George Govier, a University of Calgary professor and expert on energy resource conservation and management, former BC Hydro engineer Wayne Minion who was hired as Chair of the Petroleum Marketing Division, and many similarly qualified others. Overall, the new Lougheed cabinet and civil service were younger, better educated, and perhaps represented a wider range of the political spectrum than the Socred cabinets of the past, although this last comparison is tricky, given changes to the province's overall political demographic over time. That said, the one qualification all members of the new Tory Cabinet shared was a trusted relationship, and/or sense of priorities and directions, with Peter Lougheed himself. With a loyal team in place that appreciated his perspectives and programs, Peter quickly developed and implemented a code of ethics for his civil servants, and consultants hired by his government, that prohibited them from accepting gifts, favours, or services from individuals, organizations, or corporations. Another first priority was to review the province's finances, with a special emphasis on natural resources royalties and income.

Throughout his previous term as an MLA and Opposition leader from 1967 to 1971, and during the 1971 campaign itself, Lougheed had been very careful not to acquire political debts or accept favours that might encumber him once he became Premier. Like Trudeau, it was important for Peter Lougheed to be free to do things on his own terms, without compromises that could tie his hands. Although he was extremely courteous to his cabinet and to government officials and workers, there was little doubt in any of their minds that it was Lougheed who was in control. And, despite his general sense of propriety and fair play, he was not above using certain advantages of his office to play to his strengths and to the detriment of those who might oppose him. These were aimed primarily at the Social Credit opposition, but also included any dissenters in his own ranks. Thus, shades of Tory red were more common and prominent in a redecorated Legislative chamber, audio-video outlets were installed behind opposition benches so that cameras would face only the government side of the chamber, and detailed records were kept of legislative proceedings.

However, the main focus of Lougheed's first term as Alberta's Premier was to get greater control over the development and management of Alberta's non-renewable natural resources. To this end, he routinely demanded observer and participant status for himself and Alberta in international energy discussions, meetings, and conferences involving Canada and other nations. These were demands that were just as routinely disregarded by Trudeau's federal Liberal Energy Ministers as improper for the conduct of international negotiations, which they viewed as entirely federal matters. Announcing his desire to be fully informed about federal energy policies and decisions, Lougheed argued that "Any decision by the federal government that might limit petroleum or natural gas exports or discourage exploration and development ... will have a serious effect on Alberta's economy"[17] and Alberta must be included in such decisions.

When, at the end of November 1971, the federal government nixed Alberta's approval of a plan to sell a billion dollars worth of natural gas to the United States, Lougheed responded: "If eastern utility companies expect Albertans to just simply sit and keep its gas in the ground, surplus to the needs of the people in Alberta until they get around in eastern Canada to use and take advantage of Alberta gas, then obviously that is not a satisfactory situation."[18] Trudeau then sent a brief telegram to Lougheed stating his willingness to discuss such matters. And discuss they did. Over the next 13 years, many much more acrimonious exchanges would ensue between the two men and their ministers about Alberta's natural resources.

◆◆◆

In December 1971, the Lougheeds purchased and moved into a new home in Edmonton, and Peter began to prepare for his first sitting of the legislature as Premier. But any thoughts of governing were temporarily halted by the death of Peter's mother in February 1972. Despite her lengthy illness, her death hit Lougheed hard. Edna Bauld Lougheed, who had encouraged Peter's political ambitions, never would see her younger son as Premier in the Alberta Legislature. As the March 2, 1972 opening of the provincial legislature approached, Peter Lougheed struggled to keep his grief private amongst the pomp and ceremony that announced a significant changing of the guard in Alberta politics. A new governing dynasty was about to take power.

The new government's speech from the throne promised greater diversity and balance in the province's economy. This commitment echoed Lougheed's promise to himself not to allow his home province to experience the kind of "boom and bust" experiences he had witnessed during his summer in Tulsa, Oklahoma while studying at Harvard. But, perhaps the biggest surprise of that legislative session was Lougheed's introduction of an Alberta Bill of Rights, taken almost intact from that proposed and introduced previously by John Diefenbaker for the country as a whole, but carefully adapted to the Alberta context by Merv Leitch. Using the same language, but applying these rights to the Province of Alberta and its practices of governance, Leitch, with Lougheed's oversight, enshrined six fundamental freedoms that would apply to all Albertans "without discrimination by reason of race, national origin, colour, religion or sex": "the right to individual liberty, security of the person, and enjoyment of property; the right of the individual before the law; freedom of religion; freedom of assembly; freedom of speech; and freedom of the press."[19] Lougheed also made all decisions of the Supreme Court of Canada immediately applicable in Alberta. However, in a departure from Diefenbaker's Bill of Rights, he, at Leitch's suggestion, added a "notwithstanding clause" that reserved the right of the Alberta Legislature to exempt certain of its decrees and declarations from the Provincial Bill of Rights, foreshadowing a strategy that would prove central to the constitutional debates between Canadian federal and provincial governments in the early 1980s.

Lougheed's first legislative session as premier also saw the introduction of a program of economic nationalism that required foreign companies, including those in the oil and gas sector, to use Alberta technology, personnel, and products in future construction and expansion, including the hiring of Canadian directors and the authorization of Albertan shareholders. Further, it was proposed that any products manufactured from oil extracted should be processed in plants established in the province. In making these proposals, and also suggesting a tax on the future development of oil reserves still in the ground, Lougheed signalled that the days of treating foreign oil companies generously, so as to stimulate initial growth of the industry in Alberta, were over. Alberta had matured and so must they. Nonetheless, Lougheed did offer the oil companies various incentives to increase exploration for new fields and allowed them to deduct the new tax on their federal tax returns. Whether or not he realized at this time that he was courting a feud with Ottawa by purporting to allow such a tax is uncertain, but once again a seed for future conflict was sown.

Such moves created considerable discomfort in central Canadian financial and governmental institutions. In some such quarters, Lougheed was denounced as a "Western separatist." He responded by saying that it was necessary for Alberta and the other provinces to develop a national industrial strategy they all could agree to, one that would not isolate Alberta or any other province, so as to forestall regional alienation. He seemed to indicate that these current initiatives were just the first moves in that overall strategy, and more could be expected. Even at this early stage in his premiership, Lougheed made no secret of his vision of a Canadian federation with strong regional representation, participation, and powers.

Throughout 1972 and 1973, Lougheed continued to pursue his efforts to build a greater power base for Alberta in its dealings with the oil companies and the federal government with respect to control of, and revenue sharing of proceeds from, Alberta's oil and gas production and reserves. In this, he adopted a three-pronged strategy—courting other provinces, especially western provinces, to adopt his push for greater provincial powers; continuing his fight with Ottawa over control of, and profits from, Alberta's natural resources; and bringing large international oil companies operating in Alberta to heel.

Lougheed flexed his "province building ambitions" further by organizing what was called the Western Economic Opportunities Conference (WEOC) in Calgary in October 1973, to which he invited Pierre Trudeau to meet with him and other Western Premiers from British Columbia, Saskatchewan, and Manitoba. Still smarting from his near defeat, and demotion to leader of a minority government, in the federal election of 1972, Trudeau began by stating his desire to better understand Western concerns and ambitions. "Orchestrated by Lougheed and needing little encouragement ... the Premiers heavily criticized federal policy ... they portrayed federal transportation and economic development policies as at best indifferent to western Canadian needs." Overall, "federal policy perpetuated a division of labour between an industrial heartland and resource-producing peripheries."[20]

In the words of Allan Tupper, "the WEOC had lasting consequences." It spawned the annual Western Premiers Conferences that continue to this day, and established "a tradition of cooperation" among these provinces that has demonstrated repeatedly "the national impact of a united western Canada."[21] Of course, the WEOC also made Peter Lougheed a powerful figure within the overall landscape of Canadian politics, and displayed his trademark capabilities for disciplined organization, well-researched documentation, and, perhaps above all, team building. After this, with the other western provinces as team players, when Lougheed spoke for Alberta he increasingly was perceived as speaking for western Canada as a whole.

Another province-building initiative undertaken by Lougheed, during his first term of office as Premier, has already been mentioned but deserves greater attention. By changing and restructuring Alberta's oil and gas royalties, Lougheed not only increased Alberta's share of revenues, but also asserted and drew attention to the provincial Crown's power as landowner. Here, Lougheed's argument was crystal clear and consistent: Alberta must prepare for the time when it's non-renewable natural resources would inevitably be depleted. Therefore, it must maximize its returns, and guard against excessive development unnecessary to and beyond the province's needs of the moment, thus keeping an eye to the future.

As Premier, his personal preference was to let existing oil and gas leases on provincial crown lands lapse by simply not renewing them, and then to negotiate higher royalty rates for new leases. However, in late 1973, when the federal government announced an export tax on Alberta's oil during the height of the OPEC oil embargo on the U.S. and its allies, an act Lougheed called "the most discriminatory action by a federal government against a particular province in the entire history of Confederation,"[22] he upped his royalty demands in retaliation. He now insisted that all existing leases in Alberta also be subject to his new, higher royalty rates, angering not just the Feds, but the oil industry as well. In fighting the export tax imposed by Ottawa, Lougheed's anger and actions spilled over to include some of the other provinces. If export taxes were to apply indiscriminately to Alberta's natural resource exports, what about pulp and paper from Ontario and Quebec, lumber from BC, or potash from Saskatchewan? He eventually went as far as to cancel all existing provincial leases and to impose maximum royalties. Lougheed did not like to be pushed around, and when he considered such pushing to be unjustified, he pushed back.

Matters only got worse when, in 1974, the federal government disallowed petroleum companies from deducting provincial royalties when calculating their federal taxable income, thus increasing significantly the fiscal burden the companies already had absorbed from Lougheed's hikes in royalties. With Trudeau claiming that such a tax was necessary to protect the national fiscal regime during a time of inflationary pressure, Lougheed once again charged that Alberta was being singled out for unfair treatment. The Feds were not only interfering with his province's ownership and management of its resources, but also undercutting the energy pricing agreement that had been negotiated earlier that year. Although Lougheed later made some concessions to the oil industry, the Alberta-Ottawa feud over oil export taxation and royalty pricing and deductibility presaged a stormy next decade for intergovernmental relations between Peter Lougheed's Progressive Conservatives and Pierre Elliott Trudeau's Liberals. Neither Lougheed nor Trudeau was a bully, but they could come close if they perceived themselves to be threatened by bullying.

In his home province, despite the wariness he now inspired in many oil executives, Lougheed was increasingly viewed as standing up for Alberta's rights, and praised for his steadfast stewardship of its resources and the wellbeing of its citizens. Leading up to the next provincial election in 1975, Peter Lougheed and his PCs had not only exorcised most remnants of Social Credit political authority, but looked to most observers like the wave of the future for Alberta and Albertans. Lougheed had made it clear that "he was a formidable negotiator, a determined defender of Alberta's interests, and a person capable of decisive national action. The province builder had arrived."[23]

On February 7, 1975, provincial Finance Minister Gordon Miniely delivered in the Alberta Legislature what was clearly a pre-election budget. It was a budget that took full advantage of the flood of revenue flowing from Lougheed's new royalties and increased provincial share of profits from the petroleum industry. Spending on health, education, and welfare was increased significantly, even after provincial income taxes were lowered. And, true to Lougheed's commitment to his province and himself, the new budget was crowned by the creation of a Heritage Trust Fund intended to "ensure the prosperity of the future generations of Albertans." Although opposition parties and some of the province's newspapers found the budget overall to be "devoid of new ideas," in that "there is nothing remarkable ... about cutting taxes and increasing expenditures ... when you have more money around than you know what to do with,"[24] the fact remained that the provincial Tories were able to boast that in only three and a half years they had completely turned around the province's financial standing—to the extent that (as it was later reported) Miniely had failed to include $600 million in additional provincial revenue when drawing up his budget.

On the weekend following release of his new budget, Lougheed met with Prime Minister Trudeau, who was in Alberta to open the Canada Winter Games being held in Lethbridge. During their meeting, Lougheed realized that Trudeau was not convinced that the majority of Albertans were solidly behind his energy policies and oil royalties and prices. To demonstrate that such support did indeed exist, Lougheed, symbolically sporting a yellow (in opposition to Trudeau's trademark red) rose in his lapel, confidently announced in the Legislature on Valentine's Day, that because he needed to be certain he was backed by "the full confidence of the people"[25] before engaging in further negotiations to increase oil prices even more, he was announcing a provincial election to be held in little over a month's time, on March 26, 1975. In doing so, Lougheed also laid out the terms on which the snap election would be fought, launching what was to be a major theme in his forthcoming campaign: "You're not just voting Progressive Conservative when you vote for us. ... It's time for Albertans to stand together."[26] Against who, and for what, were by this time pretty obvious.

In the campaign itself, Lougheed overrode attempts by Strom and the Social Credit party to make the election about what they regarded as the Premier's abuse of executive power and unnecessarily heavy handedness in his dealings with the other provinces and the federal government. Lougheed also dismissed concerns expressed by Grant Notley and his NDP party about his seeming collaboration with the large petroleum company Syncrude in exploring development of the vast tar sands in the northeast of Alberta. Lougheed's primary strategy was to dwarf these and other concerns as wrongheaded and minor distractions, compared to the clear and present need to send a message to Ottawa that the voters of Alberta are fully behind their Premier, who was fighting tooth and nail for them and future generations of Albertans.

The result of the 1975 election gave Peter Lougheed all the ammunition he needed to support his royalty and pricing demands. He and his PCs received a record high 63 percent of the popular vote and elected 69 PC MLAs. The provincial Liberals were completely locked out, the once proud and seemingly invincible Socreds reduced to only four seats, and Grant Notley claimed the one and only seat for his NDP party. Even Trudeau seemed to get the message. When Lougheed arrived in Ottawa on April 9, 1975, Trudeau rewarded Lougheed's demonstration of the extent of his support in Alberta by saying, "We cannot expect Alberta to go on, year after year, selling its oil to Canadians at a price which is far below that which they could get by exporting it. We cannot expect those who search for oil—whether they be Canadians or others to look for it and develop it in Canada—if our prices are far below those in other countries."[27]

Unfortunately for Lougheed, Bill Davis, PC Premier of Ontario, could not afford to go along with him and Trudeau on any plan that might raise prices of oil and gas in Ontario, especially when he was preparing for his own provincial election in the near future. A significant rise in oil prices would inevitably translate into a major loss of jobs in Ontario, which would seal his political demise. Davis' strategy was to complain that Alberta and Ottawa were colluding to fatten their own purses at the expense of the rest of Canada. In this, he was supported by the premiers of BC, Manitoba, New Brunswick, and Nova Scotia, thus forcing a stalemate in the matter of petroleum pricing. The meeting, in many ways a portend of what was to come over the next decade, ended with Trudeau warning that if the provinces could not compromise by the end of June 1975, he and his government would have no choice but to take matters into their own hands and work out a system with the producing provinces for higher oil and gas prices nationwide.

With no compromise forthcoming, on June 23 1975, federal Finance Minister John Turner seemed to create one, when presenting his new budget to the House of Commons. He raised the well-head price of oil from six and a half to eight dollars, an amount still four dollars below the world price. However, he also increased the price of natural gas four-fold, and levied an additional dime a gallon excise tax to encourage conservation. With what promised to be an additional $500 million a year in the Alberta treasury, Lougheed accepted Turner's compromise, and announced to the Alberta Legislature that Alberta and Ottawa "are cooperating in the best interests of Canada," acknowledging "that there has been very significant progress" in their "continuing negotiations ... on energy matters. The petroleum industry at last has a sense of stability."[28] Things seemed to be looking up for many of those concerned. However, changes of circumstances are common in life, and perhaps never more so than in the realm of politics.

In 1976, Lougheed and Miniely established the Alberta Heritage Savings Trust Fund (AHSTF) they had promised in the pre-election budget speech before announcing the 1975 provincial election. The initial investment in the fund was $1.5 billion, and was followed by annual supplements equal to 30 percent of the yearly royalties earned from sales of the province's non-renewable resources. Lougheed described the AHSTF as a "rainy day fund" for a future when oil and gas no longer produced most of the province's revenue stream. With that goal in mind, the fund was "a tool to aid economic diversification and to enable Alberta to break away from its historic boom and bust cycles."[29] As a reminder of current prosperity and a promise of fiscal health in the future, the Fund became a source of pride for Lougheed and Albertans themselves—pride that was no doubt enhanced by the comparative financial struggles of the federal government during the 1970s. Throughout this decade, inflation exacted a considerable toll on Ottawa's ability to manage its existing costs, let alone expand those costs further by realizing election promises of the Trudeau federal government. Indeed, for most Canadians, Alberta's Heritage Trust Fund became a symbol of a transfer of the nation's wealth from central Canada to the west.

However, Alberta's new prosperity and its lust for additional revenues from its booming petroleum industry were not without problems of their own. One of the biggest was how to develop the province's tar sands in ways that would keep revenue flowing to support the rapid growth in population that accompanied Alberta's economic recovery. Solving the puzzle of the Athabasca oil sands, estimated to hold a third of the world's oil reserves if they could be tapped, was a tantalizing project. The puzzle was how to extract oil from the tar-like, dense bitumen of the Athabasca field, an extremely viscous form of crude oil that can be made to flow only when heated or diluted by hydrocarbons like light crude oil or natural gas condensate.

With Lougheed's encouragement, a consortium of large U.S.-controlled companies like Imperial Oil and Atlantic Richfield, and Canadian affiliates like Gulf Canada and Canada-Cities Service, had been formed to find a way of extracting tar sands oil as efficiently as possible. Calling itself Syncrude Canada, the consortium spent much of 1973 to 1975 negotiating with the Alberta government to strike a deal that would give the Government of Alberta and Albertans a healthy share of the profits that potentially could follow from

American investment in the technology required to produce useable oil from the sands. The idea was that oil extracted would flow through a new pipeline from the Athabasca tar sands to Edmonton. Don Getty, now Lougheed's Energy Minister, demanded that the Province of Alberta have a 20 percent share in Syncrude itself, 50 percent ownership of an electric generator and the pipeline that would be required to run the operation and get the product to Edmonton, and half of any future profits. When the Americans objected, Getty, with Lougheed's support, appeared perfectly willing to walk away from the talks. Eventually, a deal was struck that involved tweaking the ownership arrangements somewhat in favour of the Americans.

However, profitably getting oil to market can be a tricky business, and even more so when new technologies and operating systems are required. So, it was not entirely surprising when the Alberta government's initial arrangement with Syncrude fell apart on December 6, 1974, after Atlantic Richfield announced that it was pulling out because of soaring costs. In an attempt to salvage a viable deal, the Lougheed government now scrambled to contain costs, curtail damage to its image, and find new partners. On February 2, 1975, just before the pre-election sitting of the Alberta Legislature and delivery of the pre-election budget, Lougheed, Getty, and their Alberta team met with federal ministers Donald Macdonald and Jean Chrétien, Ontario Premier Bill Davis, and representatives of the oil companies involved, which now included Shell Oil (replacing Atlantic Richfield), to hammer out a new deal. In the end, the consortium would increase its investment to 1.4 billion dollars and keep 70 percent ownership of the entire operation. Ottawa chipped in $300 million for a 15 percent share, and agreed to allow Syncrude to sell oil extracted at the world price. Alberta reduced its ownership share from 20 to 10 percent, and contributed $200 million. Ontario added $100 million for a 5 percent share.

The CBC later aired a program based on a book by University of Alberta political scientist Larry Pratt[30] that cast Lougheed as a dupe of the oil companies involved in Syncrude, claiming that Canadians were now paying for money to flow out of the country. An outraged Lougheed sued the CBC for libel, and eventually was vindicated when, after several ups and downs, the province of Alberta began to realize large profits from the project by the early 1980s. Nonetheless, as the 1970s moved along, both close friends and casual observers noticed the toll that the oil negotiations and fights were taking on Lougheed himself. The near failures and unpredictable, sudden oscillations in oil prices seemed to have aged him considerably. As the end of the decade approached, Lougheed, perhaps sensitive to an unaccustomed flurry of negative media coverage, seemed to become less immediately accessible, not only to the media, but to the public as well.

Overall, the 1970s were years of tremendous growth in Peter Lougheed's Alberta. As the oil flowed, fortunes were made, not just in the oil patch and among its many suppliers, but in other sectors of the province as well. Most of the newly rich were delighted to showcase their wealth. When Peter Pocklington turned a modest car dealership into a multi-million dollar empire of real estate and food processing and began to spread his holdings in other ways, he basked in the glow of his various sports teams, which included the Edmonton Drillers soccer team, the Edmonton Trappers triple-A baseball team, the Kamloops Junior Oilers, and, Wayne Gretzky and the NHL champion Edmonton Oilers. It was the age of the Albertan entrepreneur.

An increasing number of Albertans who now identified as self-made successes, were not always pro-Lougheed. Some of those who attributed their successes entirely to their own initiatives began to worry that Lougheed and his progressive conservatives might be a tad too "socialistic" for them. Paradoxically, as the provincial oil industry pumped out more and more multi-millionaires, the man who many had heralded as Mr. Alberta maintained a decidedly frosty relationship with many of these nouveaux riches. They fretted about the royalties that he placed on their hard and independently earned profits, what they regarded as his big government, interventionist tactics. They also were wary of all the newcomers (including many unwanted competitors) who now flooded into the province, expecting instant riches. Nonetheless, for the most part, Lougheed continued to hold their votes and support, both of which were almost completely denied to Trudeau and his federal liberals. "He may be a son of a bitch," one oil executive told the *Globe and Mail*, "but he is our son of a bitch."[31]

As Alberta's economic growth dwarfed that of the other provinces, its population exploded, adding almost a half million people to what had been a population of 1.6 million in 1971. New suburbs spread in every direction around Edmonton and Calgary, The classic Alberta rancher gave way to fancier and larger split and multi-level homes. Bigger became synonymous with better, and with all this growth, costs began to escalate. Calgary emerged as a major financial centre. Growth in rural as well as urban areas of the province overwhelmed contractors. Previously unheard of projects, like the Ghermezian family's West Edmonton Mall, which eventually opened in 1981 as the largest indoor shopping centre in the world and remained so until 2004, became accepted as almost commonplace. Smaller cities, like Canmore, Red Deer, Medicine Hat, Lethbridge, and Fort McMurray mushroomed. Medical, educational, and health services began to falter in a tide of rising demand. Crime increased. Houses were hard to find—and for many, far too expensive to purchase if they could be located.

The newcomers flooding into the province also transformed Alberta demographically. Franco-Albertans now outnumbered those in Manitoba, long a bastion of Francophone prairie culture. New federal immigration policies welcomed many highly trained and skilled individuals from almost all points of the globe. At the end of the 1970s, Asian immigrants made up more than 50 percent of Alberta's 10,000 annual newcomers. Refugees from Uganda, Chile, and other nations experiencing violent civil strife and turmoil found or hoped to find opportunities in Alberta's economic boom. Assimilating into Alberta's traditional cultural milieu established by earlier European settlers sometimes was not easy for these newcomers. However, in contrast to many previous non-European immigrants to the prairie provinces, those who sought a better life in Alberta during the 1970s had the advantage of support from provincial and federal multiculturalism policies. In Edmonton, a large and established Ukrainian-Canadian community, which had helped to develop national and provincial policies in areas like second-language education, provided a model of acculturation for these more recent arrivals. Lougheed and his governing party, with the province's increased oil revenues and commitment to progressive social policies, were ready and able to do a great deal to accommodate the challenges posed by the population boom of the 1970s. One area in which such accommodation was particularly noteworthy was in the area of cultural growth and development.

In the artistic and cultural life of the province, Jeanne Lougheed proved to be remarkably capable and helpful to her husband. During their courtship at the University of Alberta, Jeanne had introduced Peter to the fine and performing arts. Her background as a singer and pianist was part of a wide appreciation of the arts, on behalf of which she worked tirelessly, typically in quiet and unnoticed ways. Many who have commented on the accomplishments of her husband's government have overlooked the important part played by cultural development in Lougheed's efforts to modernize Alberta. One of the first things he did following his election as Premier in 1971 was to establish a stand-alone Ministry of Culture, making Alberta the only province, other than Quebec, to do so. Throughout the 1970s, the PC's used a small, but increasing, portion of the provincial government's lottery funds to fan the cultural aspirations and achievements of Albertans active in the fine and performing arts, and to celebrate the cultural richness of Alberta's increasingly multicultural population.

Fil Fraser, an Edmonton radio and television program manager, talk show host, and member of the Canadian Association of Black Journalists, referred to the 1970s as Alberta's "Camelot years,"[32] noting that at this time Edmonton had more live theatre per capita than any other North American city. Theatre, visual arts, music, and literature all flourished as never before. Highlights included a new venue in downtown Edmonton to house the Citadel Theatre, the spawning of a large number of smaller theatres in both Calgary and Edmonton (including the Alberta Theatre Projects, the first entirely alternative theatre on the Canadian prairies), significant growth in the holdings of the Edmonton Art Gallery, the emergence of a uniquely Edmontonian form of assembled abstract sculpture, the appearance of major architectural projects by Douglas Cardinal that displayed his flowingly curvilinear, indigenous style (e.g., the Grande Prairie Regional College and the Alberta Government Services Building in Ponoka), the granting of university status to the Banff Centre (where Jeanne Lougheed had sung while attending the University of Alberta) as a year-round educational institution, the formation of the Calgary Opera Association, and many other important developments in the arts.

Matching this growth in the fine and performing arts was an incredible outburst of publishing activity throughout 1970s Alberta. More than twenty such enterprises received a combination of provincial and federal funding. In 1972, Mel Hurtig (a pioneering bookstore operator, publisher, champion of Canadian nationalism and independence, and arguably Peter Lougheed's most prominent political critic) ran the only trade publishing company with national reach (*Hurtig Publishers*) that was located outside of Toronto. By the end of the decade, independent publishers such as *Tree Frog Press* and *NeWest Press* had joined *Hurtig*, and university presses had been created at the University of Alberta and Red Deer College.

An interesting example of Lougheed's encouragement of Albertan cultural initiatives and institutions occurred in 1979. At this time, the Lougheed government created a 75 million dollar fund, fuelled by its burgeoning oil revenues, to finance projects that would celebrate Alberta's forthcoming 75th anniversary as a province in 1980. Although he had been a persistent thorn in Peter's side as a vocal critic of Lougheed's government, Alberta publisher Mel Hurtig felt he could not let such an opportunity pass. On May 29, 1979, he wrote to Peter Lougheed to suggest "the idea of a 'gift to Canada' as part of the province's celebrations."[33] The gift Hurtig had in mind was to be a three-volume *Canadian Encyclopedia* he was hoping to produce and publish if adequate financing for the project could be obtained. Describing what followed, Hurtig, in his memoirs, wrote that "I didn't think, given my deteriorating relations with the government, that there would be much likelihood of success, but why not try"? Late one afternoon during the Alberta winter of 1980, Hurtig recalled receiving a call from Bob Dowling, whom Lougheed had placed in charge of the 75th anniversary celebrations.

> He said that he had bad news and good news. He gave me the bad news first: "I'm sorry but after much careful thought we've decided that there's just no way we can give you the $2-million. We just can't do it. It's out of the question." My heart sank. Now the dream was gone forever. Dowling continued: The good news is that we

don't want you to go to Ottawa. We don't want any other government involved. We're going to give you all of the $4-million.[34]

In the end, Lougheed and his government underwrote Hurtig's research and development costs for the *Encyclopedia* to the tune of 3.4 million dollars and used the remaining $600,000 to purchase 25,000 copies of the *Encyclopedia* for Alberta schools, libraries, colleges, and universities. To do so, Peter Lougheed had to buck significant resistance from his cabinet and caucus. In Hurtig's words, Lougheed "graciously overlooked years of criticism from me ... and made the final decision himself. Peter and I had fought even before he had become premier in 1971. But nevertheless, there was some long-term degree of mutual respect."

I admired his energy, his communication skills, his hard work, and hands-on approach to governing the province. Conversely, one Sunday afternoon at a summer party at Pigeon Lake, Peter had given me the ultimate compliment. "Hurtig, you're the one person I know who I'm darn glad didn't get directly involved in Alberta politics."[35]

In many ways, Hurtig's reminiscences about Peter Lougheed, in this and other sections of his memoirs, capture nicely Lougheed's approach to life and politics. "Peter always fought the good fight, but when all was said and done, he held few grudges and was willing to find common ground and to compromise. He was courteous in victory and in defeat."[36]

In addition to book publishing, several literary and political magazines were established in Alberta during the 1970s. These included *The White Pelican* and *Saint John's Report* (both Edmonton and Calgary versions of which were combined in 1979 as *Alberta Report*). By the end of the 1970s, a veritable flood of novelists, investigative journalists, playwrights, and poets provided a steady stream of input to the new magazines and publishing houses. Many (like Douglas Barbour, E. D. Blodgett, W. P. Kinsella, Robert Kroetsch, Miriam Mandel, George Ryga, Aritha van Herk, Sharon Pollock Walsh, and Rudy Wiebe) received national and international awards and recognition for their works.

Cultural advances under Lougheed's PCs during the 1970s were significant. However, there can be little doubt that Peter's first two terms as Premier of Alberta (1971-1975 and 1975-1979) were dominated by two issues that defined his premiership and continue to feature prominently in contemporary relations between the province of Alberta and the federation of Canada: oil and the Canadian Constitution. Much already has been said about tensions during the 1970s between Alberta and Ottawa, and between Lougheed and Trudeau, over oil. Although it certainly is true that intergovernmental relations between Alberta and Ottawa during this time inevitably intersected with the securing, pricing, and marketing of petroleum, debates between Lougheed and Trudeau over the respective powers of the Canadian provinces and the federal government went far beyond oil alone.

Constitutional disagreements between our two protagonists reflected two distinctive and oppositional views concerning the very nature of Canada as a federation sand nation. Trudeau's position was grounded in his philosophy of personalism, joined to a Laskian conception of federalism. He championed the sovereignty of "a people with a collective will to live as a nation, seeking a common good throughout the country and governing themselves under a federative form of constitution"—a view he contrasted disparagingly with one that understood the Canadian federal government as "the creature of ten provinces, dependent on them for its existence and governed by the consensus of its eleven governments—ten provincial and one federal."[37] Lougheed's position favoured a decentralized federalism "providing for a much greater degree of co-operation between provincial administrations,"[38] all duly elected to represent the interests of their citizens—without assuming that such interests always would be held in common or would yield to a central government's interpretation of what was good for all.

The original constitution of Canada was the British North America Act of 1867, a document that had been signed by representatives of Upper and Lower Canada, Nova Scotia, and New Brunswick, and legislated by the British House of Commons, because Canada was then a colony of Britain. Since then, efforts to alter and amend the BNA Act, to reflect better and more specifically the existence of the majority of provincial governments that had come into being after 1867, had failed. When Pierre Trudeau became Prime Minister, the patriation of the Constitution from Britain was one of his primary goals. With patriation, the Constitution would be truly Canadian and could be amended in Canada by the Canadian Parliament and provincial legislatures to reflect contemporary realities and desires. No longer would Canadian prime ministers need to go hat in hand to London, England seeking constitutional reform or update.

In the summer of 1971 in Victoria, BC, Trudeau and the ten premiers, with Harry Strom representing Alberta, put together a package of proposed changes to the Canadian Constitution that became known as the Victoria Charter. It's key elements included a list of fundamental freedoms and political rights (including language rights) for all Canadians, a proposal for the make-up of the Supreme Court of Canada, measures to ensure income security, and a constitutional amending formula. As discussed and tentatively agreed to, the Victoria Charter also would have abolished federal powers to over-ride or disallow provincial legislation, committed all parties to reduce social and economic disparities among provinces, and set annual conferences of the Premiers and the Prime Minister.

Lougheed, then still in his role as Leader of the Official Opposition in the Alberta Legislature but sensing a likely win in the 1971 Alberta election set for August 30, agreed with aspects of the Victoria Charter, such as the abolition of the federal veto over provincial legislation. However, he was incensed by Strom's endorsement of the amending formula proposed as part of the Victoria package. That formula stipulated that a majority approval authorizing any amendments must include the agreement of Ontario, Quebec, at least two Atlantic provinces, and at least two western province with fifty percent of the West's population. What appalled Lougheed was that under these terms, the other provinces would hypothetically be able to rob Alberta of its control of its natural resources, as the population of British Columbia and Manitoba combined would meet the criterion of fifty percent of the population of the western provinces. Vowing to pull out of the tentative Victoria Charter agreement became a prominent plank in Lougheed's 1971 election campaign. However, in the end, Robert Bourassa, Premier of Quebec, vetoed the Victoria Charter and its amending formula by withdrawing from the agreement because he regarded it as supplying insufficient provincial authority over social policy in Quebec.

With his federal majority reduced to a minority government in 1972, Trudeau temporarily shelved further attempts to repatriate and amend the Constitution. But, when his Liberals were returned to a majority position in 1974, he tried again, going so far as to threaten the provinces that if they had not come to an agreement about patriation by September 15, 1976, he would ask the federal parliament to act on its own and unilaterally get the job done. Lougheed, now Alberta's premier and concerned about the possibility of Trudeau enacting an amending formula like the one in the Victoria Charter that would leave Alberta out in the cold at the mercy of the other provinces and the federal government, quickly became an active participant in meetings with the other premiers. In these meetings, he attempted to stitch together a constitutional proposal and amending formula on which they could agree unanimously. Of course, his constant condition was that any such agreement adequately serve his aim of enhancing Alberta's control over its own resources, and of its fate more generally.

Two such meetings, one in Edmonton and one in Toronto, occurred in 1976. At the first meeting in Edmonton, Premier Frank Moores of Newfoundland was charged with coordinating position papers from each of the provinces that had been endorsed by the provincial attorneys-general, thus boding well for a possibly successful agreement. However, the day after the meeting adjourned, during a follow-up session in Banff, Lougheed, supported by William Bennett of British Columbia, insisted that the amending formula require unanimous consent from all the provinces. On this, he was unwilling to compromise, despite a near consensus among the majority of the other premiers (and the national and Alberta media) to the effect that he was being overly rigid and demanding—"selfish" being implied if not stated explicitly.

At the next meeting in Toronto on October 1, 1976, Lougheed, who now stood alone against the other premiers, seemed to change tactics slightly, insisting that what Alberta was really against was any suggestion that there would be two classes of provinces under a revised constitution—such as proposed in the Victoria Charter—that would see Ontario and Quebec with vetoes and the others without the ability to unilaterally stop any constitutional change with which they might disagree. He also insisted that there be no erosion of existing provincial powers. Once again, Lougheed was pilloried in the press, with Geoffrey Stevens of the *Globe and Mail* railing that "The country has been treated to the parochial obstinacy of Peter Lougheed. To hell with national concerns. To hell with trying to create a sounder framework for a healthy federation. ... More for Alberta is his slogan and they love him back home for every elbow delivered to the eye of an Easterner."[39]

Picking up on the idea that Lougheed was more concerned about gaining powers for Alberta than repatriating and revising the constitution, Trudeau wrote to Lougheed, informing him that "I cannot consider myself committed in advance to anything the premiers seem to have agreed upon when the points of agreement are entirely apart from the central exercise."[40] Of course, for Trudeau the "central" exercise was exactly that—i.e., to retain, and hopefully extend, the power and thus capability of the central federal government to pursue its agendas for the nation as a whole without being encumbered further by the provincial governments.

In the Spring of 1978, Trudeau, making good on his threat to act unilaterally, unveiled a discussion paper entitled "A Time for Change," in which he outlined plans to amend federal powers by July 1, 1979, and work out a new division of powers with the provinces by July 1, 1981. In a speech delivered on the occasion of the opening of the 1978 Commonwealth Games in Edmonton, a diplomatic Queen Elizabeth, reading a speech prepared by the Lougheed government (on the evening of August 2) endorsed Lougheed's constitutional visions that included "a society where the individual can find full expression in an atmosphere of tolerance, cooperation, and harmony,"[41] a view with which Lougheed knew Trudeau would agree. However, on the night thereafter, perhaps not to be seen as taking sides, the Queen seemed to endorse indirectly aspects of Prime Minister Trudeau's vision of constitutional change, with which Lougheed clearly did not agree.

On October 20, 1978, the Alberta government released its own blueprint for constitutional change, entitled "Harmony and Diversity: A New Federalism for Canada," prepared by Peter Meekison, Deputy Minister of Alberta's Department of Federal and Intergovernmental

Relations. "Harmony" was far from the tone of the document, which demanded the elimination of almost all the federal government's emergency powers, proposed a complicated "constitutional court," insisted on a greater role for the provinces in international relations, and generally limited many of Ottawa's powers or demanded that they be shared with the provinces. The *Calgary Albertan* described it as "unacceptable," "a daring raid on the federal political arsenal; a design for deconfederation that is *provincial* in the worst sense of the word."[42]

At a federal-provincial conference in Ottawa a week later, Lougheed threatened to call a provincial election on questions related to the constitution. Speaking directly to Trudeau, and dispensing with a prepared text, Peter described his government as "committed to the view that Canada requires both a strong federal government and strong provincial governments,"[43] to safeguard the individual freedom of Canadians. Surprisingly, Trudeau adopted a conciliatory tone throughout the conference, willingly discussing several matters of federal power in relation to the provinces, including the control, management, and taxation of natural resources, regulation of interprovincial trade, and cooperation on infrastructure and public works. Even René Lévesque, Quebec's Premier and leader of the separatist Parti Québécois since November 15, 1976, left the conference with a feeling that things were beginning to change. Lougheed seemed to be the only premier who smelled a rat.

Of course, it was Lévesque's election as PQ Premier of Quebec in 1976 that had put a new wind of urgency in the country's constitutional talks. Lougheed sympathized with some of Lévesque's concerns and continued to support additional powers for all provinces, but, being committed to his own vision of federalism, was suspicious of Lévesque and the possibility that he would shift Ottawa's focus more fully away from Alberta. Lougheed knew well where more of Trudeau's own concerns and attention rested. As it turned out, Lougheed himself was once more the outcast, and once again the object of media ridicule, with the *Edmonton Journal* chastising him—"Alberta's suspicion of Ottawa should know some bounds."[44] Peter's reaction to all the criticism typically was to continue to tie his constitutional objections to his concern that Alberta be the beneficiary of its petroleum riches: "If Ontario owned the oil you can be assured that we in Alberta would be buying it at the world price."[45]

Of course, some, but certainly not all, of Peter Lougheed's fiery rhetoric, as 1978 came to a close, was in anticipation of the third provincial election battle he would fight in 1979. If Lougheed himself was judged by some Albertans and many other Canadians to be getting a bit carried away in his war of words with the federal government and the Canadian media, he still had a long way to go before he could compete with a growing number of right-wing Albertans like Milt Harradence, prominent Calgary lawyer and leader of the Alberta PCs from 1962 to 1965, who had encouraged Lougheed to run for leader of the Alberta PCs in the first place. Increasingly incensed over the way in which he believed Alberta was being robbed blind by Ottawa, Harradence called Pierre Trudeau a "crypto Communist," being supported by his "almost socialist" dupe, Peter Lougheed.[46] By hammering away at Ottawa, Lougheed ensured that he would not be outflanked by the more extreme rhetoric of Harradence and those who supported some version of Alberta separation that would rival what was going on in Quebec. For despite his championing of Alberta, Lougheed was a committed federalist, of a different stripe from Trudeau, but equally strong in his identity as a Canadian. And, in this, he was like the vast majority of Albertans. In the words of the *Calgary Herald*'s Bill Gold, Alberta had "five separatists with $100,000 each, while in Quebec there were 100,000 separatists with $5 each."[47] Nonetheless, given that a 1976 survey showed some 75 percent of Albertans in support of beliefs such as "The economic policies of the federal government seem to help Quebec and Ontario at the expense of Alberta," Lougheed could hardly afford to "go soft" on Trudeau and the national government.

Although many Albertans had fallen for the charming Pierre Trudeau during the 1968 federal election, the romance was not widespread, and proved to be short-lived. There was not a single Liberal MLA or Liberal MP elected in Alberta during the three provincial and three federal elections contested during the 1970s. Darryl Raymaker, author of *Trudeau's Tango: Alberta Meets Pierre Elliott Trudeau, 1968-1972,* offers a detailed description of Trudeau's personal fall from grace in Alberta. At the height of Trudeaumania in the 1968 federal election, Trudeau and his federal Liberal Party had won only 4 of 19 federal seats in Alberta, but they had received 36 percent of the popular vote in the province. In the 1972 federal election only 25 percent of the popular vote in Alberta went to the Liberals, without a single MP elected. Raymaker maintains that Trudeau's support in Alberta peaked just after the 1970 October

Crisis. Many Albertans were impressed by how he had stood unflinchingly at the barricades and stared down the rioting mobs, momentarily emerging as the quintessentially strong leader in most parts of Canada, including the western provinces. Raymaker suggests that if a federal election had been held late in 1970, Liberal support would have been strong in Alberta. That Trudeau did not take advantage of this opportunity, Raymaker considers to have been his worst moment politically, but his finest moment as a man of principle and honour.

After that, Trudeau's Alberta fortunes plummeted. His government was hit with the crosswinds of inflation and unemployment. When serious cutbacks and price controls were enacted, matters only worsened. In western Canada, falling grain prices brought farmers and their tractors to demonstrations and protests, at the same time that the oil patch demanded retaliation against OPEC for its embargo and the US for its surcharges. All of this stoked talk of western alienation, which was fanned further by attacks on foreign ownership of the province's natural resources by Albertans like Mel Hurtig. Trudeau became a target for Albertans of all political stripes.

According to Raymaker, Lougheed's political ascendency in Alberta also was a major factor in Trudeau's Alberta downfall:

> While Lougheed launched progressive policies on a host of issues, Trudeau was stuck with a fight against inflation and consequent unemployment. All of this helped Lougheed glom onto the affections of disaffected or uncertain Liberals and turn them into Tories. Whereas Lougheed

was visible everywhere and every day in Alberta, Trudeau was generally seen only from a distance and most of the time portrayed negatively as a foe of the province. Whereas Lougheed was set on improving the province's standing in the country, economically and politically, Trudeau was perceived to be standing in his way.[48]

In late 1978, Lougheed went into his now well-rehearsed pre-election mode of rewarding Albertans for their faithfulness by dispensing an array of goodies that included a $750 million project in support of municipal transportation and infrastructure, a billion dollars to help reduce municipal civic debt, and the creation of the Alberta Heritage Foundation for Medical Research, with a price tag of $300 million. When the election was held on March 14, 1979, Lougheed's PCs grabbed 74 of the 79 available seats, but with a reduced popular vote total that dropped from 63 to 57 percent. What remained of the Social Credit Party controlled 4 seats, and Grant Notley retained his sole NDP seat in the Alberta Legislature.

Lougheed's third election victory for the Tories in Alberta preceded, by a little more than two months, fellow Albertan and federal Tory leader Joe Clark's narrow victory over Trudeau's stagnating Liberals on May 22, 1979. What transpired over the seven months that followed reveals a good deal about the social, political nature of the ongoing battles between Ottawa and Alberta. With Clark's victory, many assumed that the intersecting issues of resource revenue sharing and constitutional reform would finally be resolved. After all, Clark had made it clear in his parliamentary exchanges with

Trudeau leading up to the 1979 federal election that he favoured a much more decentralized federal system that would recognize the provinces as distinct communities and presumably allow them to develop as such, a view that Trudeau had derided as a dreamy and unrealistic "community of communities," but with which Lougheed strongly agreed. What then was to stop the two Albertans, Clark and Lougheed, from getting along famously and soothing Lougheed's and Alberta's upsets?

In the build-up to Clark's victory over Trudeau in May 1979, it was clear that Alberta oil might play a big role in determining the outcome of that federal election. In consequence, Lougheed and his Energy Minister Don Getty decided it would be best to "play nice" with Trudeau, so as not to give him a "political club with which to hammer Joe Clark in Central Canada." "Letters of sweetness, light and all accord ... agreeing to hold any increase [to oil prices] in abeyance for six months,"[49] were exchanged between Getty and Trudeau's federal Minister of Energy, Mines, and Resources Alastair Gillespie.

Unfortunately, once he was elected as Prime Minister, Clark and his newly appointed energy minister Ray Hnatyshyn (a Saskatchewan MP whom Lougheed did not know and worried might know little about the oil industry) somehow failed to appreciate the magnitude of Lougheed's and Gillespie's gift. A moment's thought should have told them that they would have been unlikely to have won the election if there had been an increase in the price of oil from Clark's home province during the just completed election campaign. Needless to say, their apparent blindness in this regard did not please Lougheed, who believed strongly in principles of team loyalty and support, which he found sorely lacking in Clark's and Hnatyshyn's behaviour. Lougheed wrote to Clark on June 22, 1979, telling him that in his view, "The principal domestic energy requirement is for a commitment to move Canadian oil prices expeditiously towards world prices," and that "to subsidize oil prices in an energy shortage was foolish domestic policy." Clark's response in a letter to Lougheed dated July 9 was that "we must make a major effort to expand our energy supplies,"[50] which Lougheed interpreted positively as in agreement with his own views.

However, Lougheed's concern that Ray Hnatyshyn knew little about oil pricing and did not appreciate his and Getty's arguments proved to be accurate. Given his lack of experience in his new role, "Ray's [Energy Department] officials had him closeted for briefings almost every day and night for three months. Ray didn't have one minute to come up for air."[51] Eventually, Hnatyshyn's advisors, who included several of the same individuals who would draft the National Energy Program of the federal government in the early 1980s, convinced him to accept the oil policies they had prepared for Trudeau. [It is quite common in Canadian federal politics for ministerial officials and civil servants to carry on in their roles across successive administrations of different political parties.]

Meanwhile, Premier Bill Davis of Ontario, another ex-university football player who also had appointed several of his former teammates to his cabinet and other government positions, released what Lougheed read as an anti-Alberta diatribe, entitled *Oil Pricing and Security: A Policy Framework for Canada.* In it, Davis demanded, as premier of Canada's highest oil consuming province, to have a say in any future negotiations between Ottawa and Alberta. Almost as if the usually more collected Davis was out to create chaos, the document also suggested that Alberta's Heritage Trust Fund be shuttered to allow for the "shifting [of] new money from provincial royalties into the federal treasury."[52] In this context, Lougheed's response to Clark, bypassing Hnatyshyn, was immediate, predictable, and forceful: "Joe, we're going to have a wholesale battle, and it's one I didn't start."[53]

It was more than a little ironic that Lougheed now found himself fighting fellow progressive conservatives over Alberta's oil revenues in general and the Heritage Trust Fund in particular. Shortly after the establishment of the HTF in 1976, Lougheed had created a semi-secret committee of several of his closest and most trusted Ministers to strategize about how best to fight Trudeau's federal government over oil revenues.[54] Peter and other members of his inner circle knew that the Feds had the upper hand when it came to provincial-federal negotiations. Faced with this reality, the Lougheed government's general strategy was to talk tough and do whatever they could to prevent relations between Ottawa and the other provinces from becoming too cozy. One obvious way of doing this was to use the HTF to lend money to the other provinces in competition with federally determined equalization payments. In doing so, Peter was skating close to the edge of what was permissible under existing federal-provincial constitutional powers, and both he and his secret committee knew it.

Caught between Lougheed and Davis (given the diametrically opposed negative reactions of Albertans and positive reactions of

Ontarians to Davis' *Oil Pricing and Security*), Clark tried desperately to find some way to compromise. He met with Lougheed face to face, after a federal cabinet retreat to Jasper, and subsequently met with Davis, and Premiers Peckford (Newfoundland) and MacLean (PEI), both with off-shore oil interests of their own. While this was going on, Lougheed met with Alberta's federal MPs and castigated them for letting their positions and responsibilities as MPs representing Alberta to be taken over by federal bureaucrats who were effectively taking instruction from Davis.

When Peter Lougheed headed to Ottawa for a First Ministers' Conference on Energy convened by Prime Minister Clark in November 1979, things initially went well, with the other eight premiers, except Ontario, taking Alberta's side. But then, all hell broke lose when, without Clark's or federal cabinet approval, federal energy mandarins Ian Stewart and Ed Clark (two of Hnatyshyn's backroom boys, apparently acting without his okay) released to the media a call for the institution of a federal wellhead tax on oil. Despite many attempts to remedy and resolve matters during the remaining days of the First Ministers' Energy Conference, the damage had been done and distrust was heightened. Since neither Stewart nor Clark were dismissed or demoted, subsequent attempts to reach a compromise between Alberta and Ontario were unsuccessful.

During his fateful budget speech in the House of Commons on the evening of December 11, 1979, Clark's Finance Minister John Crosbie, in the absence of an agreement on oil pricing, said the Clark government was "prepared, once full agreement is reached with the producing provinces, to permit oil prices to rise in stages, by four dollars and fifty cents a barrel."[55] Crosbie then proceeded to introduce a federal tax of eighteen cents a gallon on gas poured from the pump. Having alienated Lougheed, the Clark government was caught between wreaking havoc on the national economy with large price increases for oil, and its own need for an increased share of petroleum revenues to meet its federal responsibilities. Crosbie's attempt at compromise in the face of these conflicting concerns proved futile, and played right into the machinations of Liberal strategy gurus Jim Coutts and Keith Davey, who had been busy setting traps for Clark so as to create an opportunity for Trudeau to return as leader of the Liberal Party of Canada and lead it to victory. With the defeat of Crosbie's budget on December 11, 1979 constituting a vote of non-confidence, the short-lived and ill-fated Clark government came to an embarrassing end. With Clark thus defeated, Lougheed commented tersely, "We have taken all the offers off the table. We start again from scratch,"[56] thereby clearing the decks for future battles with Trudeau and his new majority government, elected on February 18, 1980.

When the Trudeau government announced *The National Energy Program* in its budget of October 1980, the oil wars, which had simmered and flared throughout the 1970s, became fully engaged. To add to Lougheed's disgust and ensure that the gloves were off, two of the most senior bureaucrats who put together the details of the *NEP* (under the general direction of Trudeau, his Minister of Energy, Mines, and Resources Marc Lalonde, and his Deputy Prime Minister and Minister of Finance Allan MacEachen) were Ian Stewart (Deputy Minister of Finance) and Ed Clark (senior

Assistant Deputy Minister for Policy in Energy, Mines, and Resources). These were the very same mandarins who had scuttled a possible deal between Lougheed and Clark by releasing to the Ottawa press their unauthorized and unofficial announcement of a federally imposed wellhead tax on oil during the First Ministers' Energy Conference of November, 1979. The stage was set for what now would become the most significant battles between Peter Lougheed and Pierre Trudeau over provincial versus federal control of natural resources and the constitutional powers of Canada's provincial and federal governments.

In the Spring of 2012, *Policy Options* (published by the Institute for Research on Public Policy, an independent, non-profit group) asked an expert panel of thirty historians, political scientists, economists, journalists, and policy advisors across Canada to rank order lists of their top five choices for the best Canadian provincial Premier from 1972 to the then present. All members of the panel were extremely distinguished for their work in governmental, academic, and public service capacities. Peter Lougheed won in a landslide, reminiscent of his victories in the four Alberta elections he contested in 1971, 1975, 1979, and 1982. He was the only premier ranked by all 30 experts and he was ranked first by 21 of them. Voters from all regions of Canada cast ballots for Lougheed.

To ascertain the possible reasons for the panellists' selections, they also were asked to rank the premiers on nine aspects of leadership: winnability, communicator, vision, fiscal frameworks, the economy, infrastructure, interprovincial relations, federal-provincial relations, and legacy. Lougheed was rated first on all aspects of leadership considered. His lowest ranking (although still higher than that of any other candidate) was on interprovincial relations. His highest ranking was on his ability to win voters and elections. It is worth mentioning that one of two advisors who assisted the staff of *Policy Options* in devising and organizing this exercise was Thomas Axworthy, a Winnipeg native, who served as Pierre Trudeau's senior policy director and principal secretary, before resigning when Trudeau himself left politics in 1984. Lougheed followed them into retirement in 1985.

In summarizing the reasons for Lougheed's high rankings and selection as the top Canadian premier of "the past 40 years," *Policy Options Magazine (POM)* stated:

Lougheed was quite simply the builder of modern Alberta, from better roads to higher education. During the four terms and 14 years of his premiership, Alberta played a leadership role in the Canadian federation as it has at no time since. Not only did he defend the interests of Alberta on the ownership of its resources, he created the Heritage Savings Trust Fund to save for a rainy day. And there would have been no agreement on patriating the Constitution with an entrenched Charter of Rights in 1981 had Ottawa not accepted Lougheed's general "7/50" amending formula requiring the consent of Ottawa and seven provinces representing 50 percent of the population, as well as the notwithstanding clause providing a legislative override clause to Parliament and the legislatures. Though never invoked by Ottawa, it was a deal maker at the federal-provincial constitutional table in November 1981.[57]

Interestingly, the premier who came second in the *PO* expert poll was Bill Davis. Although Davis received no first-place votes, he was a consensus choice of the panel for second position. Both Davis and Lougheed led their respective provinces of Ontario and Alberta from 1971 to 1985. Like Lougheed, Davis was a fierce defender of the rights and interests of the people of his province, and was a highly successful premier, adept at positioning himself and his party so as to maintain the support of voters and a diversity of corporate and public firms and agencies.

Peter Lougheed's popularity during his 14 years at the helm of Alberta's government undoubtedly was based on public acceptance of his stance as a staunch defender of Albertan interests, a position secured by his unshakable strategy of using the wealth generated from the province's natural resources to benefit all Albertans, not just those in the business community. This was a commitment that distinguished Lougheed from more ideological conservatives, like Milt Harradence, who preceded him as leader of the Progressive Conservative Party of Alberta, and several of his successors, like Jason Kenny. Like Ernest Manning, another long-serving Premier of Alberta, Lougheed, despite his commitments to teambuilding and teamwork, stood apart from his government in the public's perception.

But, also like Manning, the longer he was in office, the more truth there seemed to be in Albertan NDP leader Grant Notley's contentions that Lougheed became more secretive and began to keep things undercover through closed door dealings. Certainly, it became much more difficult for many citizens, especially critics, to access Peter directly toward the end of his time as Premier. And, again like Manning, while continuing to maintain in public that MLAs were free to exercise their own judgement, he showed little tolerance to those of his party who broke ranks with him on matters he considered to be central to his plans and vision. On another front, despite his establishment of the Heritage Trust Fund, a growing group of environmentalists and others still awaited the day when Alberta's finances might be less dependent on oil and decried the lack of concrete evidence to support Lougheed's claim to be securing alternative sources of provincial wealth through the establishment of secondary industries and other areas of economic development independent of the oil patch.

Feminists, whose political activity in Alberta will forever be marked by the victory of the "famous five" (Henrietta Muir Edwards, Nellie McClung, Louise McKinney, Emily Murphy, and Irene Parlby) in the Persons Case of 1929, which recognized women as persons and therefore able to sit in the Canadian Senate, also were growing restless. They increasingly railed against what they regarded as significant barriers to female political participation and influence erected and maintained within the province's predominately conservative culture. Journalist Christina Newman had begun to denounce Lougheed's political practices as examples of what she called "aggressive conservatism."

Indigenous Albertans and their leaders also contested Lougheed's claims to have benefited all Albertans. Harold Cardinal, who had published his book *The Unjust Society* in 1969[58] and lambasted the federal government's treatment of Indigenous Peoples as nothing short of cultural genocide, didn't have much good to say about Lougheed either. So despite his many successes, as the 1980s approached, Peter Lougheed certainly was not immune from criticism in his home province.

Unlike Trudeau's biographers, those who have written about Lougheed tend not to engage in much psychobiography, limiting their discussions to his political dealings and public acts and pronouncements. Even those who do venture to comment on aspects of his personality and possible links between his childhood and adulthood are rather, and perhaps appropriately, cautious in treading such waters. It also seems possible that Peter Lougheed's much more conventional life, in private and in public, doesn't invite psychological perusal and analysis, in the way that Trudeau's much less conventional life has seemed to do.

Nonetheless, Lougheed biographer Allan Hustak does draw a clear link between Peter's childhood experience of his family's loss of status and what he regards as Lougheed's subsequent strivings to reverse such perceptions and circumstances. Hustak also makes some interesting observations about Lougheed's possible psychological makeup in a final chapter of his biography, which he begins by writing "To understand Peter Lougheed is to understand

Alberta, for more than any other Canadian Premier ... Lougheed is his constituency."[59]

Sometimes referred to as Mr. Alberta, Peter Lougheed often has been portrayed as captivated by a politics of resentment and frustration that has its sources in the experiences of his own family during the 1930s, when his parents suffered a downturn in family income and influence, symbolized by the loss of his grandparents' beloved Beaulieu residence—a resentment and frustration that are cast in a narrative similar to that said to have been experienced by generations of Albertans dismissed by self-important and peacock-clad Easterners as second-tier dirt farmers and cowboys with dung on their boots.

But, for the most part, Lougheed's personality was not replete with spite and vengefulness. Yes, he had a deep distaste for what he regarded as unfair and unjust treatment, and for those unable to see different perspectives and points of view, but this is not the same thing as desiring to deliver comeuppance. Being unstintingly positive about and promoting of Alberta and its people was part and parcel with Peter Lougheed's way of living. His power and will derived from being an agent of planned change, not one of getting even. His desire to have Ottawa better understand and recognize Alberta's grievances and perspectives was not a fight or an end in itself. It was an integral part of his overall vision of Canadian federation as a functioning partnership of provinces with greater powers of governance that would allow them to stand up to and overcome existing tendencies to federal paternalism that he believed negatively affect and stifle both provincial and Canadian wellbeing in general.

Lougheed had little sympathy for western separatism of any sort. He was a committed Canadian and a proud Albertan. He may not have always been diplomatic in pursuit of his ambitions for both Alberta and Canada, but his core impulse was to organize and unite for change. His strengths were a combination of robust self-sufficiency that sought out unanimity of purpose, plans, and goals, with a view to changing things for the better. He was always looking forward. "The way I look at it, is some day I'll walk into my office and I won't be trying to change things. I'll find I'm trying to protect what I've done and I know that's the day I'll start planning to leave."[60] Yet, in many ways, Lougheed was a manager, not an innovator. He was not an inspirational speaker, but he possessed a boyish charm that smoothed over much of his bureaucratic tenacity. Often impatient with the contrivances of politics, he tried to keep his political mind uncluttered and efficiently targeted.

According to Richard Gwyn, Trudeau biographer and newspaper columnist, "There are really two Lougheeds. One is the brilliant manager and organizer, the visionary, the Alberta patriot. The other is the little guy who made it to the top and who still can't quite believe it, wary, humourless, crushed by criticism," basically shy and at his best in his office "where the blueprints that will shape Alberta's future are drawn."[61]

Lougheed's politics were like his personality in one important respect—both were, and are, difficult to categorize. He and his administration were much more moderate than many of his government's elected representatives, some of whom were prone to extreme and occasionally insulting remarks and slights. Lougheed himself did not suffer slights lightly and more than a few of those he worked with have remarked his sometimes fiery temper. However, in the end, his desire to move forward in pursuit of his goals for Alberta and Canada usually trumped any momentary and shorter-term annoyances and upsets. Perhaps Lougheed's greatest gift was his ability to work closely with loyal colleagues and companions to whom he returned loyalty and support. In this, he was fortunate, both in his political and domestic life. Jeanne Lougheed no doubt helped him greatly to separate his public from his private life. As friend Peter Macdonnell noted "No matter how difficult his day as Premier may have been, he leaves his office completely behind him once he walks through the door of his house. His transformation from politician to father is remarkable. His dedication to his family is absolute."[62]

Having followed the lives of our two protagonists from childhood, through their educations and pre-political adult lives, to their political lives from the late 1960s and throughout the 1970s, the stage has been set for what many consider to be two of the most important events in the history of Canada and Alberta. These were events with consequences that continue to reverberate into the present—the fights between Peter Lougheed and Pierre Trudeau over the federal government's National Energy Program, imposed in October, 1980 (and lasting until 1985) and the constitutional talks during the First Ministers' Meeting in the early days of November 1981, which led to the patriation of the Canadian Constitution and added the Canadian Charter of Rights and Freedoms on March 29, 1982. Although the nine other provincial premiers, and many others (mostly behind the scenes), played important, even critical roles in both these national dramas, Trudeau and Lougheed were undoubtedly central players—the former as the Prime Minister of Canada, who favoured a centralized form of the Canadian federation; the latter as the chief proponent of a competing vision of the Canadian federation as much more decentralized and regional.

At the time Trudeau and Lougheed entered into these nation forming contests, both were at the top of their political careers as individual leaders, with the strong backing of their parties and carefully selected and loyal negotiating teams and support personnel, well prepared and versed in the complex issues and implications of these two essential matters that would have lasting effects on Canada and Alberta. Despite their differences, both had now reached a point in their political lives where they were well positioned not only to fight for their competing visions of Canada, but to do so on their own, relatively unfettered terms, as architects of their political success in pursuit of long and strongly held aspirations for the country and provinces they loved.

Chapter Six: Battles over the NEP and the Constitution
(1980-1982)

It is no exaggeration to suggest that the 1980-1982 clashes between Alberta and Ottawa over ownership and control of natural resources on the one hand, and patriation of the Canadian Constitution on the other, were amongst the most important in the entire history of the Canadian federation. Indeed, it was the contested nature of the federation itself that was both cause and effect of these battles. To Pierre Trudeau, federalism, to be successful, required a centrally controlled process of planning and implementation, undertaken and overseen by a strong central government. If the provinces and territories could not come together, the federal government must be able to act unilaterally to ensure the national interest and wellbeing of all Canadians. This view was in direct opposition to that held by some of the provincial premiers, particularly the view of Peter Lougheed. In Lougheed's opinion, a successful federation required that the provinces must be granted clear areas of regional authority that were essential to their flourishing. Centralized unilateralism by Ottawa must be fettered by a respectful understanding of regional circumstances and needs, and mediated by reasonable negotiation between federal and provincial governments in light of those circumstances and needs.

Alberta owned and regulated natural resources on its provincial crown land, but Ottawa had the constitutional right to regulate commerce and trade across provincial and international borders. During the 1970s, the default strategy of the Trudeau federal government for getting what it regarded as its rightful share of revenues from Alberta's petroleum industry was to price and tax Alberta oil flowing to the rest of Canada and elsewhere, in ways favourable to federal coffers. Alberta's method of insisting that its rights be respected, and retaliating against what Lougheed regarded as Trudeau's intrusion on those rights, was to place provincial royalties, payable solely to the Alberta government, on the procurement, with intent to export, of the oil it owned. This allowed the Lougheed provincial government to take much of what it regarded as Alberta's rightful share of its oil and natural gas revenues, before its petroleum products moved beyond Alberta's boundaries.

Lougheed's overall goals in his energy and resource battles with Trudeau were to use revenue from Alberta's natural resources to improve and diversify the province's economy for the benefit of Albertans, but he also believed that in doing so he would help to make Canada stronger by encouraging other provinces to take similar steps to secure their own resources and to forge and implement mutually beneficial interprovincial agreements. Trudeau's goals were to increase the authority of the federal government over trade and commerce and to exercise this authority to ensure the economic health of the country as a whole through diversification and profit-sharing nation wide. More specifically, a greater share of the wealth flowing from Alberta's natural resources would allow Ottawa to subsidize Canadian consumers in other provinces who relied on higher-priced imported oil, to finance its own development plans and programs (including equalization payments), and to reduce the federal deficit.

But, using oil revenue to enable and further their own plans for Canada was not the only reason for Ottawa's intransigence in its energy wars with Alberta. Trudeau and his government also felt threatened by the greater political clout an oil-rich Alberta could muster. In particular, under Lougheed, Alberta had started to provide financing to other provinces, which Ottawa interpreted as eroding federal systems of equalization payments that supposedly spread the country's wealth across all the provinces in ways consistent with federal government goals and priorities. Under these conditions, conflict had been and would continue to be inevitable.

When the Liberals were returned to power in 1980, federal Minister of Energy Marc Lalonde proposed a comprehensive energy program as part of Trudeau's renewed efforts at nation building, which were intended to revitalize federalism as he understood it. Lalonde introduced the NEP as an entirely budgetary matter, so that it hopefully would not be perceived in the context of ongoing federal-provincial interactions over constitutional powers and the patriation of the constitution. Lalonde knew that modernizing the Canadian Constitution was a central priority for Trudeau. Both he and Trudeau were therefore anxious that whatever transpired in their fight with Alberta and Lougheed over oil revenues not derail their constitutional plans. From their point of view, if they could work out an agreement with the Lougheed government that transferred some of Alberta's oil-related wealth and power to Ottawa, in a way that would be viewed as reasonable and justifiable by most Canadians and their provincial leaders, their chances of negotiating a new constitutional deal with the provinces would be significantly enhanced.

Tabled as part of the Liberal's federal budget delivered in October 1981, the NEP promised, by 1990, to achieve energy "self sufficiency through increasing domestic oil production, energy substitution and conservation programs." It also promised to give "Canadians the opportunity to participate in the petroleum industry through a Canadianization program aiming at 50 percent of Canadian ownership by 1990, [and] a petroleum pricing and revenue-sharing regime that would be fair to all Canadians, as well as to the federal and provincial governments."[1] In well-rehearsed rhetoric aimed at garnering public support, the Government of Canada's carefully prepared brochure, *The National Energy Program,* set out three goals: "energy security, the opportunity [for Canadians] to participate in energy development, and fairness in the manner in which the benefits of the nation's rich resources are shared." The rationale for a fair distribution of such benefits was that at present "one provincial government—not all, and not the national government—enjoys most of the windfall, under current policies. These policies are no longer compatible with the national interest." Currently, "Alberta, with 10 percent of Canada's population, received over 80 percent of the petroleum revenues gained by provinces."[2] The document then went on to call for a new agreement that would give the federal government a greater share of petroleum revenues so that it might distribute them more fairly across the nation and increase Canadians' ownership of the petroleum industry through the vehicle of the national petroleum company, Petro-Canada.

Other details in the report that were not emphasized in the budget papers of October, 1980, or in most other government documents, were that a significant part of the energy self-sufficiency promised would be achieved by encouraging "new discoveries on Canada Lands, that is, in federally controlled areas such as the Northwest Territories or offshore, rather than in provinces." In effect, by a combination of taxation changes and generous federal grants to explore and develop oil reserves on federal government lands, oil revenue "was [to be] diverted from Alberta and the other producing provinces to areas under federal control."[3] In addition, any companies holding interests or agreements in federal Crown land would be required to return half of the land thus controlled to federal Crown land reserves, without compensation. An additional 25 percent interest in what remained was to be given freely to Petro-Canada, then a federal crown corporation. With respect to the pricing of oil, it would be kept under 85 percent of the world price, starting considerably lower and rising to that level incrementally over the years of the NEP agreement.

The immediate effect of the "pricing and revenue-sharing regime that would be fair to all Canadians, as well as to the federal and provincial governments," coupled with "the reservation of a 25 percent Crown share in frontier lands"[4] was to increase significantly the federal government's share of revenue from oil and gas and to reduce Alberta's share, which infuriated Lougheed and his Alberta Tories. The immediate effect of the Canadianization program was to enrage Alberta's American-owned oil companies because of the advantages it gave, not just to Canadian companies, but to the very large advantage it gave to Petro-Canada, the country's state-run oil company. Many Albertans not directly connected to the oil sector reacted against the unilateral imposition of the NEP arrangements and policies on a province that was not represented by the governing federal Liberals, who had no elected Alberta MPs in their ranks.

What distinguished the NEP from previous phases in the fights between Ottawa and Alberta over oil pricing, royalties, and revenues was that in instituting the NEP, Trudeau and Lalonde had forsaken any attempt at a negotiated settlement and opted for a unilateral imposition, one that also promised to be permanent (as opposed to earlier temporary policies). Although Alberta often has been cast as intransigent and unwilling to compromise in its dealings with the federal government over oil, Tammy Nemeth, in her review of federal documents declassified in the early 2000s, revealed the contents of an April 16, 1980 memo written by Deputy Minister of Finance Ian Stewart. The date of this memorandum precedes any negotiations between the newly elected Trudeau Liberals and Lougheed's Alberta Government over oil and energy policy. In fact, before this memo was written, there had been no negotiations attempted, following Lougheed's declaration that "We have taken all the offers off the table. We start again from scratch,"[5] when his negotiations with the Clark government had collapsed on December 8, 1979, well before Trudeau was re-elected with a new majority government on February 18, 1980.

In his April 16, 1980 memorandum, Stewart writes: "Mr. Lalonde, correctly in our view, points out that his basic proposals are incompatible with the views that Mr. Lougheed has been expressing, and that there is, therefore, little hope of a negotiated settlement.

Implicit in the proposed strategy is the assumption [that] at the end of the day the government will, if necessary, be prepared to impose a solution unilaterally." Of particular interest, are Stewart's own interpretations of Lalonde's strategy: "the energy proposals as they now stand, would be seen by many to be the biggest revenue grab in the history of the country," and "would allow eastern oil and gas consumers to continue enjoying massive rents (via lower prices) and the federal treasury to collect billions from a gas export tax, both of which would reinforce western alienation." To combat such an outcome, Stewart goes on to recommend a package of western-based development initiatives, conceding that "it will be difficult to develop a credible list of initiatives, and the cost of some of them could be high."[6]

Yet despite knowing and planning all of this, Lalonde did not meet with Alberta Minister of Energy and Natural Resources Mervin Leitch until May of 1980 to outline some of his thinking in person. After doing so, he issued no request for a formal response from Leitch. In a later meeting in June, Lalonde formally presented his proposals to Leitch and requested a response, which he and Trudeau then rejected. Subsequently, two more meetings were held, with no agreement emerging. The extent of Trudeau's direct involvement in Lalonde's negotiations with Alberta in the Spring of 1980, leading into the federal budget of October 1980, was probably little, given his understandable, full engagement with the Quebec referendum on sovereignty association, on which he had gambled much of his own credibility and legacy.

Nonetheless, Lalonde's general lack of urgency in negotiating a new oil agreement with Alberta during the Spring and Summer of

1980 lends considerable credence to Tammy Nemeth's conclusion that all the available evidence "suggests that the suspicions of the Alberta government were correct: Lalonde, and his officials, had no intention of seriously negotiating with Alberta and planned from the start to impose an energy package unilaterally." In reaching this conclusion, Nemeth not only relies on memoranda such as the April 16 internal missive written by Ian Stewart, but on a strategy outlined by Lalonde himself in a May meeting of the Federal Cabinet. In this Cabinet session, Lalonde laid out a "federal strategy to isolate Alberta by soliciting support from the other provinces so that Alberta's position would appear inflexible and unreasonable compared to the others—a tactic that Alberta also employed the next year during negotiations on the constitution."[7]

In fact, despite their different views of federalism and some key differences in their approaches to leadership, there were many similarities between Trudeau and the equally strong-willed Lougheed.

> Although many Albertans would not like to admit it, ... both employed similar tactics and strategies and had similar goals. Both, for example, attempted to mobilize popular opinion to support their aims through rhetoric and other means. Most importantly, both saw oil and gas resources as a means to increase and diversify economic development. Lougheed, however, wanted to use the province's resources to achieve that end for Alberta, whereas Trudeau wanted to use revenue from Alberta's

resources to promote economic development and diversification wherever the federal government saw fit.[8]

Anyone familiar with the referendum on Quebec's "sovereignty" on May 20, 1980 (and the build-up to it) will understand where most of Pierre Trudeau's time and energies were directed from the time of his re-election as Prime Minister of Canada on February 18, 1980 until the May 20th Quebec referendum. One of Trudeau's primary reasons for entering federal politics as a rookie MP in 1965 was to work toward a strong federal government that would counter the nationalist and separatist tendencies of a growing number of Quebec leaders and intellectuals. Trudeau believed that a modern and vibrant Quebec only could develop as such within a strong and progressive Canada. He viewed past (including his own youthful nationalist sentiments and activities) and present calls for a Quebec sovereign nation separate from Canada as regressive and ultimately destructive for the wellbeing of his home province and its people.

Joe Clark's short-lived tenure as Prime Minister in 1979 was marked in part by his seeming indifference to what was happening in Quebec. In fact, neither Clark nor his Cabinet were equipped with the understanding and ability to intervene and resist what by the end of 1979 appeared to be an increasing certainty that Quebec might vote to demand a new form of Canadian federalism, and/or separate from the country. To Trudeau, for whom the status of Quebec within Canada and matters of constitutional patriation and reform always had been front and centre in his political thinking and concern, Clark's passivity in the face of the situation in Quebec was the source of immense frustration. The prospect of erasing what he saw as Clark's weakness in the face of Lévesque's resolve undoubtedly figured in Pierre's decision on the morning of December 18, 1979 to re-enter federal politics and once again lead the Liberal Party of Canada.

Two days later, on December 20, 1979, Lévesque announced the question he would put to Quebecers on May 20, 1980:

> The government of Quebec has made public its proposal to negotiate a new agreement with the rest of Canada, based on the equality of nations. This agreement would enable Quebec to acquire the exclusive power to make its laws, administer its taxes and establish relations abroad—in other words, sovereignty—and at the same time to maintain with Canada an economic association including a common currency. Any change in political status resulting from these negotiations will be submitted to the people through a referendum.
>
> On these terms, do you agree to give the government the mandate to negotiate the proposed agreement between Quebec and Canada? [9]

When Trudeau was back in power, as of February 18, 1980, he immediately named Jean Chrétien (his newly appointed Minister of Justice and Attorney General) as federal representative on the forthcoming Quebec referendum, telling him to "Get in there a bit more vigorously. Play whatever role you want."[10] With his best street fighter in the mix, and while Lalonde (Minister of Energy, Mines and Resources) was handling the Alberta file, Trudeau, on April 4 informed leader of the Liberal Party of Quebec, Claude Ryan, that he himself would now play a direct role in battling the referendum question to encourage a "No" vote, doing whatever he could to defeat Lévesque. What happened next is recounted in detail in the National Film Board of Canada's *The Champions*, in which previous battles between Lévesque and Trudeau, dating from their days as TV personality and political journal editor respectively, are revisited. In this film, their spring 1980 referendum duels are portrayed as the continuation of a long, personal fight for the hearts of Quebecers and Canadians. Recalling Lévesque's statement that Trudeau had an "inborn talent for making you want to slap his face,"[11] and various other exchanges between the two men, the documentary film captures vividly the historical and political context in which the two leaders "deftly jabbed, dodged, bobbed, and weaved as they jousted with each other."[12]

On April 15, 1980, Trudeau rose in the House of Commons, speaking in a solemn and decisive manner, mostly without referring to his notes, to accuse Lévesque and his supporters of dishonesty in framing such a misleading and insulting question, with the very future of Quebec and Canada at stake. As an oddly quiet House listened, he made it crystal clear that he would not negotiate sovereignty association with Quebec if the referendum vote was "Yes." He also reassured Quebecers that a "No" vote would not result in federal complacency, but that he and his government would strive to secure a "Parliament that would become more effective in representing the interests of all Canadians, as it must."[13]

In Montreal's Paul Sauvé Arena on May 14, six days before the referendum vote, Pierre Trudeau gave the final speech of his referendum campaign. Beginning by stating that all federal parties were united against separatism and stating his desire to renew Canadian federalism, he lectured Lévesque about the illogic of his referendum proposal:

> Mr. Lévesque, there will be no association. Now, if you want to speak of sovereignty, let me say that you have no mandate to negotiate that, because you did not ask Quebecers if they wanted sovereignty pure and simple. You said: Do you want sovereignty on the condition that there is also association? So, with no association, you have no mandate to negotiate sovereignty; you do not have the key to open that door, and neither do I ... What we are criticizing the Parti Québécois for is for not having the courage to ask: INDEPENDENCE, YES or NO? YES or NO?[14]

After voting in his own riding of Mount Royal, on May 20, Trudeau returned to Ottawa to watch the results with a small group of colleagues and friends. By evening's end, 86 percent of the citizens of Quebec had cast votes, and 59 percent of them had voted "no" to Lévesque's sovereignty association. Trudeau's public comments immediately following the vote avoided gloating and seemed to express some sympathy for Lévesque himself, if not for his cause. He ended with "Never have I felt so proud to be a Quebecer and Canadian."[15]

The next day, Trudeau began to tackle the challenge of keeping his promise that a "no" vote, would not deter him from pursuing a renewed and strengthened federalism that would have no place for a return to the status quo. However, as 1980 continued into late Fall, there was little to indicate a significant change of direction in his and his government's dealings with Quebec. Indeed, several Francophones, like André Burelle, Trudeau's political advisor and speechwriter from 1977 to 1984, have subsequently written eloquently about the extent of the betrayal they experienced at the hands of Trudeau after the sovereignty referendum of 1980.[16] Many Albertans were to feel equally snubbed by Trudeau's unwillingness to change his inconsistent, fluctuating, yet mostly adversarial, approach to Alberta with respect to the production and pricing of its natural resources.

Soon after the tabling of the NEP as part of the federal budget in October 1980, Lougheed predictably reacted furiously to it. In his typically multi-pronged, combative posture, he "took legal action, mobilized other Premiers, prepared fall-back positions, and rallied his fellow Albertans."[17] On October 30, 1980, in a half-hour television broadcast, he announced that beginning March 1, 1981 Alberta was going to reduce out-of-province oil shipments to Eastern Canada by 60,000 barrels a day, in three stages, to a maximum of 180,000 barrels. Using one of his most powerful lines, he reiterated that: "if the oil and gas industry was located in Ontario, the country would be paying world prices," and closed with these words:

> Who will ultimately decide? It won't be Peter or Pierre—it will be you, as Albertans. You will determine whether or not you want to see more and more of your lives directed and controlled in Ottawa or whether you want to see a fair portion of the decision-making determined by Albertans in Alberta. If you choose the

latter, I believe, over time, we will have a strong Canada and a better Canada.[18]

Elsewhere in his remarks, Lougheed announced that Alberta would not approve any new projects in the oil sands and that it would launch a challenge in court to the NEP's "Natural Gas and Gas Liquids Tax (NGGLT)." He also questioned the legality of a second NEP tax called the "Petroleum and Gas Revenue Tax (PGRT)."

The PGRT was an eight percent tax on gross revenues and was not income tax deductible. Calling it a federal royalty on Alberta's provincial resources, Lougheed maintained that the PGRT not only encroached on the Province's constitutional jurisdiction, but also would have the effect of stifling investment in exploration and development, especially by smaller Canadian companies, which the Feds claimed to want to help. In effect, because oil and gas companies could not absorb both this new non-refundable tax and existing provincial royalties, the new federal "royalty" prevented Alberta from continuing to impose its own royalties on its own natural resources, as it was perfectly within its constitutional rights to do. In fact, in Alberta, the vast majority of oil and gas extraction is undertaken on provincial crown (or public) land, which is leased by the province to petroleum companies

As bad as the PGRT was for Alberta, the NGGLT was arguably worse and certainly more annoying. Unlike oil, there was no shortage of natural gas and a large portion of Alberta's 1970s natural resource revenues came from exporting natural gas to the United States. As such, the NGGLT was seen by Lougheed to be a bald money grab by the Trudeau government, a blatant attempt to fatten its own "coffers by redirecting revenue from a previously untapped source into its own treasury."[19] Because this seemed to be the only motive for introducing the NGGLT, it was interpreted by Lougheed as an unwarranted attack on the constitutional principle of provincial ownership of resources. Consequently, Lougheed's legal challenge was directed initially at it.

To reinforce Lougheed's October 30, 1980 televised reaction to the NEP and to ensure public support, the Alberta government distributed a 10-page pamphlet to the province's households that outlined its views and positions on energy and the constitution. In doing so, Lougheed was explicitly telling Trudeau that trouble on the energy front would mean trouble on the constitutional front. As 1981 got underway, in his annual New Year newspaper column, Peter Lougheed informed Albertans that he was resolved to pursue positions and policies in his relations with the federal government that demanded "fairness, equity and the recognition of our aspirations."[20]

As it turned out, Albertans required little convincing. For this reason, many scholars, members of the media, and other professional observers have tended to dismiss Peter Lougheed's reaction to the NEP as first announced in the federal 1980 budget, as a manipulation and aggravation of Albertan resentment of central Canada. However, others have pointed to evidence that the sharp downturn in Alberta's economy that followed in the mid-1980s could be traced directly to the NEP, and estimate "that upwards of $70 billion was lost to the Alberta economy in the first few years of the NEP."[21] In light of this fact, it can be argued that whatever the sources of past grievances with Ottawa, Albertans hardly could be accused of reacting negatively to the NEP without reasonable cause.

For many Albertans, Lalonde's and Trudeau's rhetoric of fairness and sharing as they lowered the NEP boom was both insulting and familiar. As a newly minted province in 1905, Alberta was a sparsely populated, undeveloped corner of the Canadian federation, without an established record of contributing to the Canadian economy and way of life. The mere fact of its existence hardly had registered with most Canadians east of the Manitoba-Ontario border, before the depression of the 1930s laid waste to the Canadian prairies. Although widely called the Great Depression, the depression was significantly greater on the prairies than in much of the rest of the nation.

As the 1930s unfolded, the Canadian plains were hit by a triple whammy. Following the stock market crash of 1929, many European nations who had been major importers of Canadian grain, especially wheat, enacted embargoes and quotas to protect their own farmers. At the same time, huge increases in worldwide grain production from new agricultural exporters like Australia and Argentina led to enormous surpluses that could not be shipped for lack of buyers. A bushel of number one Northern dropped from $1.03 in 1928 to 29 cents by 1932. The average income of an Alberta farm was more than halved. To top things off, by 1936 a combination of dust storms, drought, and scorching winds resulted in dried lakes, swarms of locusts, and exploding populations of gophers that destroyed millions of acres of prairie land—its topsoil eroded and blown away.

Mortgages on these depleted lands, the homes they contained, and the businesses that supplied them were dropped like hotcakes by central Canadian bankers and investors. With such memories of bad treatment firmly entrenched, and refreshed as they were from one generation of Albertans to the next, the very idea of good, fair, and equitable intentions on the part of the federal government was a tough sell.

These were the muddy waters into which Pierre Trudeau strode in the summer of 1980 when he insisted that Albertans must "exercise a sense of sharing" and went on to accuse their Premier of always wanting more. "I think, after I'd offer him again more, at some point he'll say, 'Enough, enough. I don't want the Canadian consumer to be strangled just to give a few more billion dollars to Alberta.'"[22] For most Albertans, fed up with what they regarded as easterners' whining whenever things didn't go their way, as they most often did, Trudeau's flippancy about ongoing negotiations with Alberta and Lougheed was unforgiveable. For many of them it wasn't hard to imagine, with Lévesque, giving a slap to the face of someone arrogant enough to deliver such lines.

Nonetheless, politicians, perhaps unlike many of those who elect them, must have a short memory for posturing, exaggeration, and insult. Behind the scenes of the ongoing NEP flare-ups that followed the 1980 October budget, both Trudeau and Lougheed were concerned that they had let things go too far. After all, "Trudeau cared more about the Constitution than the NEP, and he urged Lalonde to reach an agreement with the producing provinces."[23] For his part, Lougheed was concerned that his exchanges with Trudeau were becoming bitter and personal in a way that was not good for the country. Although profoundly angry with Ottawa, Peter Lougheed possessed a love for Canada that never was in doubt, and had a strong distaste for any hint of western separatism. When Don Braid of the Edmonton Journal reported on January 6, 1981 that several of Alberta's Conservative MPs had begun to talk openly about leaving Canada, Lougheed quietly confided his concerns to his friend and Minister of Energy, Merv Leitch, and suggested that it would be best to work out an agreement with Ottawa on revenue sharing.

Lougheed also was well aware of goings on in the Alberta oil patch's executive quarters and knew where the real loyalties of many oil barons lay. He worried that some of the biggest players, like Dome Petroleum and Nova, might be enticed by the NEP's provisions to acquire some of the foreign owned companies operating in Alberta and move more of their operations to federal Crown lands in the North West Territories. For his part, Trudeau was increasingly concerned that tensions arising from fights over the NEP were likely to sour forthcoming constitutional talks. By the late spring of 1981, both Lougheed and Trudeau, who actually did respect each other, seemed ready to retire their barbed arrows, and began to seek a compromise. However, things would continue to get worse before they got better.

In March 1981, the Alberta Court of Appeal ruled that the NGGLT (the federal excise tax on natural gas) was outside of federal jurisdiction, a decision that was immediately appealed by Ottawa. Then, in April, Alberta enacted the first leg of its promise to cut production and export of oil to Central Canada. The Feds responded with what became known as the "Lougheed levy," a half a cent per litre tax on gasoline and other petroleum products. To avoid further escalation, and on strict instructions from their bosses to bargain in good faith, Lalonde and Leitch met to negotiate over 100 specific items in the NEP that divided their governments. However, even as these negotiations were progressing, the summer of 1981 was about to prove unkind to their efforts.

On July 9, 1980, Imperial Oil suspended work on a major project near Cold Lake in the Alberta oil sands. Initially saying they would not be blackmailed into sweetening the deal by increasing the loan they had already given to Imperial, Lalonde and Trudeau later backed away from this strong stance. In the interim, they had been informed by Dome and Nova executives that federal grants to encourage "frontier exploration" were inadequate. Polls conducted in Alberta continued to show strong support for Lougheed's tough stance against the Liberals' NEP. To keep pressure on the Lalonde-Leitch negotiations, Alberta cut oil production once more in June 1981, just as Lougheed had promised in his October 30, 1980 television broadcast. With a third cut scheduled for September, Ottawa responded with an additional 1.6 percent a litre gasoline tax.

With these last flare-ups, things finally had become too volatile to continue and both sides gave up the game. Ottawa ceased its attempts to tax natural gas exports. Canadian oil moved closer to the world price, in a complicated manner that distinguished between "old" oil already in production, and "new" oil extracted from oil sands, offshore, and Artic deposits. In return, the federal government secured much of the additional revenue it sought. Trudeau commented that "in keeping with the long tradition of Canadian federalism, we've bargained hard and we've reached a compromise— a good Canadian term—a compromise which is to the advantage of both the people of Alberta and the people of Canada."[24] In his memoirs, Trudeau added that in his view, Lougheed "was just doing his job. ... His focus was on what is good for Alberta ... and it was my job to think of the whole country first."[25] As finalized, the agreement would greatly benefit the federal government's pocket book if the price of oil continued to rise. However, if it began to fall, it would be the federal purse that would empty the most. Trudeau now shifted his focus fully to his primary concern—the forthcoming constitutional talks with the ten provincial premiers about patriating and amending the Canadian Constitution.

Trudeau had entered federal politics in 1965 as a novice MP representing the Quebec riding of Montreal Mount Royal, with the intention of contributing to a stronger national government that could enable a progressive modernization of all regions of Canada, but with a particular focus on his own home province of Quebec. Under the Lesage provincial Liberals, Quebec had begun a "quiet revolution," and was beginning to emerge from its historical subjugation under the triumvirate of its powerful Catholic clergy, American and other out-of-province corporate interests, and the traditionalist government of Maurice Duplessis' Union Nationale Party. This period of Quebec history, often referred to as "the Great Darkness," ran from 1936 to 1958, almost without interruption.

Perhaps the fact that Trudeau himself, as an older adolescent and young adult, had once been embroiled in right-wing corporatism through his Brébeuf education, added a touch of personal redemption to his genuine and heartfelt concern to help bring his home province into the modern world. This goal was still at the top of his "to do" list when he decided to stay on as leader of the Liberal Party of Canada at the end of 1979. It provided a big part of his motivation to create a constitutional framework in which the people of Quebec and the other provinces could be protected from political and economic forces that eroded their fundamental rights and freedoms.

Lougheed's motivations for entering Alberta politics, as the MLA for Calgary-West, were not that dissimilar to those of Trudeau. In fact, Lougheed's initial political interests as an adolescent and young adult had been focused on a potential involvement in federal politics, following the examples of his grandfather, Sir James and his grandmother's uncles, Lord Strathcona and Richard Hardisty. Both Sir James and Senator Hardisty had been strong advocates for western Canadian interests in the Canadian Senate, and when it was clear that Peter's best opportunity for a future political career was at the provincial level in Alberta, he became focused on bringing Alberta into a more progressive and modern style of governance and social development than it had experienced under Social Credit rule from 1935 to 1971.

Lougheed's primary focus, given the realities of the Albertan economy and his direct experience of the boom-and-bust cycles of Tulsa, Oklahoma, while studying for his MBA at Harvard, was on protecting and allowing his province to benefit from its rich natural resources. However, he also was concerned with protecting the rights and freedoms of the citizens of Alberta whom he represented. Both Lougheed and Trudeau were avid defenders of individual rights. One of Lougheed's first acts, after being elected as Premier of Alberta in 1971, was to institute a provincial bill of rights modeled after John Diefenbaker's federal statute. At that time it was Lougheed's attorney general, Mervin Leitch, who had suggested that they include a notwithstanding clause in the provincial bill of rights that would allow the government to propose legislation contrary to the rights protected in the bill should the need ever arise to do so. Lougheed, always the pragmatist, saw no harm in this. Given the strength of his commitment to protecting citizen's rights and freedoms, he doubted that any such need ever would arise. Even so, it was never possible to predict with accuracy all events and circumstances that might attend the future, and it made sense to Lougheed to give himself and his government some room to manoeuvre if absolutely necessary and defensible.

Managing the economy and general good governance aside, three of the most vexatious issues that had dominated Pierre Trudeau's previous terms as Prime Minister (1968-1972, 1972-1974, and 1974-1979) were Quebec separatism, energy and natural resources, and the patriation and reform of the Canadian Constitution. With the narrow defeat of Lévesque's sovereignty association in the referendum of May 1980, Trudeau was left to juggle the priorities of oil and the constitution, while simultaneously attempting somehow to patch up a weakening Canadian economy that continued to suffer inflationary pressures—pressures made worse by the sad state of federal financial coffers. Finances, oil, and the constitution all required intricate intergovernmental negotiations between the provinces and Ottawa. Trudeau and his cabinet were forced to walk a strategic tightrope that could be kept aloft only if how they acted on the energy end did not impede their actions at the constitutional end. With the Quebec referendum behind him and having made it clear to Lalonde that he wanted the heat from the energy file turned down, Trudeau, in the summer of 1981, turned his attention to what he hoped would become the jewel in his political legacy, the patriation of the Canadian Constitution with a new Charter of Rights and Freedoms that satisfied his personal, political, and philosophical penchants.

Since he was first elected as Prime Minister in 1968, Pierre Trudeau had made no secret of his plans to bring Canada's constitution home from Great Britain. He, like most Quebecers, viewed the fact that the Canadian constitution remained an act of the British Parliament as a humiliation that symbolized Canada's continuing colonial status. Having made limited progress on the constitutional file during his previous terms as prime minister, Pierre knew that time was running out if he wanted patriation of the constitution to be part of his legacy to his country. Most Canadians were strongly in favour of being able to govern themselves in both name and fact. So were the vast majority of the country's politicians and governmental officials. However, most of the provincial premiers also saw constitutional talks as a chance to gain more powers relative to those wielded by the federal government, and consequently resisted patriation without a restructuring of intergovernmental power differentials. The resultant stalemates continued a pattern of failed attempts to bring the constitution home that had occurred regularly since the 1920s.

In October 1980, following a particularly non-productive meeting with the premiers in September, Trudeau decided he had had enough of the premiers' demanding and stalling, and warned them that he was prepared to act unilaterally to get the job done. To this end, he proposed an amending formula that ultimately would empower the nation's citizens to decide, by citizen referendums, contested matters concerning constitutional change. He also introduced a Charter of Rights and Freedoms as a guard against abuse by all Canadian governments, provincial and federal. His primary motive for introducing the charter was undoubtedly to enshrine in Canadian society his deeply and sincerely held commitments to the equal protection of the individual rights of all Canadian citizens, under the rule of law. However, he also knew that most of the premiers would not want to be constrained by such a charter or by the constant threat of citizens' referendums, but would be reluctant to go against either, with polls showing very strong public support of such initiatives. In effect, Trudeau quite happily used his proposed charter and citizen referendums as means of garnering public support for his proposal to patriate the constitution unilaterally, or, failing that, to bring the premiers, properly chastened, to the negotiating table he had prepared for them. But Peter Lougheed and several of the other premiers still had a few cards of their own to play.

In the months that followed Trudeau's announcement of his unilateral intentions concerning the constitution and charter, Ontario and New Brunswick indicated a willingness to support Trudeau's patriation plan (what he called the *People's Package)*, but the rest of the provinces (the so-called *Gang of Eight*) resisted for a variety of political, regionally specific, and personal reasons. These mostly concerned their fears about a possible shifting of power from the provinces to the federal government and to the country's law courts. In the words of Ron Graham, author of the award winning 2012 book *The Last Act: Pierre Trudeau, the Gang of Eight, and the Fight for Canada,* throughout most of 1980 and 1981, "in the midst of the worst economic downturn since the Depression, the prime minister and the premiers warred like the gods on Mount Olympus in a battle over their vision of Canada."[26] In the House of Commons, the opposition parties exhausted their array of delay and derail tactics. The Supreme Court described the Government's unilateral approach, although technically legal, as a violation of constitutional convention, and the Gang of Eight, led by Peter Lougheed and Sterling Lyon of Manitoba, continued to dig in their heels.

On April 16, 1981, the Gang of Eight held a news conference at which they announced their own proposal for patriating the constitution. Their plan did not include a charter of rights, but did include an amending formula. Under this formula, future constitutional changes would require the support of the federal government and seven provinces, totalling 50 percent of the population of Canada. In addition, the provinces would have the right to opt out of any provisions affecting provincial jurisdiction with a simple majority vote of their legislatures. In supporting the Gang's proposal, Peter Lougheed cautioned Trudeau with the words: "To suggest that the Prime Minister or the federal government can ignore what is happening here this morning defies the reality of Canada."[27] Nonetheless, Jean Chrétien (Trudeau's Minister of Justice and Attorney General) and Trudeau himself reacted immediately and unequivocally to the Gang's proposal. For them, the opting out clause and the absence of a charter were non-starters. A Charter of Rights and Freedoms was at the very heart of Trudeau's political philosophy of personalism, and the opting out clause proposed by the Gang was so extensive and easily invoked that it could apply to other cherished Liberal values such as language rights.

Heated debate over these and related matters boiled over into rancour at the First Ministers' meeting of September 1981, giving Trudeau little chance of claiming any significant provincial support for his unilateral patriation plans. Later that same month, on September 28th, the Supreme Court of Canada ruled that unilateral patriation of the constitution by the federal government would be legal, but ill advised. Proceeding in this way would violate time honoured practices and conventions of Canadian governance. There also were increasing signs from the UK that the British parliament and Queen were wary of a patriation proposal from Canada that did not have overwhelming support from both the Canadian public and from most of the provinces.

In light of these events, Trudeau decided to take one last stab at securing a constitutional deal with the provincial premiers, a possibility he had kept open as a "Plan B." So it came to pass that, during the first week of November 1981, Pierre Trudeau presided over the eleventh first ministers' summit on the constitution—the first had been held in 1927. With Canada in its worst recession since the 1930s, Canadian home prices falling, and unemployment going through the roof, most premiers wanted to be on their home turf attending to these matters, as many of their citizens were demanding. But Pierre Trudeau was, by this point, as one of his advisors described him, beyond "obsessed … he's monomaniacal."[28] Although he too thought the meeting ill-timed, Peter Lougheed seemed just as committed to resisting Trudeau's unilateralism on the constitutional file, as he had recently done on the oil file.

As reported by John English, "when the premiers and the prime minister gathered in Ottawa for their first ministers' conference, … Mervin Leitch engaged Lougheed in a private discussion, suggesting that he 'intervene by proposing a notwithstanding clause along the lines of section 2 of the *Alberta Bill of Rights.*' It was a crucial intervention, even though Lougheed discovered that most of his fellow premiers had no idea what he was talking about."[29] Ron Graham's *The Last Act* paints a detailed portrait of the 24 hours between the morning of November 4th and the morning of November 5th, 1981. Graham describes just how "crucial" Lougheed's "notwithstanding" proposal proved to be during this nation-determining summit. He also reveals a great deal about Pierre Trudeau and Peter Lougheed, their visions of Canada, and just how far they were prepared to go to secure a constitutional deal that did not contradict their core political and personal values.

◆◆◆

Two days earlier, on the morning of Monday, November 2, 1981, our two protagonists, together with the other provincial premiers, accompanied by some of the most powerful provincial and federal ministers and officials of the land, entered the Centennial Room of Ottawa's Government Conference Centre, in what once had been the city's railway station, to determine the future of the Canadian federation. They were there at Pierre Trudeau's invitation to settle the matter of constitutional partriation and reform, once and for all. The premiers, all conservatives (including Social Credit Premier Bill Bennett of BC) other than René Lévesque (Parti Québécois) and Allan Blakeney (Saskatchewan NDP), were united in their anger at Trudeau for issuing an ultimatum to attend this undesired meeting at a time when their electorates were clamouring for action on the economic front. Certain that they would be asked to give up some of their existing provincial powers to the federal government, they were angered further by Trudeau's public plea for them to resist trying to use the talks to advance their own provincial agendas and powers. Only Bill Davis of Ontario and Richard Hatfield of New Brunswick found any merit at all in the pre-conference proposals and documents circulated by the federal government. Many of them, led by Peter Lougheed and Sterling Lyon of Manitoba, objected strongly to the peremptory tone and manner, the threats and ultimatums, which had trapped them into participating in what they regarded as Trudeau's pursuit of his personal goals for the country. "They didn't see themselves as provincial satraps journeying to the capital to render homage to the grand potentate in exchange for favours and rank."[30]

The first day of the conference on Monday, November 2 was surprisingly civil, perhaps because the morning session was carried live on television and consisted mostly of prepared, opening statements from each leader.

Trudeau, as Prime Minister and chair of the meeting, outlined three questions that would guide deliberations during the conference. Speaking in French, he began by saying that:

> We are here to search for an agreement and that agreement will be possible to the extent that all of us are prepared to compromise. ... We have to respond to three questions. The first: do we want to patriate the Canadian Constitution ... to put an end to the colonial statute of Great Britain that we have had since 1867. ... The second question: should we find an amending formula or do we want a rigid, status quo constitution that most Canadians would like to escape. ... (switching to English) The third question is should we have a Charter of Rights for all Canadians binding on all governments of Canada or do we remain in a country where the federal government has its bill of rights, each of the provinces has a Charter of Rights or a Bill of Human Rights, but there is no Charter of Rights for all Canadians, no common values that we can say we all hold in common and which are written into our constitution?[31]

Trudeau went on to say that he hoped the first question could be dealt with quickly to signal to Canadians that we will have our own constitution in Canada, and "to that extent be nation-builders and settle the problem that has been plaguing us for many, many years." With respect to the second question concerning an amending formula, Trudeau offered to move away from the Victoria formula that Lougheed and others had disagreed with, saying that "We are prepared to look at any other number of formulas … There is no desire on our part, and I state it unequivocally, to impose an amending formula on Canadians." Regarding the third question concerning the Charter of Rights, Trudeau offered his strong views in support of a common Charter of Rights and Freedoms for all Canadians, but also indicated that he and his government were willing to negotiate further "on the substance of the Charter and on the timing of its implementation." He then added: "but we cannot be flexible on the principle of the Charter itself, no more than you have been in your various provinces."[32]

In stating Alberta's position, Peter Lougheed opened by acknowledging the usefulness of the conference as providing an opportunity for "the Canadian people to hear the views expressed by the First Ministers on this important subject in this particular setting," adding that: "I don't think it is overly dramatic to say that this is a very important cross roads for our confederation." He continued: "The federal government can try and press on and change our constitution without the agreement of the provinces, with all the division and the antagonism that will result, not for a short time but for many years." Or, "it can sincerely sit down and work out our differences without threats but in an atmosphere of negotiation." He then very briefly revisited the controversies and negotiations between Alberta and Ottawa over energy resources, exchanges that had been necessary after "the federal government acted unilaterally," but which nonetheless resulted in "a negotiated settlement," such that hopefully "differences of the past can now be put aside and governments can now work together to achieve the common goal of energy self-sufficiency."[33] Lougheed went on to express the hope that having "realized that unilateral action would not work" in the case of energy negotiations, the federal government will come to the same realization with respect to the ongoing constitutional negotiations they were here to attempt to put an end to.

In the rest of his lengthy opening remarks, Lougheed repeatedly chastised the Trudeau government for abruptly abandoning constitutional talks after they were last attempted with the provinces in September of 1980, only to renew them now, after the Feds had been reprimanded by the Supreme Court for acting in ways that, although technically legal, were considered inappropriate and highly unconventional. Lougheed reminded everyone that "The Supreme Court stated in unmistakable language that some of the unwritten rules are more important than the written ones, even if the court cannot prevent their breach," and gave the example of "the unwritten rule that a Prime Minister must resign or call an election when defeated on a major matter in Parliament."[34]

After saying that "Alberta ... fully supports the objective of patriation of the Canadian constitution," Lougheed responded to the second of the two questions framed in Trudeau's opening remarks by saying that "from the perspective of Alberta, any amending formula that is devised must incorporate the principle of provincial equality and reflect the need to protect existing provincial legislative powers, rights and privileges."[35] He then placed this demand in recent and historical context by referring to previous debates between the two of them concerning "a lack of comprehension of the people of Alberta" and their sense "validly or otherwise, that the nature of government and the history of Canadian development to this point has favoured those parts of the country where there are large populations, … the central provinces, in fact. … They feel they have been hindered in their progress to being a full member in Confederation as a result of" this imbalance.[36] Having dug in his heels against any amending formula that would give (directly or indirectly) the central provinces the ability to veto the desires and wishes of the other provinces, Lougheed ended his opening remarks by again deploring the divisive consequences of federal unilateral action on energy and constitutional matters, concluding with "Alberta's overriding objective is to preserve and protect the federal principle of [a united] Canada which is the very foundation of our constitution."[37]

The only concrete concessions contained in any of the opening statements were in those of Trudeau (Ottawa), Bill Davis (Ontario), and Richard Hatfield (New Brunswick). Davis's concession had been prearranged with Trudeau, and appeared, on the surface, to be a significant one. In response to the question about the amending formula, Davis indicated a willingness to drop his demand that Ontario, as one of the two oldest and most populous provinces, have a veto on any constitutional change. Hatfield's concession was more minor, involving the timing of introducing a Charter of Rights in New Brunswick, but nonetheless responded to Trudeau's attempt to introduce a spirit of compromise into the proceedings. During the afternoon session, the leaders probed each others' positions, hoping to uncover signs or signals of weakness and gauging levels of commitment, and circled the ring, with occasional sharp exchanges. A harbinger of things to come was the Gang of Eight's refusal to accept an invitation to lunch with Trudeau, in favour of using the lunch break to discuss their own strategic plans and moves.

By Tuesday, things became much more heated and personal, with Trudeau briefly storming out in frustration, and the conference breaking up at noon. After that, the Gang of Eight once again huddled in a Château Laurier suite across the street from the Conference Centre to produce a proposed settlement, which included forming a commission to examine Trudeau's Charter of Rights and report recommendations at a later date. When presented with this proposal by B.C.'s Bill Bennett, in consultation with Lougheed and Buchanan, later that afternoon, Trudeau rejected it out of hand in an angry exchange, casting a pall that Allan Blakeney later described as "a general discouragement that anything would ever be agreed to."[38] As the glum mood settled in, private discussions continued into the evening, searching for ways to prolong the talks in hope of some kind of agreement, but ideas seemed few and far between.

The final 24 hours began on Wednesday morning, with a grim Pierre Trudeau in full professorial mode as an expert in constitutional law (which he was), calmly, but with hints of anger, chastising his student premiers for being petty and self-interested, while further admonishing them with sternly disapproving looks for their inadequate work. He also reminded them that this is a "final attempt" and that "I can't be party to a waiting game."[39] By this time, Quebec Premier René Lévesque, obviously furious, threatened to leave the conference—to "quit this circus" as he put it, to return to Quebec for the opening session of the Quebec National Assembly, which he did not want to postpone for what was "going on here."

Trudeau already knew that Lévesque would be most unlikely to want to renew a federation he was trying to separate from, but nonetheless hoped he would stay on, for appearances if nothing else, especially since Sterling Lyon, Premier of Manitoba, had left after breakfast that morning. Lyon did not like Trudeau and was anxious to return to a heated provincial election campaign he had reluctantly left for two days already. It was clear that Lyon was unlikely to agree to anything Trudeau would be satisfied with as an outcome of the conference. Trudeau and Lyon, who considered Trudeau to be a French socialist trying to subvert the British parliamentary tradition, already had locked horns on the first day of the conference on Monday.

The other western premiers were more difficult to figure out. Trudeau sensed some flexibility in Allan Blakeney of Saskatchewan and Bill Bennett of BC, but doubted that either of them would abandon Lougheed. And, Lougheed, much less ideological than Lyon, clearly was smarting from their many recent skirmishes over oil pricing. Although Trudeau and Lougheed respected each other, they appeared to be on very different tracks when it came to intergovernmental sharing of constitutional powers. Perhaps disappointing their teacher most were those he took to be his allies, Davis and Hatfield, both progressive conservatives. The two hadn't weighed in as Trudeau had hoped they might do after giving their muted consent to his plans as outlined in the pre-conference materials. But then, Trudeau was prepared for most of this.

In fact, Trudeau had come into the final constitutional conference:

> ... aiming at one of two outcomes: I could either prove to the Canadian public that the Eight were being completely unreasonable and then go ahead alone, legally but perhaps unconventionally. Or I could break the solidarity among the Eight and go to London with the support of a substantial number of premiers, which I supposed would be anywhere between five and nine of them. Lévesque's goal was to keep the Gang of Eight intact to thwart me, and mine was to make a certain number of concessions that would split their ranks and bring some of the others onside.[40]

When Lévesque decided to stay, it was a seemingly off-the-cuff remark by Trudeau during the Wednesday meetings that suddenly got things moving again, in what, for many attendees, was an unanticipated and highly surprising way. In some frustration, Trudeau expressed the view that perhaps a referendum was the only way of resolving the stalemate that seemed to have griped the conference. This remark suggested a way that Lévesque might extradite himself from the proceedings without further loss of face. For various and probably somewhat different reasons, Trudeau's remark also engaged the Gang of Eight to the extent that it became the main topic of conversation for the rest of the day.

Ron Graham provides a useful description of what happened on Wednesday to break the stalemate. In the midst of things seeming to bog down, suddenly:

> Trudeau saw an opening, his best chance, his last card. For two days he had tried to split the Gang of Eight, to pull enough provinces out of the common front to give him the number he needed to satisfy the Supreme Court's constitutional convention. Now he seized the moment. "Rather than break up in disarray and continue our fight on the doorstep of the British Parliament," Trudeau asked the premiers, "why don't we get patriation first—nobody can object to that—then give ourselves two years to solve our problems over the amending formula and the Charter, and failing that consult the people in a referendum? There, that's a new offer. The thrust of it is to do with the Charter what we did with the amending formula. I believe we have to have an end to this, a binding process."[41]

In fact, what appeared to many around the table to be a spontaneous thought of the moment, had been well rehearsed by Pierre Trudeau in a slightly different context. As he revealed in his *Memoirs*: "I decided it was a good time to try a fall-back position that I had had in mind for quite a different purpose. I had been thinking that if it became necessary to go to London unilaterally and the British showed any reluctance to cooperate, I might"[42] do exactly what he now suggested to the premiers.

At first, all the premiers were unimpressed by this way of proceeding. Most of them found it out of step with the parliamentary system, and Lévesque had little interest in agreeing with any suggestion made by Trudeau. However, during a coffee break, Pierre began to chide Lévesque, raising the matter of the recent Quebec referendum and asking why a great democrat like him should be worried about taking the matter directly to the people in a referendum, something that hadn't bothered him in the past. Rising to the bait, and seeming to forget he was part of the Gang of Eight (although only strategically), and perhaps sensing a possibility of giving Trudeau a comeuppance of the kind he himself had suffered when the results of the Quebec referendum on sovereignty association were returned, Lévesque, according to Trudeau, eventually replied "I would like to fight the charter."[43]

After the coffee beak, when the Wednesday conference session resumed, Lévesque declared "I think we should consult with the people. It's not the end of the world," Lougheed immediately jumped in to say, "I think you're wrong. It's very divisive."[44] Of course, the other Gang members were equally furious with Lévesque for breaking ranks. They were perhaps even more riled by the possibility that they now might have to oppose and fight the Charter of Rights openly in a completely unanticipated referendum, which would further distract them and the Canadian public from the country's financial woes. Later, when Lévesque realized the magnitude of his mistake, Trudeau already had announced to the press that "The cat is among the pigeons," and mischievously referred to "an alliance" he now had with Quebec, in so far as Lévesque and he both had expressed a possible interest in a referendum to decide the matter of a charter. It then was too late for Lévesque's denials and back-pedaling. "His 'alliance' of a few hours had blown what remained of the Gang of Eight apart."[45]

As he walked away from the morning session on Wednesday, November 4, Lougheed declared that if a referendum was going to occur "We'll fight and we'll win."[46] Privately he was appalled at the morning's events and the possibility of a referendum, but his competitiveness had been aroused and Trudeau's Liberals had no federal seats in Alberta. He knew that however much Albertans might want patriation and a charter, they also liked him and his government and were completely onside with his tough stance against Trudeau on the NEP. "If the gunslinger from the East wanted a shootout, Lougheed would be ready and waiting at the O.K. Corral. He suited the part, with his handsome features and the physique of an aging athlete. Short, tough, laconic, he was a Marlboro Man who had traded his horse, his Stetson, and his home on the range for law school, a Harvard MBA, and a corner office downtown."[47]

Like Trudeau, Lougheed certainly didn't lack toughness, nor was he known to compromise his principles. Yet, there also was an attractive boyishness in his manner "that suggested a shy, sensitive, slightly insecure but fundamentally decent soul protected by a steely resolve—very much like Pierre Trudeau, in fact, which is what made them such well-matched protagonists."[48] Of course, what separated the two were very different backgrounds and visions of Canada, which sprang from their life-long participation in the very different historical and social cultural milieus of Alberta and Quebec. Trudeau was a national politician who saw the world in terms of his philosophical and personal principles, filtered through his Quebec-Ottawa experience. Lougheed was a provincial politician who saw the world through Albertan eyes, informed by his compelling sense of practical necessity and loyalty to the province's people and land. Trudeau's centrist federalism and Lougheed's regional federalism were directly connected to their backgrounds and personalities. What they had in common, in addition to some shared dispositions and talents, was a great love for their country and a strong belief in their visions for it, as different as those might be.

Lougheed had told the other members of the Gang of Eight at a pre-conference meeting on Sunday evening, November 1, 1981 that he strongly believed Trudeau would be forced to back down from his unilateral patriation plan if all of them held firm and did not break their alliance. To try and ensure the continuity of their agreement, given the likelihood that unforeseen events might occur in the next few days to invite reconsideration or change in their strategy, he suggested that they agree to discuss any possible changes in their views with each other before acting on them in the conference sessions themselves. Obviously, Lévesque had not gotten the message, or more likely had forgotten it in the heat of battle, when Trudeau had succeeded in triggering René's lingering animosity from their recent referendum combat in Quebec.

As a progressive conservative, Peter Lougheed was not like prairie populists of the past. For him, Parliament (or in the case of

Alberta, the Legislative Assembly) was supreme and constitutional matters should be left to governments. Although there may be a place very occasionally for plebiscites, negotiated compromises amongst elected officials were strongly preferred. What Trudeau had done and Lévesque had accepted, at least long enough to break the trust that had held the Gang of Eight together, was anathema to Lougheed's parliamentarianism and blatantly destructive to his cause of the moment. Across the country, Canadians were overwhelmingly in support of patriating the constitution and in having a Charter of Rights and Freedoms to curb governmental excess. No sane person, let alone premier, wanted to campaign against the people's will and the idea of a just society. Under these conditions, Lougheed's confidence that the Gang would win was suddenly in tatters. Trudeau now seemed to have all the cards.

Suddenly backed into a corner, Lougheed returned to the conference meetings on Wednesday afternoon anxious to know the exact rules and wording of any proposed referendum about patriation, the Charter, and an amending formula. When it became clear that Trudeau was only going to accept an amending formula based on regional approval from Ontario, Quebec, the West, and the East, with referendums and constitutional amendments requiring the support of all four regions, Lougheed responded forcefully. "Any referendum that ignores the views of the provinces and deals with regions is fundamentally opposed to our view of Canada. It's not a nation of regions; it's a nation of provinces."[49]

Trudeau, however, had no intention of further empowering the West and the East by giving each of them four provincial possibilities for vetoing or forcing amendments to any resolutions that the two most heavily populated and historically dominant provinces of Ontario and Quebec might agree to. Knowing that the citizens of all provinces, including Alberta, were strongly in favour of both a Charter and patriation, and that Lougheed or any other premier who might appear to obstruct either or both these ends would pay a price in public opinion, he threatened once more to use the vehicle of referendum to let the Canadian people decide. As the afternoon meeting droned on, with the western and eastern premiers railing against the idea of a referendum and Lévesque content, despite his blunder, to watch the entire show deteriorate, Trudeau brought the afternoon session to a close. "Well, we've tried everything. Screw it, I think we should be prepared to meet the television cameras at five and tell them we couldn't agree."[50]

With the "last chance" Wednesday afternoon session apparently concluded, the premiers, their ministers, and senior federal and provincial officials leaped into a frenzy of activity. Federal Minister of Justice Jean Chrétien talked to anyone who would listen, warning that a referendum was inevitable if they did not make concessions, and that a failure to compromise risked damage to their careers and their country. Saskatchewan's Attorney General, Roy Romanow and his Ontario counterpart, Roy McMurtry, were receptive to Chrétien's overtures and threats. Retiring to a kitchenette not far from the conference meeting room, the three of them drew up a plan in which they tried to give Trudeau and the western premiers much of what they wanted but also required them to compromise on other matters. As Trudeau later described the deal in his memoirs, "It involved swapping provincial acceptance of a charter of rights, but with a notwithstanding legislative override clause, for the Alberta amending formula, but without fiscal compensation for provinces that opted out." Trudeau went on to say that "My first reaction was to say, 'Oh, no, no, the Alberta amending formula is terrible, and as far as the charter is concerned, there isn't going to be any watering down'."[51]

But, eventually, Trudeau came around. In his memoirs he provides a clear and insightful look into his metamorphosis from a hardline opponent of what has subsequently been labeled "The Kitchen Accord," to a still reluctant but, without other alternatives, confirmed supporter of the "Kitchen" compromise.

The notwithstanding clause violated my sense of justice: it seemed wrong that any province could decide to suspend any part of the charter ... I saw the charter as an expression of my long-held view that the subject of law must be the individual human being; the law must permit the individual to fulfill himself or herself to the utmost. Therefore the individual has certain basic rights that cannot be taken away by any government, ... liberty, equality, and the rights of association that Canadians from coast to coast could share. ... With the charter in place, we can now say that Canada is a society where all people are equal and where they share some fundamental values based on freedom. ... With these beliefs, I had little sympathy for provincial demands for an override by means of this mealy-mouthed 'notwithstanding' clause. Just as I was saying that I didn't want to make these concessions, the phone rang; it was Ontario premier Bill Davis.[52]

Trudeau then goes on to describe how, during that phone call, the usually unruffled Davis, who sometimes seemed to avoid direct conflict, came right to the point, saying "No, look, Pierre, I think we have to tell you that this is a good compromise from our point of view. Rather than fight this thing to the bitter end, we have to tell you that we wouldn't go to London supporting you as we have until now if you don't accept some compromise of this nature."[53] After talking to Davis, Trudeau hung up and turned to his ministers and advisors to say "I think we may have to go for the compromise solution even though I don't like it—because otherwise now we'd be going to London alone."[54]

Throughout the night and into the early hours of Thursday, November 5, several conference participants met to debate and prepare final wording of what they hoped would be an agreement based on the Kitchen compromise, while others slept fitfully, if at all. To one such meeting, at the invitation of Allan Blakeney of Saskatchewan, Lougheed and Brian Peckford of Newfoundland, the two most entrenched members of the Gang, sent Peter Meekison and Cy Abery, respectively their top negotiators, to meet with their Saskatchewan counterpart Howard Leeson and several legal and constitutional advisors. Blakeney's purpose in arranging this meeting was to see if Lougheed and Peckford could be convinced to accept some version of the Kitchen deal. By the time Blakeney himself joined the meeting around ten o'clock, he and Meekison faced off over whether or not Alberta would agree to exempt the application of its notwithstanding clause to the fundamental freedoms that Trudeau regarded as inviolate. When Blakeney insisted, despite Meekison's protests, that they phone Lougheed to ask him once again about this matter, a sleepy Lougheed testily growled at Meekison, saying, "My answer stays, and don't call me again."[55] When Peter's response was reported to Davis by Blakeney, Bill responded by saying, "We have to get the prime minister onside. I think I'll have a little talk with him."[56] As Trudeau's account of that conversation in his memoirs confirms, that telephone call was successful in convincing him to bow to Lougheed's demand.

The one additional feature that Trudeau insisted upon in his telephone conversation with Bill Davis was that in the case of minority-language education rights, nothing would be applied in any part of Canada without the agreement of all the provincial premiers. Davis communicated this last piece of the plan to Blakeney when the latter called him after midnight. By one a.m. on Thursday, November 5, 1981, it looked like Blakeney and Davis, with the assistance of Brian Peckford, had convinced almost all the premiers or their representatives that they had a tentative deal. Only René Lévesque or any of his Quebec delegation had not been consulted or informed.

By the time Jean Chrétien was on the phone before sunrise, seven of the provinces were clearly on board with the agreement. Unbeknown to the provincial premiers, this was the minimum number that Trudeau had told Chrétien he believed he must have committed to his patriation proposal so that the demand of the Supreme Court of Canada for demonstrated provincial support could be met. Knowing this, in his early morning call to Trudeau, Chrétien said, "Mr. Prime Minister, if you agree now with what you agreed last night, then we have a new constitution." To which, Trudeau replied, "Jean, if you were here, I'd give you a hug." Such apparently were the rewards of compromise. With these words exchanged, the two men agreed to a breakfast meeting with a few of their senior officials to give the proposal a final consideration before any formal announcements.

Around the same time, Lougheed's two top officials, Peter Meekison and Dick Johnston, arrived at their boss' suite in the Château Laurier to tell him that Trudeau had agreed to Alberta's twin objectives of an amending formula based on a greater equality of the provinces and an override provision in the charter. A draft of the deal was about to be circulated at the Gang of Eight's regular breakfast meeting that was set for eight o'clock. Peter Lougheed was pleased with the news, although not to the point of hugging its messengers. He then got on the telephone to share several concerns with Manitoba's Sterling Lyon, with whom he had maintained contact following the latter's departure from the constitutional talks. Both men worried that Trudeau's charter would give too much power to Ottawa, unelected judges, and be difficult to amend as provincial concerns might demand. However, unlike Lyon, Lougheed had conceded to his closest confidants that he could live with the charter if it was balanced by inclusion of the amending formula and notwithstanding clause he insisted upon. At the end of the conference, Lougheed confessed, "I have been very silent properly on the whole question of the charter of rights. ... It's useful to hold a few things in reserve."[57]

When Lévesque arrived at the breakfast meeting on the morning of Thursday, November 5, 1981 and read the constitutional deal that had been circulated, he exploded in fury, railing that all of this had been done behind his back and that he had been double-crossed by Ottawa and the rest of the Gang, which indeed he had. Quebec would receive no compensation for opting out of the agreement and he was left with a charter that he viewed as an infringement on Quebec's rights. As the others slipped away from the uncomfortable scene to prepare for the closing session and announcements, Lougheed stayed behind with Lévesque to talk about what had occurred since yesterday afternoon.

Peter Lougheed and René Lévesque had developed an unusual camaraderie as they had gotten to know each other during previous conferences and gatherings. Recognizing the validity of Alberta's regional concerns as a western version of his own concerns about and for Quebec, Lévesque considered Lougheed to be "the most remarkable man on the Prairies in his time, ... passionately concerned about sovereignty in his own way that, even though opposing us, he can understand our position."[58] For his part, Lougheed saw Lévesque as "shrewd, affable and naturally friendly. ... He saw me as an ally ... But, dealing with a separatist ... made me uneasy about where we were at and where we would end up."[59]

After the others had left the breakfast table, Peter explained to Lévesque that he had not participated in any of the late night sessions, and had only agreed to the draft proposal a few moments ago at breakfast. He also said that Lyon of Manitoba had not been informed, until he did so that morning. Lougheed suggested there was still time to have financial compensation for Quebec inserted into the proposal and to raise questions about charter rights. He also showed some surprise at Lévesque's reaction, since it was his understanding that Quebec already had decided not to sign any agreement. In the end, the exchange proved awkward and fruitless, but nonetheless demonstrated Lougheed's genuine concern about Lévesque's feelings of betrayal. Lougheed then telephoned Sterling Lyon once more to tell him that "We only can get what we want if we swallow the charter, [but] the notwithstanding clause would let him [Lyon] argue that Parliament was still supreme."[60]

When the final in camera session began at 9:25 a.m. on Thursday, November 5, 1981, Brian Peckford read out the agreement and called on each premier in turn to voice reactions. When it was Alberta's turn, Peter Lougheed agreed to the text, but made it clear that Alberta had to take "a great swallow" on language rights. As the last to agree, following Quebec's statement of discontent as the only disagreement, Pierre Trudeau, ever the dramatist, maintained to the very end a grumpy expression before declaring "Not bad, nice work. It makes a lot of sense."[61]

So, what were the feelings of our two protagonists once the conference ended? Lougheed was conflicted: "I regret that Quebec has not been able to accept the constitutional resolution, and I fully accept Quebec's position. However, my recollections clearly show that there was no breach of understanding or commitment by the other Premiers. ... Nor did the consensus of November 5 evolve with any thought or desire of excluding Quebec. On the contrary, I believe the other nine provinces very much wished Quebec to join with them."[62] Still suspicious of Trudeau as wanting to turn Canada into a unitary state, Lougheed, a staunch defender of a federalism in which the provinces had clear constitutional responsibilities in areas like education and language rights, also sympathized with Quebec's sense of injustice over federal intrusion into these areas, thinking that Trudeau had not lived up to his post-sovereignty referendum promise to Quebecers to protect their rights and freedoms. He left the conference feeling that "isolating Quebec at this point in history would damage national unity in the long term."[63]

For his part, Trudeau had achieved the great aim of his political life—a Canadian Constitution that belonged to the nation of Canada and its people, with a Charter of Rights and Freedoms, that despite Lougheed's notwithstanding clause, promised to protect the fundamental rights of all Canadians as equal participants in a single Canadian community, at least with respect to fundamental matters of individual freedom. This was Trudeau's most cherished political and personal goal. The Cyrano in him undoubtedly rejoiced, even as the mantle of this particular compromise sat somewhat uneasily on his shoulders. However, in the end, he saw little merit in the manner of the struggle just concluded. "Let's face it, it was a mean process,"[64] he remarked to one of his staffers.

Late in November 1981, Trudeau and Lougheed sat side by side at the traditional Canadian Football League's Grey Cup game, a mere three weeks after the historic constitutional conference, watching the Ottawa Rough Riders and Edmonton Eskimos contest for the oldest sporting trophy in North America, Lord Grey's Cup. Ottawa led 17-1 at halftime, causing Trudeau to turn to Lougheed and say, "What's this, Peter? A replay of the constitutional game"?[65] only to see Edmonton storm back in the second half to win.

The Constitution Act of 1982 was proclaimed on April 17, in an outdoors ceremony in front of the Canadian Parliament Buildings in Ottawa. Trudeau and all the provincial premiers, with the exception of René Lévesque, witnessed Queen Elizabeth II's formal signing of the Constitutional Proclamation. The "mean process" of the constitutional talks of November 2-5, 1981 had signalled the political demise of a dispirited and angry Lévesque, who resigned as leader of the PQ in June of 1985 and died of a heart attack two years later.

In his memoirs, Trudeau signals his resignation to and general acceptance of what had occurred during the first week of November 1981.

> It [The Constitutional Act] was not perfect. I would have much preferred not to have included the notwithstanding clause that limited the charter of rights. But I certainly prefer a charter with the notwithstanding clause than no charter at all. ... On the whole, the Constitution Act largely enshrined the values I had been advocating since I wrote my first article in *Cité libre* in 1950. And, most important, it meant that no longer would there be an easy way for provinces to blackmail the federal government by holding out more and more powers in exchange for allowing patriation.[66]

As Trudeau approached the last two years of his final term as Prime Minister, which ended with his resignation from politics on February 29, 1984, he had finally drunk from his charter victor's cup, although not exactly in the heroic way he had imagined.

By the start of 1982, Alberta's oil boom had come to an end. Expansion of world oil reserves in combination with a global recession had caused oil prices to begin a slow decline and Alberta's unemployment rate to climb. Under these conditions, the rationale for the NEP had all but vanished, and by 1984, Jean Chrétien, Trudeau's Minister of Energy, Mines and Resources, began a phased shutdown of the program. When conservative Brian Mulroney defeated new Liberal leader John Turner in the 1984 federal election to become Canada's 18th Prime Minister, he gradually removed the last vestiges of the NEP, which eventually was replaced by a new "Western Accord on Energy" on June 1, 1985. On June 27, Peter Lougheed resigned as Premier and leader of the Progressive Conservative Party of Alberta.

To compensate for declining oil and gas revenues, Lougheed raised Alberta's personal income taxes by 13 percent in 1983, and scaled back public expectations by promising a "smaller is beautiful" period of gradual recovery and steady growth in the near future. In the months leading up to his retirement from politics, Lougheed had prepared a white paper proposing an industrial and science strategy for his province, advocated for a "back-to-basics" educational approach in the province's schools, and joined Mulroney in calling for a free-trade agreement with the United States. In his final year as

Premier, and with the provincial economy looking more promising although far from its halcyon days of the early 1970s, Lougheed was careful to avoid controversy or the introduction of major projects, as he cleared a path for an orderly succession that would leave Alberta's next premier, Don Getty, with a relatively free hand to determine future directions.

After more than 20 years at the helm of Alberta's provincial government, Peter Lougheed was ready to move on. Less than three years after the intensity and unnerving unpredictability of their heated jousts over the NEP and the Canadian Constitution, both Trudeau and Lougheed were gone from the Canadian political scene. With the retirements of Trudeau and Bill Davis in 1984, followed by the retirements of Lévesque and Lougheed in 1985, a generation of influential Canadian politicians who had dominated the nation's affairs since the mid 1960s had come to an end.

Chapter Seven: Lives, Legacies, and Visions

Many contrasts have been made in previous chapters between Alberta and Ottawa, between western and eastern Canada, and between our two protagonists, their backgrounds, life experiences, and visions of Canada. Having traced the life trajectories of Pierre Trudeau and Peter Lougheed allows us to consider the numerous, and sometimes complex and conflicting, ways in which their personalities, motivations, goals, and perspectives emerged, stabilized, and occasionally changed over the course of their lives. In doing so, we inevitably confront one of the most basic conundrums of human life: how much weight reasonably can be placed on life experiences and contexts versus personal characteristics, temperaments, and dispositions in explaining and understanding lives and life accomplishments? In tackling this question, it is not necessary, and certainly not helpful, to draw a hard line between life circumstances and personality or character. Much of the latter surely is generated by experience in the former. If this seemingly self-evident assertion is granted, the task pursued in this final chapter, is to revisit what has been said so far about our leading men and attempt to stitch together patterns and trajectories of personal development and conduct as these emerged during the experiences, contexts, and courses of their lives as actually lived.

Theirs were lives of striving, animated by ambitions and visions for themselves and their country—the Canada into which they were born, to which they contributed much of their life energies, and which we contemporary Canadians have inherited and inhabit in ways that shape our own personalities and characters. Throughout this final chapter, their visions and legacies are explored further and some of their later life activities after leaving politics are recounted. Particular attention is paid to their ability, not only to engage in passionate and forceful disagreement, but to do so in a manner that retained ingredients of respect and compromise that allowed them to move forward, across the circumstances and perspectives that divided them.

Both Trudeau and Lougheed have been described as having a definite "presence" in interpersonal, social contexts and both performed well and communicated effectively on television. This said, there can be no doubt that Trudeau had a celebrity status that eclipsed Lougheed's political gravitas. Many who knew them have remarked the seriousness, and often humourless, demeanour of the determined and focused Lougheed, in contrast to the dramatically oscillating playfulness and steely determination of Trudeau. Indeed, an important part of Trudeau's charismatic attraction was his unpredictability, something that hardly can be said of the "I am as you see me" Lougheed. Yes, Lougheed's handsome, blue-eyed visage often hinted at boyishness, a feature that softened, even disarmed, some of his supporters and adversaries. But he was not in Trudeau's league when it came to a genuine aura of mystery that many found compelling. Lougheed displayed considerable personal and interpersonal talents, but couldn't match the enigmatic Trudeau in the fascination department.

The simple fact is that few public figures in Canada ever have projected the multifaceted, contradictory, and inscrutable persona that Trudeau presented to his audience. Alternating between performance artist and withdrawn loner, passionate believer and icy cynic, professorial scholar and ruggedly athletic outdoorsman, generous friend and petty enemy, Trudeau combined the rigid discipline and asceticism of a multilingual Catholic intellectual with the occasional sybaritic immaturity of a Don Juan and the risk-taking adventurousness of a Cyrano de Bergerac. He had few peers, even amongst other limelighters, in politics or other fields of endeavour. His carefully crafted cultivation of a European manner and elocution, his rhetorical and theatrical flair, and an impeccable sense of timing and style played a huge role in his personal and political life. In a truly Nietzschean manner, he purposefully presented himself to the world as "a work of art." He spent long, studious hours memorizing poetry and classical passages, perfecting accents and performance talents, honing rhetorical tricks and oratorical turns. Trudeau was formidably equipped for both combat and romance. Few to whom his characteristic icy stare, sartorial and refined charm, or playful goofiness were directed remained unaffected and unimpressed by the experience, although not always in favourable ways.

This entire personal armoury was made even more formidable by the rapidity with which Trudeau could, and often did, flip from seeming semi-somnolence to animated flashes of pique, from an inattentive ennui to a quick quip to dissolve or promote tension. His characteristically dismissive shrug and frown could give way instantaneously to unexpected displays of genuine interest, and vice versa. The net effect on others was to keep them off balance, continually anticipating something unusual but not knowing what or when it might occur. As a means of holding the spotlight and maintaining dominance and control, Trudeau's self-presentation was unparalleled. What was going on in his head? Was he crying wolf, faking injury, serious or only feigning, about to make a deal or walk away? Who knew? With such a repertoire of moves and possibilities, Trudeau styled himself as a camera-ready political conjurer.

And yet, despite all of his apparent contradictions and unpredictability, Trudeau was not inconsistent or changeable in his core mission and his vision of Canada. He had entered politics with strongly held views and principles and a powerful desire to do great things with them. Despite his many ups and downs, including some almost inconceivably self-inflicted misfires, he stuck to his guns with a tenacity and unswerving consistency from the time he entered politics in 1965 until his 1984 retirement. When he finally quit, he left the political scene mostly on his own terms, having accomplished much of what he wanted to do. True, he had squandered the opportunity he had been given by the Canadian electorate during his 1974-1979 majority government, due to a combination of fiscal difficulties (inflationary pressures and economic mismanagement) coupled with personal problems (the painful breaking up of his marriage). But, after a brief period of dejection in which he announced what turned out to be his very brief resignation as leader of the Liberal Party of Canada in November of 1979, he came roaring back to lead the Liberals to another majority federal government in February 1980. After that, he did not take his eye off his two major political aims—helping Quebec to prosper within the Canadian Confederation and patriating the Canadian Constitution, with his Charter of Rights and Freedoms attached.

Nonetheless, the outcomes of Trudeau's time as Prime Minister, and the many constitutional and intergovernmental battles he engaged, were and continue to be much debated. His reckless gamble of threatening the premiers with unilateral federal action on the constitution came very close to preventing the compromised constitutional deal he eventually achieved in November of 1981, and then only at the price of leaving Quebec unappeased and in many ways outside of that deal. His threats of similar unilateral action in his dealings with Alberta over the NEP not only added to the difficulty of achieving his constitutional ambitions, but undoubtedly contributed to a growing sense of alienation in Alberta and elsewhere in western Canada. Trudeau got much of what he wanted, but at times the manner of the getting was nothing to celebrate. And, of course, how well he served Quebec as Prime Minister has been and is likely to remain a hot topic of controversy in that province.

In comparison to Trudeau, Lougheed presented a much more consistent, uncomplicated, and less colourful personal style. His was a way of operating that left little doubt that he was a demanding (even if supportive) friend and formidably persistent foe. If Trudeau was the high achiever who liked to present an image of spontaneous creativity and easy perspicuity, Lougheed made no attempt to hide his painstaking preparations and attention to detail. He trumpeted what he took to be his embodiment of basic and essential habits of hard work. On the playing field or in the political arena, he was nothing if not well rehearsed and knowledgeable. Even when he occasionally made a show of tossing away his notes and appearing to speak extemporaneously, he could do so quite easily because of the depth and breadth of his preparedness. As a leader, he was not satisfied with being briefed, but devoured documents in whole. He rarely adopted the common politician's habit of browsing only the executive summaries of reports and proposals.

Lougheed most often spoke directly and clearly to issues at hand. He was a good listener, but seldom was unprepared to offer his own views and opinions. As a result, friends, colleagues, and co-workers had little choice but to do likewise. In this and many other ways, Lougheed led by example, inspiring others to make similar efforts. The only times that saw him completely relax his iron will and self-control—his competitive edge—were spent with family and close friends. Jeanne and his children were his top priority when he was at home and out of his home office. Later in the evenings, when their four children had retired, he often returned to work. When her help was solicited, Jeanne was a competent and insightful sounding board, loyal but quite willing to offer suggestions and raise concerns.

Where Trudeau kept people off-guard, Lougheed kept them on-guard. In this and other ways, his personality and personal characteristics reflected the values and traditions of his home province, where straight-forwardness, hard work, economy, and loyalty were admired and frequently practiced. Lougheed came to leadership easily, knowing that it was expected of him and that he was up to the challenge. Although initially attracted to federal politics, he was quick to seize provincial opportunities that opened for him. When Lougheed saw a leadership void, in his Calgary high school, at the University of Alberta, or in provincial politics, he saw an opportunity to be the leader he knew he could be, for his high school, his university, his province, and his country.

Lougheed's approach to leadership required working closely with others as a team, a simple and powerful commitment that animated his days as a football player and his years as the Premier of Alberta. Although sometimes perceived as selfish, especially by central and eastern Canadians during his battles with Trudeau over control and development of Alberta's petroleum industry, Lougheed seldom displayed a personal selfishness. If he was selfish, it was a selfishness exercised with others (e.g., his sport or political team) on behalf of others (the fans or public). He typically made sure that he was the best-prepared and most goal-focused member of whatever team he led. If he was leader of his pack, it was because he knew the lay of the land and what was at stake. He seldom lost sight of the goals he wanted to achieve. In this way, he inspired the confidence, loyalty, and hard work of other members of his team. His preparedness, his organization, and his teambuilding ensured that his goals were accompanied by clear and concrete plans to achieve them, plans in which all his players knew their parts. As situations changed, his plans usually contained contingencies that made them adaptable, but his goals seldom varied.

Later in his career, Lougheed was accused by some of becoming more arrogantly aloof and less accessible. There undoubtedly is some truth to these later-career allegations, particularly when he refused to hold regular news briefings with reporters, and began to rely more on members of his cabinet and their departmental officials, especially those who had proven their loyalty and competence to his satisfaction. The gruelling schedule of official duties, appearances, and the daily grind of governing, almost inevitably erode an appetite for accessibility as years of public service accumulate. Perhaps also fuelling criticism, like Trudeau, Lougheed was always very sure of himself. Nonetheless, inaccessibility and arrogance certainly were not hallmarks of Lougheed's typical political style. He was well aware of how arrogant inattention typically was viewed by Albertans and he shared their opinion.

Like most politicians, Lougheed was less analytical, more spontaneous, and more sentimental with family and close friends than he was at the office. Yet overall, with Lougheed, what you saw was what you got. There was little dissembling in his personal or political life and usually little oscillation in his workmanlike demeanour. Yes, he could explode with anger, frustration, or exasperation, but for the most part he succeeded in giving the impression of solid, stable, and sincere commitment and leadership to the people of his province because this was truly how he was.

A strong and effective advocate for the interests of his province of Alberta and its people, Lougheed also was a strongly committed Canadian, whose allegiance to Canada as a nation was never in doubt. A dual commitment to his home province and nation also pervaded the vision of Canada held by Pierre Trudeau. Both men wanted a Canadian Federation that effectively attended to both regional and national interests. Such a balance required ongoing negotiation to keep the country strong and united—negotiation that recognized and supported the distinctiveness and diversity of its regions. Both men wanted a central government that was sufficiently strong and sensitive to the different life conditions of all its citizens. Where they differed was in their views of how best to structure powers and conduct negotiations between the provincial governments and the national government to achieve this end. Nonetheless, both wanted a country that did not hold together in spite of its regional differences, but held together because of these differences.

The trick was somehow to achieve, for as many citizens as possible, strong commitments to neighbourhoods, municipalities, and provinces that connected to a strong commitment to the nation overall. What was to be avoided was feeble, ineffective governance at any of these levels that failed to represent citizens' interests and prevented effective action on their part and on their behalf. For example, Canada as a nation must have the active support of its citizens when negotiating international trade agreements and political alliances, while provinces must have the active support of their citizens with respect to representing and pursuing their interests at both provincial and national levels. To these ends, both Trudeau and Lougheed supported the idea of equalization payments among the provinces, overseen by the federal government, although Lougheed wanted such oversight to include input from the provinces that was taken seriously by the Feds, and was not above poking Ottawa by offering his own financial inducements to other provinces.

Both men recognized the need for mutual respect, trust, and understanding in support of the inevitable necessity of trade-offs among provincial and federal leaders and members of their governments—a state of affairs often referred to as the Canadian tradition of compromise. Clearly it is the job of premiers to champion and fight for the best interests of the citizens who elected them—i.e., those living in and contributing directly to the provinces they lead. Equally clearly, it is the job of the federal government to enact laws, policies, and structures to ensure that all Canadians benefit as much, and as equally as possible, from the country's social, economic, and political resources, arrangements, and practices. Because any such broad agreements always play out in particular circumstances, and these circumstances are subject to change, close monitoring of and sensitivity to the concerns and needs of different regions in the Canadian federation are constantly required.

Despite sharing a common understanding of the foregoing aspects of Canadian federalism, there should be no doubt that Trudeau championed a stronger central government with powers of unilateral discretion that were unacceptable to Lougheed. A primary goal in Trudeau's political thinking and acting was to maintain a federal government that was powerful enough to oversee an equitable distribution of the nation's resources and revenues. This was an objective that remained constant across his political life. It was grounded in ideas central to his philosophy of personalism and in the appreciation of pluralism he had acquired during his graduate studies at Harvard, Sciences Po, and especially at the London School of Economics.

Trudeau believed that society is essential to human fulfillment and that individual freedom only could be achieved through coexistence with others in a society that enabled sufficient cooperation and collaboration to secure and protect conditions required for the pursuit of individual and collective goals. Such a society required and enabled the exercise of certain basic freedoms by all its members—freedoms of thought, belief, opinion, and expression; freedom of the press and other communicative media; freedom of peaceful assembly; freedom of association; and freedom of conscience and religion, as laid out in the 1982 Canadian Constitution and Charter of Rights and Freedoms. However, for Trudeau, acting freely never could be equated with doing whatever one wanted. All such freedoms must be subject to the rule of law. It is lawfulness that prevents infringement on the exercise of basic freedoms and rights, including infringement by governments.

Pierre Trudeau was especially concerned that the state or particular communities and groups not impose measures or encourage actions that diminished the dignity, uniqueness, indisputable moral worth, and universal rights of any of the nation's citizens. This was the first commandment of his philosophical personalism. Given the facts that all persons develop within society and that society is inevitably plural in its make up (consisting of a variety of communities of people from different backgrounds), Trudeau was a staunch defender of multiculturalism. Indeed, his support of multiculturalism was guided by his belief that the variety of different cultures in Canada contributed to its prosperity. Trudeau asserted that a vigorous policy of multiculturalism would create a society in which all could participate on equal and fair terms. This was a pluralism that went beyond mere tolerance of differences to encompass opportunities for creative self-expression that grew out of the richness and variety of the Canadian multicultural mix.

Nonetheless, it was the rights of individual citizens not communities of citizens that Trudeau enshrined in the Canadian Charter of Rights and Freedoms. He often spoke of the undesirability of uniformity in a nation the size of Canada, and disparaged the idea of a model or ideal Canadian, holding that such an emphasis on uniformity is likely to breed intolerance and hate. Like Canada, its various cultures, societies, and communities are not uniform and should not be allowed to enforce uniformity through coercion or in other ways that violate individual rights and freedoms.

Thus, in his political thought, Trudeau did not envision a combination of personalism and pluralism that eulogized an average or even prototypic individual citizen. He equated such an idea with mediocrity at both personal and societal levels. He believed in the dignity, uniqueness, and moral standing of all people, together with a social context supportive of such diversity. Trudeau's defense of the fundamental rights of all Canadians was a testimony to the intrinsic worth of the individual within a society that shared human values of understanding and compassion, even of love.

Of course, political theory does not always translate directly or easily into practice, produce widely shared acceptance of any particular philosophy or political creed, or ensure unanimity amongst citizens concerning what is desirable or acceptable. So it should come as no surprise that not all Canadians believed that Trudeau was committed to treating all them and regions of the country equally. Certainly, any such claim would have been hotly disputed by many Albertans during the

1970s and early 1980s, including their premier. For them and for many other Canadians, there was a suspicion that behind Trudeau's formidable education and his rhetoric of inclusivity and justice, there lurked a man too enamoured with his own points of view.

If Trudeau's vision of Canada was grounded in philosophical reasoning, Lougheed's vision of the Canadian federation was born of a lifetime of practical interactivity with others in leadership roles, tempered and tested in the Harvard classrooms of his MBA case study debates and in the real world of his legal and corporate experience. At Harvard, Lougheed had taken a class with Nobel Prize winning economist Paul Samuelson in which they had sparred over the effectiveness of government intervention as a major factor in national economies. Granting the point that government intervention was sometimes necessary and useful, Lougheed argued that in the long run it wasn't likely to be decisive. Lougheed believed that the interventions of a central federal government were occasionally necessary and useful when provinces were unable to reach agreements amongst themselves. However, in such cases, it was crucially important that the interventions be carefully planned and negotiated between federal and provincial leaders and officials. Unilateral actions by one or the other level of government in such circumstances were a recipe for current disaster and future distrust. Indeed, it was the unilateralism of Trudeau, his willingness to act without what Lougheed considered to be adequate forewarning, briefing, negotiation, and above all agreement, which probably offended Peter most in his dealings with Pierre and his government.

Given the heat and intensity of their battles over natural resources and the constitution, it is surprising that the political views of Lougheed and Trudeau were most often not that far apart. Both were located toward the middle of the classic political spectrum of left versus right, with Lougheed more to the conservative side. Moreover, both were quite willing to challenge the views and actions of powerful corporate entities (whether they be oil companies in Alberta, mining operations in Quebec, or financial firms in Ontario) if their actions were detrimental to public wellbeing. Both had a clear appreciation for the necessity of maintaining a common good through a delicate balancing of corporate and public interests.

After Trudeau's tendency to unilateralism, the other main sources of their disagreements and political battles were more a matter of differing positions and interests than strictly political and philosophical differences. Indeed, much of their occasional enmity resulted from their failure to appreciate the extent of the differences between Albertans and central Canadians. Trudeau had a much better understanding of the latter (including the many deep divisions between Ontario and Quebec) than did Lougheed. But, Lougheed's comparative ignorance of Canada's centre paled in comparison to Trudeau's ignorance of western Canada, and Alberta in particular. It was this gulf in understanding, when set alongside their differing visions of Canada as a more or less undifferentiated nation versus a confederation of regions, which was a major cause of most of their disagreements and contests. Such imbalances in understanding could, and did, easily spill over into their personal exchanges, especially given their combative, competitive natures and personalities.

A strong case can be made that even their different visions of the Canadian federation were grounded in their different sociocultural backgrounds and contexts. These were differences that often were amplified and exaggerated through media coverage in the nation and its regions. Against this background, Lougheed's advocacy for a federation of distinct and powerful provinces to offset and balance the might of the federal government was completely understandable. Even if it is assumed that Trudeau genuinely wanted citizens in all Canadian provinces to achieve a similar level of flourishing and fulfillment, it is not unreasonable to ask, as Lougheed constantly did, if such equality could spring from an unequal appreciation of the needs and requirements of distinctive provinces. What Peter Lougheed wanted, but often did not get, was recognition by Pierre Trudeau of these differences in a way that clearly factored into federal decision-making.

Lougheed's vision for Canada was yoked to his vision of himself and Albertans as a whole. When he was referred to as Mr. Alberta, his sense of what he was doing was affirmed. He saw himself as standing up for Alberta and Albertans, and was ready to take on all comers in the process—Trudeau, oil patch executives, or any others who might threaten the progress and future of his province and its people. In doing so, he was quite willing to yield the same rights to the other provinces, subject to negotiations that could be conducted in an atmosphere of mutual respect and understanding.

Trudeau's more centralized vision of Canadian federalism was acquired during his schooling and higher education, but was fostered by his experiential understanding of the Quebec society of his youth, and the seeming difficulties of bringing it into the modern era. These were difficulties that he believed only could be solved by wrenching the province from its traditional leadership triumvirate of church, state, and outside corporate interests. When unable to gain traction for this overhaul in his home province, Trudeau made the decision to do what he could to achieve this end from outside Quebec, in nearby Ottawa. From his privy council, functionary days to the final hours of his Prime Ministership, a primary goal was to revitalize Quebec as a progressive modern society within an increasingly multicultural Canada.

Lougheed's project for Alberta and Trudeau's project for Quebec were similar in many ways. However, where Lougheed's efforts at province building were conducted within the corridors of governmental power in Alberta, Trudeau's efforts at province building were conducted outside the Legislative Assembly of Quebec. This difference proved hugely important in maintaining the different visions of Canada toward which they directed significant portions of their life energies. As Prime Minister, Trudeau wielded powers that could influence both Canada and Quebec. As Premier of Alberta, Lougheed could influence Alberta, but not Canada as a whole, at least not directly. Yet both had strong ideas about how their home provinces and the Canadian confederation should be governed.

One other matter that helps to explain the tensions between Trudeau and Lougheed was reflected in significant differences between the attitudes of Albertans and central Canadians with respect to free enterprise. Neither Trudeau nor Lougheed was naïve about the powers wielded by large corporations or the monetary self-interest that often crept into, even dominated, their dealings. After all, theirs was an age during which the now common refrain of "We always must act in the best interests of our shareholders," was being refined and rehearsed by many CEOs, in the petroleum industry and elsewhere. Nonetheless, Lougheed, although always cautious, shared much more of the free enterprise ideal than did Trudeau, who was not only cautious, but inclined to deep skepticism about many things. His view of capitalism had been partially forged in conversations with his socialist professor Harold Laski at the London School of Economics, and Trudeau liked to think of himself as a left of centre politician.

Anyone who could comfortably share a laugh and a dance floor with Fidel Castro was not the kind of free enterpriser esteemed by most Albertans, and certainly not by their American colleagues in the oil patch. Lougheed, on the other hand, had cut his corporate teeth as a Calgary lawyer and executive with Fred Mannix's construction company. He knew first hand how vital Canadian business and CEOs were to the wellbeing of his province and nation. He also had insider knowledge of the many ways in which corporate power can be leveraged. In his dealings with Alberta corporations as Premier of Alberta, Lougheed took a balanced approach that shifted to stronger corporate support when his goals and vision for his province aligned with certain business interests. For the most part, he maintained a good working relationship with corporate Alberta and Canada.

The trust and respect much of the corporate sector extended to Peter Lougheed, especially that given by Alberta's free enterprisers, was seldom granted to Pierre Trudeau. Nonetheless, in central Canada, Trudeau maintained considerable, traditionally liberal, corporate support. Indeed, as Christo Aivalis noted in his reflections on Trudeau's political career: "on the question of economic democracy and social equality, Trudeau's legacy is a conservative one, ... an agenda only marginally to the left of that of the Conservatives themselves."[1] Once again, differences between Mr. Alberta and the Quebec-born Citizen of the World, may not have been as deep and insurmountable as many assumed. Yet, the perception of most Canadians was that Lougheed was stridently pro-business, with Trudeau lagging well behind in this respect.

Several psychological interpretations have been offered to explain Trudeau's and Lougheed's personal and political development. These include the Jungian idea that Trudeau could be described as a perpetual youth (a *puer aeternus*), a kind of child-god who is forever young, and who, on Jung's interpretation, has both positive and negative qualities. The positive is cast as a creative potential for newness and growth, linked to a hopeful future brought about by heroic efforts and conquests. In these terms, Trudeau's constant efforts to develop himself as a strongly independent, self-sufficient, and dramatic, charismatic figure might signal the positive side of being perpetually youthful. On the negative side, is the child-man—a person who never wants to grow up and face life head-on. This is a person who often escapes from tricky and potentially self-diminishing situations, waiting for fate to intervene to resolve his dilemmas and set him on the path to heroic accomplishment. In the meantime, he prefers a self-centered fantasy in which a desirable life is free from commitments and bonds, perhaps other than a mother's enduring love. Those who have made allusions to what they see as Trudeau's puzzling inconsistencies, his tendencies to tease and skip playfully from one project to another, to affect a disarming coyness and otherwise keep others wondering about him, might find the *puer aeternus* attractive as an interpretation and explanation for such aspects of Trudeau's character and personality.

Another, less colourful, interpretation that has been offered for what have been seen as salient aspects of Trudeau's character is in terms of the life-span developmental theorizing of Jerome Kagan. In the late 1930s and early 1940s, before leaving Montreal for Harvard, Trudeau displayed many typically adolescent inconsistencies between ambition and timidity, strength and weakness, individual aspiration and group affiliation. For Kagan, many such oppositional tendencies are associated with figuring out one's own identity, beliefs, and causes. Trudeau's temporary youthful involvement in radical corporatist and nationalistic groups and activities, his Brébeuf declarations that he was committed to French Canadian and Catholic causes, and his extreme competitiveness in academics and athletics might be seen to fit the broad idea of experimenting with and developing his identity.

Still others, who have taken a more Freudian interpretation of Pierre's development, have pointed to the significance of his father's early death, which possibly left young Trudeau with unresolved *Oedipal* issues. These might have included uncertainties about his new role in relationship to his mother and siblings, and feelings of inadequacy about filling the shoes of the *pater familias,* which may have contributed to a "stalling" in his psychological and personal development. Evidence of such a developmental and psychological "delay" might include Trudeau's living under the same roof as his mother until he entered his thirties and his eventual marriage to the much younger Margaret Sinclair.

Not only do such attempts to psychologize Trudeau's life experience differ considerably in style and conclusions, they selectively attend to and prioritize the significance of somewhat different events in his life. They also, given that they often rely on assumed psychic aspects of his mind and private life, run the risk of offering more or less exotic accounts that don't really explain his experience and behaviour as much as simply re-describe them and attribute them to purported inner causes. For example, does the idea of a perpetual youth explain what might be seen as Trudeau's extended adolescence, or is it merely another description of it? In a similar vein, what does Freudian Oedipal language actually add to the obvious fact that Trudeau probably struggled to sort out his new role in his family following his father's death? Although Kagan's developmental theorizing is more directly grounded in well-known teenage inconsistencies and struggles to grow up and figure out what one wants to be and do, what does it add to the detailed descriptions of his adolescent life provided by Trudeau's many biographers? Do any of these psychological explanations outweigh the likely impact of non-psychological factors such as Trudeau's inherited wealth, which probably removed any urgency he might otherwise have felt to get a job and leave home at an earlier age?

This is not to deny the possible importance of psychological factors in any human life; only to put them into perspective in an attempt to ensure that they do not obscure powerful factors of how one is positioned in life by one's socioeconomic and material circumstances. As several of his friends were quick to point out, as an adolescent and young adult, Pierre Elliott Trudeau had resources at his disposal that pretty much allowed him to do whatever he wanted to do, burden or liberation that such assets might prove to be.

Turning to Lougheed, much has been made of the scene in which he apparently secretly observed the auctioning of the household contents of his grandparents' Calgary mansion, a time that showcased his father's impotence and steeled the young Lougheed's resolve. Yet it seems overly simplistic to trace all or most of Lougheed's subsequent life goals and accomplishments to the psychic ramifications of this one early event in his life. It certainly seems possible that this was a highly significant harbinger of things to come, but very probably not by itself. Much the same might be said about the motivation of Lougheed's ambitions and achievements that is sometimes attributed to the influence of his father's more protracted failure to restore the family's holdings and good name. Both of these speculations reside in popular storylines of the supposed psychological impact of traumatic and highly memorable occurrences in life that evoke ideas and promises of restoration and redemption in those they afflict.

At a more technical, and some might say scientific, level of psychological theory and practice, Lougheed's high school scores on a standardized psychological measure of vocationally relevant, personality traits (probably the *Strong Vocational Interest Inventory*) have been posited as an explanation for his amply demonstrated talents for organization, persuasiveness, and leadership. Does this supposed connection between inventory scores and subsequent life events demonstrate the predictive, explanatory power of a scientific psychological technology or simply indicate that the adolescent Lougheed had a pretty good sense of what he was good at and acted with purpose to use these talents in his life? None of this seems to get us especially close to understanding how Lougheed developed the personal abilities and characteristics he put to such good effect in his legal, corporate, and political life.

An alternative, less psychological and more biographical consideration of the personal development of both Trudeau and Lougheed has been offered throughout this book. A biographical approach to understanding our protagonists, their development, actions, and visions is grounded in the concrete particulars of their everyday lives and life experiences. The biographical information included herein, and in the sources referenced in the endnotes, provides detailed considerations of the positions, perspectives, and possibilities that attended our protagonists' development from infants, to precocious teenagers, to successful and at times controversial political leaders. In what follows, biographical particulars discussed in the preceding chapters are summarized in ways that might explain some important influences on the development and lives of Pierre Trudeau and Peter Lougheed, two of Canada's most prominent and important political leaders during the second half of the twentieth century.

◆◆◆

Both Trudeau and Lougheed were born into families with significant social and financial resources to support them and ensure requisite lifestyle, developmental, and educational opportunities for successful lives. Although Lougheed's family fortunes were considerably reduced by the time he entered his teenage years, they were still more than sufficient to provide him with a comfortable, secure, and stimulating home and school environment. Trudeau's early lot in life easily provided him with such assets, including an elite education at the Jesuit Brébeuf College. In short, both enjoyed the advantages of childhoods free from social and financial deprivation. Lougheed's upbringing was less privileged than Trudeau's but any imbalance in this regard was perhaps offset by the social status bequeathed by his distinguished grandfather, Senator Sir James Lougheed, one of Alberta's most prominent citizens, entrepreneurs, and politicians at the time it was recognized as a province of the Dominion of Canada. Suffice it to say that both Pierre and Peter were well positioned for success, given their early life situations.

Their fathers were dissimilar in terms of their overall life trajectories. Edgar Lougheed presided over a significant decline in his family's financial and social prominence, while Charlie Trudeau was a self-made entrepreneur whose business undertakings and investments provided Pierre and his siblings with lifetime financial security. Both Edgar and Charles were highly sociable men with many friends and acquaintances, and a taste for the good life. Their wives, Edna and Grace, were devoted to their children, lavishing them with love, while demanding decency and respectability in return. This said,

Grace Trudeau seems to have been more permissive and tolerant of Pierre's occasional misbehaviour than was Edna Lougheed of Peter's.

In the Trudeau household, it was Charlie who was the disciplinarian, despite his frequent absences from home in the evenings and on business. In the Lougheed home, Edna took most of the responsibility for the children's behaviour. Charlie and Edna also were the primary sources for directly instilling a strong sense of personal independence and responsibility in their sons, although their respective spouses also often modeled such virtues in their everyday interactions. In Pierre's case, Charlie's advice and admonishment advocated being independently minded and strong in body and spirit, overcoming weakness, and developing a dominant social presence. In Peter's case, Edna's counsel emphasized a competitive independence and strength that was balanced by decency and concern for the wellbeing of others. Winning was important to both boys, but it had to be accomplished with style and flair (Charlie's demands for Pierre) and by decency and civility (Edna's demands for Peter). Hard work and achievement were expected and assumed by both boys' fathers and mothers.

Pierre and Peter were close to their mothers and it was to them that they were most likely to turn when they felt the need for supportive care and affection. After his father's death, Pierre and his mother relied on each other. She was his biggest fan, and he, her constant companion and protector. Peter was similarly protective of his mother, whose counsel and social sensibilities he mostly respected.

Both boys had more ambivalent relationships with their fathers. The sudden and unexpected death of Charlie Trudeau was certainly a major event in Pierre's life, but probably prevented what promised to be many clashes between the increasingly strong-willed adolescent Trudeau and his equally pugnacious father. Peter's ambivalence was more specific and tied mostly to his father's drinking, which perhaps also signalled a kind of capitulation. Fortunately, Edgar mostly was not a difficult drinker and had some strongly redeeming qualities. Later in life, Peter often commented on his father's humility and sociability with a wide range of others, irrespective of social standing, tendencies that Peter himself came to share.

When Peter's father was unavailable, his older brother Don was a constant presence and source of competition, support, and encouragement. Don and Peter moved in similar and overlapping school and athletic groups. They shared many mutual friends and acquaintances. Pierre's older sister, Suzette, was usually available for additional "motherly" advice and his relationships with her and his younger brother Tip were mostly harmonious. Pierre's siblings were quite happy to accept his taking the role of the "man of the house" when his father died.

Both childhood environments offered a combination of support and challenge that is frequently found in the homes of highly successful people. Nonetheless, significant differences in their parents' interactions with them probably contributed to certain tensions in their characters and personalities. For Trudeau, these took the form of oppositional tendencies with respect to the quietude and calm of his mother versus the boisterousness and excitability of his father. These were tensions further supported by sociocultural differences associated with the Francophone Quebec of his father and the Anglophone Quebec of his mother. For Lougheed, his mother's insistence on social acceptability and concern with what others thought vied with his father's general affability and laissez faire attitude.

It was during their adolescence that significant differences in their social and personal lives became more pronounced and visible in their interactions with their classmates and others. Both played and excelled at various sports. However, Trudeau, although a very good hockey and team sport player more generally, became increasingly interested in individual sports like diving, skiing, canoeing, and hiking. Lougheed enjoyed all forms of physical activity, but he, almost exclusively, enjoyed team sports, where he could enhance his and his teammates enjoyment and success by organizing, strategizing, and motivating his side to greater effort and victory. For him, there was always something special and deeply rewarding about being an integral part of a team that performed well. Don and his friends, although older than Peter and his buddies, seemed quite content to let Peter make arrangements for practices and games, and tended to defer to his plans, suggestions, and strategies. Pierre, on the other hand, always seemed happy to head off by himself, occasionally accompanied by a friend or two, for arduous wilderness trips by canoe, foot, or bike. It was almost as if he needed time away from others so that he could test his stamina, strength, and endurance, learning about himself and how to overcome his weaknesses in the process.

Their non-athletic time and activities followed a similar pattern. Trudeau edited the Brébeuf student newspaper and exhorted his fellow students to think and act in ways he regarded as progressive and necessary for future citizens and leaders of what he hoped would be a more progressive Quebec. Lougheed also wrote and edited for the University of Alberta's *Gateway* student paper, but mostly reported on university sports, especially football. Otherwise, in high school and university, he preferred to be involved in school organizations through which he could work closely with and lead others. Nowhere was the difference in their social lives more evident than in the contrast between Lougheed's fraternity living quarters in his late teens and early twenties and Trudeau's living arrangements in his mother's home while attending Brébeuf and finishing law school. For those who knew them, it would be impossible to imagine either of them in the other's situation during this stage of their lives.

In their graduate studies at Harvard, Trudeau was a solitary figure, focused on his studies and working through major changes in his philosophical understandings of politics and his own life. Harvard had some of this effect on Lougheed as well, but with Jeanne he already had embarked on the next phase of his life as a married man who needed to provide for his wife and future family. Trudeau, of course, never had any reason to be concerned about his financial security and it would be many years before he married Margaret Sinclair.

Throughout their childhoods and educations, Trudeau's and Lougheed's talents were nurtured and recognized by parents and teachers who tagged them for success. Siblings, fellow students, and friends supported and furthered Trudeau's personal aspirations and development by expecting and accepting his leadership and approval. Peter Lougheed seemed always to be positioned within his family, athletic teams, student associations, and other groups as a leader and prime mover. The overall comparative picture that develops during their early years is one of many similarities and advantages, but with one major contrast. This was a striking difference between Trudeau's more solitary personal development and Lougheed's highly social development. Trudeau was, by choice and temperament, comparatively isolated from the constant immersion in everyday engagements that Lougheed enjoyed with his peers. Trudeau's goals and projects attended his personal development and growth; Lougheed's goals and projects emerged out of interactions and activities he shared with others. Trudeau's development and plans for his future certainly involved others, but seemed to emerge more from his reflective aloofness than from the active interpersonal engagement that typified Lougheed's adolescent and young adult life. As a consequence, Lougheed's personal agency was much more collectively forged and developed compared to Trudeau's more obviously self-determined preparation for leadership.

Of course, another major difference was between the life contexts and lifestyles that Trudeau experienced as a fluently bilingual and bicultural native son of Quebec compared to those Lougheed imbibed as the scion of one of Alberta's most prominent social and political families in a province that did not take kindly to anyone "putting on airs." Here again, it would be impossible to imagine any successful exchange of Trudeau's cultivated polish and self-importance as a young man with Lougheed's matter-of-fact, one-of-the-boys demeanour.

After Harvard, Lougheed briefly practiced law in Calgary before becoming enmeshed in the Mannix Corporation, where he quickly built enduring corporate and political connections that would serve him well in the future. Trudeau continued his graduate studies at Sciences Po in Paris and the London School of Economics, honing his rhetorical and rational analytic capabilities and insights into political and economic theories. Afterwards, he escaped all familiar surroundings to test his mettle through an adventurous and occasionally dangerous solo trip through Europe and Asia. Lougheed displayed comparatively little penchant for such undertakings. His pursuit of knowledge and his testing of his own capabilities and mettle were much more pragmatically engaged, with a view to gaining practical understanding, know-how, and resolve for the political career and challenges he knew lay ahead. Where Pierre Trudeau walked a wandering path through theoretical studies and aesthetic experiences, Peter Lougheed moved in a direct line to acquire the contacts and hone the abilities he needed to position himself as a future political leader.

Trudeau lived the first four decades of his life developing himself for a vaguely anticipated political life that seemed always to take second place to his own self-development. His wealth and inclination seemed always to offer a getaway when he felt the need to be alone and contemplate his existence and life direction. Anyone who knew Lougheed, even from a distance, understood that his future lay in politics. Most who knew Trudeau, and they were mostly at some distance, wondered and perhaps worried about what he was up to and where it would lead. Nonetheless, when unexpected opportunities eventually arose in their lives to make the jump into political life, both men took the plunge. True to form, Lougheed made the most of a possibility others might not have seen or been willing to take. Trudeau eventually was coaxed (or so it seemed) to do so at the behest of Marchand and Pelletier, who were among those who worried that Trudeau, left to his own devices, might well miss his opportunity to lead his province and his nation. There was no similar possibility of inaction for Lougheed. It may well be the case that Trudeau's typical games of "cat and mouse" and "the reluctant bride" were carefully and cleverly orchestrated, but as with so many things about Trudeau, it is hard to be sure. With Lougheed, there is little room for doubt.

It is worth dwelling a bit on the differences that characterized Trudeau's and Lougheed's entries into formal political life because they reveal a great deal about their personal inclinations and life strategies. So different were these political beginnings that it is possible to say with considerable certainty that Trudeau never would have followed Lougheed's entry strategy and that Lougheed never would have waited for what happened to initiate Trudeau's political career.

In 1965, when Peter Lougheed was first elected as a member of the Legislative Assembly of Alberta representing the provincial constituency of Calgary West, he had already assumed the mantle of leader of the Progressive Conservative Party of Alberta. At that time, the Alberta PCs were a fringe party in a province that the Alberta Social Credit Party, led by William Aberhart and Ernest Manning, had dominated for 30 years. When first asked to consider taking over the leadership of the Alberta PCs, Lougheed had not even been inside the Provincial Legislative Assembly in Edmonton. Never had he witnessed an actual session of that Assembly in action. Other than his experience as a student union president in his Calgary high school and at the University of Alberta, he was a complete political rookie. Yes, he had contacts in Alberta's legal and corporate sectors and a growing reputation as an "up and comer." But otherwise, he was taking a big leap into the unknown.

Trusting his sense that all was not well with the long-standing Social Credit political machine in his home province, Lougheed was ready to provide an alternative for Alberta voters. To do so, he took over and rebuilt the Progressive Conservative Party of Alberta, which had failed to elect a single MLA in the last provincial election of 1963. Despite his unpredictability and risk-taking, adventurous inclinations, Pierre Trudeau never would have considered such a blatantly "dead-end" move. But where Trudeau had bided his time looking for the right invitation to enter the political fray on a winning side, Lougheed was quite happy to engineer his own entry.

The fact that Lougheed jumped in where Trudeau would never have ventured tells a great deal about what separated the two men with respect to their life orientations and self-perceived talents. Although both had strong desires to become influential political leaders, only Lougheed was prepared to build his own political party from scratch. Why? Because only Lougheed had complete confidence in his own organizational and persuasive capabilities. He knew he could transform the completely disorganized and inept Alberta Progressive Conservative Party into a dominant political force. He knew because he had done similar things before. On the playing field, he had basked in the role of the hard-working, "never say die" leader of his teams. In high school, he not only had become president of his school union, he had created the institution of a student union at his school in the first place. At Mannix Corp., he had risen quickly through the ranks to positions of power and influence over company directions. Lougheed didn't need a hand up because he knew that he was fully capable of providing whatever lift might be needed. And, he knew this not only because of his knowledge of himself, but even more importantly, his knowledge of others from his lifelong immersion in interpersonal, social contexts and contests. Putting together his self understanding and his understanding of others, he knew that he was capable of recruiting, leading, and motivating others to join him and share in what he was up to. And he certainly proved himself "up to" transforming the Alberta PCs. In amazingly short order, he took them from near political oblivion in the 1963 provincial election to six seats in the 1967 Alberta election, and then to a strong majority government of 49 seats (to the Socreds' 25) in 1971.

Trudeau's equally precipitous rise to political power as Prime Minister of Canada was an entirely different matter, requiring a very different set of capabilities and inclinations. Where Lougheed was nothing if not steady, reliable, and predictable in ways that were immediately perceptible to others, Trudeau appeared to be almost the exact opposite. Although both men shared a social presence and charisma that belied their physical statures, as well as an almost unrivalled competitiveness, Trudeau's friends had almost given up on his ever amounting to much. He seemed to be throwing his widely perceived talents and potential away during the 1950s and early 1960s, writing editorials for *Cité libre*, dropping in and out of various

Quebec political movements as his moods dictated, and wandering away for solitary or romantic adventures that followed no obvious schedule. Even after securing a long sought professorship at the Université de Montréal in the early 1960s, Pierre Trudeau seemed incapable of using it to advance his own political aspirations. He clearly was not going to "pull a Lougheed" and build his own political future from the ground up. His strengths were in dazzling and charming others, not in building and moulding them into an organized group ready and willing to do battle on his behalf.

Fortunately for Trudeau, the impressive and charismatic sides of his character and talents could be harnessed to long, hard hours of focused and creative work. These were the qualities that were readily apparent and highly valued by his most trusted and influential allies. Such individuals included Jean Marchand and Gérard Pelletier, without whose encouragement and support Trudeau might never have taken advantage of key opportunities they helped to create for themselves and for him. Of course, the most important of these was when they convinced him to join them as "the three wise men" from Quebec who moved together from Montreal to Lester Pearson's Liberal Party of Canada, and were elected in 1967 as Liberal MPs. Even then, Marchand had to work hard to keep Trudeau's penchants for solitary getaways, irreverent quips, and pursuing his own agendas sufficiently under wraps to warrant the support of more traditional and longer-serving members of the Liberal establishment in Ottawa, including Lester Pearson himself. But there could be no gainsaying Trudeau's brilliance and capacity for prolonged and intensive work when he was focused on matters of interest to him, as he quickly showed when Pearson made him federal Minister of Justice.

Although Trudeau may have dithered, twisted, and delayed, once he was positioned within the inner circle of the Liberal Party of Canada in Ottawa, with ready access to its extensive resources, support structures, and political mandarins, he clearly was in his element. From then on, his considerable capabilities and talents were unleashed in ways that secured and extended his political capital and aspirations. Many of those personality quirks and oddities that made people wonder about his commitments and intentions in the past now served to enhance and enchant, more than annoy and confuse.

Once their political careers were launched, it took surprisingly little time for Pierre Trudeau and Peter Lougheed to ascend to and maintain the offices that would define their lives and legacies—the former as Canada's third longest serving Prime Minister (from 1968-1979 and 1980-1984); the latter as Alberta's second longest serving Premier (from 1971-1985).

By the time that our two leading men squared off over the NEP and the Canadian Constitution in the early 1980s, both were veteran campaigners and strategists. Both had accumulated impressive records of accomplishment that also included missed opportunities, especially in the case of Pierre Trudeau. Where Peter Lougheed had mostly succeeded in obtaining for Albertans a more powerful role in the political and economic corridors of power in Canada and in securing greater control over and benefit from their natural resources, Pierre Trudeau had struggled to advance the interests and sense of belonging of Quebecers within the Canadian federation. For him, much more remained to be accomplished if he was to leave his political and philosophical mark on the nation. As he approached his final few years as Prime Minister, he was intensely focussed on patriating the Canadian Constitution from the UK and embellishing it with what he regarded as his signature Charter of Rights and Freedoms.

Nowhere were the many similarities and the striking differences between Trudeau and Lougheed more apparent than in the four days in Ottawa from November 2-5, 1981 when Pierre Trudeau bobbed and weaved his way to an eventual compromise with the bull-headed Peter Lougheed, who, still smarting from Trudeau's and Lalonde's unilateral implementation of the NEP, appeared unwilling to accept any fait accompli on the constitutional front. In consequence, Trudeau had little choice but to accept Lougheed's Alberta Amending Formula and a notwithstanding clause insisted upon by Lougheed and his two fellow prairie premiers, Allan Blakeney and Sterling Lyon. But, even as Trudeau bowed to these necessities, he was beset by fears that the accommodations he had been forced to make to Lougheed and the other premiers would never allow his dreams of a just society to flourish. In the end, Trudeau felt that he could live with the amending formula, but was left wondering how effective his Charter would actually be at ensuring Canadians' rights and freedoms if federal and provincial governments could effectively invoke the notwithstanding clause to pass legislation that would override particular rights in the Charter.

Even so, having muddled through the oil wars with Lougheed over the NEP and patriated the Canadian Constitution with its new

Charter of Rights and Freedoms, Trudeau ought to have been riding high as the last two years of what would prove to be his final term as Prime Minister approached. However, the Canadian economy was still digging its way out of the recession of the early 1980s. It was sluggishly lagging behind that of the U.S. and the U.K., which had been stimulated by the tax cuts of Ronald Reagan and Margaret Thatcher. Worried about the inequities of such cuts, the Trudeau government refused to follow their example. But with no clear and consistent thrust, the scattered economic policies of the Trudeau Liberals were attracting considerable corporate and public heat.

In September 1982, Trudeau handed the country's finance portfolio to Marc Lalonde. On April 19, 1983, Lalonde, sticking to his Keynesian guns, said that he would not cut deeply into government funding or attempt to strangle inflation in ways that would do more harm to the vulnerable, so as to court the votes of the affluent. Trudeau endorsed Lalonde's approach and attempted to recapture public support with a return to progressive social programs. These included the Canada Health Act, to protect access to health services for all Canadians without financial or other barriers, and a major initiative intended to preserve world peace, reviving tactics of the Pearson Liberals he had replaced in 1968. But with the NEP falling apart, costs of financing the national debt soaring, and Brian Mulroney, the new federal Tory leader, nipping at his heels by unexpectedly supporting some of Trudeau's more progressive bills, Trudeau's days as PM appeared to be numbered. Neither the praise of John Lennon and Yoko Ono for Trudeau's attempts to give peace a chance, nor a new bevy of attractive female companions like Margot Kidder and Kim Cattrall, could help revive the old magic of Trudeaumania.

Pierre Trudeau announced his retirement from politics on February 28, 1984, following his final Prime Ministerial "walk in the snow." Peter Lougheed, whom Trudeau had come to respect and admire during the course of their battles, as a man of principles committed to his province and to Canada, was generous and gracious. He offered his "sincere appreciation [for Trudeau's] long career in the public service of the country."[2] A year later, in 1985, Lougheed himself stepped down from his lengthy reign as Premier of Alberta to return to private life, his law practice, and to various business and philanthropic ventures. By this time, it was clear to him that the Red Tory, progressive conservativism he so valued, along with its tradition of compromise after heated and heartfelt debate and argument, was beginning to wane in Alberta and across the nation.

A final clash between Trudeau and Lougheed occurred in the context of attempts by the Mulroney government to renegotiate the Canadian Constitution in ways that would involve and recognize Quebec as an active member of a revamped constitutional arrangement. When the first attempt to do so, *The Meech Lake Accord* of 1987, had been agreed by Mulroney and the ten premiers (including Robert Bourassa of Quebec), Trudeau argued vehemently and eloquently against the new arrangement. With the support of some feminist and Indigenous groups, he maintained that Canadian citizens had not been properly informed and involved during the drafting of the new accord and that it would weaken the federal government in ways that would harm the country. Eventually, the Meech Lake Accord failed because it was not ratified by Manitoba and Newfoundland.

Undeterred, Mulroney handed the portfolio to Joe Clark, now point man for Mulroney on constitutional matters. Clark's efforts eventually led to a renewed agreement struck in Charlottetown, PEI in late August 1992, with the unanimous agreement of the premiers, Indigenous and territorial leaders, and heads of the three major national political parties (Tories, Grits, and NDP). Like the Meech Lake agreement, the Charlottetown Accord, promised "distinct society" status to Quebec, with an amending formula that gave a veto power to the province.

Whether or not to adopt the Charlottetown Accord would be decided by a national referendum of the Canadian people set for October 26, 1992. Trudeau spoke out forcefully against the new Accord in print and interview, calling the proposed deal "an unprecedented abdication of sovereign powers by the federal government."[3] Lougheed responded by telling the Canadian public that a new deal, fully signed and authorized by all provincial parties, was necessary to bring Quebec more fully into the constitutional family. Questioning the legitimacy of a constitution without Quebec's formal and free agreement, which Lougheed called "a wrong imposed by Pierre Trudeau," he also endorsed the provisions of the new agreement that promised "a right and fair treatment of our aboriginal peoples."[4] Once again, however, Trudeau prevailed. In the referendum, the Charlottetown Accord was defeated nationally 54.3 to 45.7 percent. The fight against the Charlottetown accord was Trudeau's final public performance.

Trudeau spent the remaining years of his life with close friends, companions, and, of course, his children, to whom he was deeply committed. He published his memoirs in 1993, and engaged in a few additional writing projects. He mostly stayed on the sidelines and watched dejectedly as Jacques Parizeau's Parti Québécois came within a whisker of pulling Quebec out of the Canadian federation on October 30, 1995. The dangerously close decision to stay in Canada (50.6 to 49.4 percent of ballots cast) caused Trudeau to retreat even further into his inner circle of family and friends, which now included Deborah Coyne and their daughter Sarah. As his memory began gradually to fail him in the late 1990s, Trudeau suffered the deaths of close friends like Gérard Pelletier. He also was devastated by the loss of his youngest son Michel, who drowned in a wilderness skiing mishap in Kokanee Glacier Park in BC. His faith shaken, diagnosed with Parkinson's disease, and his cancer spreading, he began to say his goodbyes to those who mattered most to him.

Throughout the rest of the 1980s, 1990s, and into the new century, Peter Lougheed, nine years younger than Trudeau, continued to serve his province and country by heading and chairing various initiatives that promised freer trade between Canada and the U.S., even as he continued to worry about the imposition of American values on Canada. From 1996 to 2002, he served as the 11th Chancellor of Queen's University in Kingston, Ontario, where he began to raise concerns about protecting Canada's freshwater, arguing that it was time for the Alberta government to treat water as its number one asset, and to resist temptations to commodify and export it. Also in 2002, Lougheed was appointed to the inaugural board of directors for the Pierre Elliott Trudeau Foundation.

At the end of his life, Trudeau remained a controversial figure capable of inspiring both eulogies and denunciations. His detractors, including authors André Burelle, Guy Laforest,[5] and Bob Plamondon, have excoriated Trudeau as having been a failure as a leader—the man who effectively put an end to the Canadian dream by treacherously betraying French Canadians, and who came within a hair's breath of ruining the country with his school boy financial policies and flippant gambling with the country's fate during the constitutional talks. Future Prime Minister Stephen Harper, never one to shy away from Liberal skewering, summed up what he took to be Trudeau's mischievous legacy:

> Only a bastardized version of his unity vision remains and his other policies have been rejected and repealed by even his own Liberal party. His definition of Canadian nationalism—centralism, socialism, bilingualism—is the polar opposite of the trends in Canadian history that are now triumphing—regionalism, globalization, Québec particularism—in no small measure a reaction to the policies Mr. Trudeau practiced.[6]

And yet, no less a conservative figure than Conrad Black, while announcing his opposition to Trudeau's left of centre, state interventionist leanings, offered a less politicized, more balanced, and more personal view of Trudeau's legacy:

He was a contrarian, and as his public demeanour often demonstrated, he was even suspicious of groups that were too admiring of him. He resolutely defended his position, but with that slightly ironic countenance the Canadian public came to know. He was much more endearing in person than on television, and he possessed the sort of high intelligence that was stimulated, rather than affronted, by a good verbal joust. ... Once he was familiar with the burdens and restraints of high office, it was difficult to separate Trudeau the sly political tactician from the upholder of the principles he had championed as an academic and journalist. Yet he dealt effectively with the greatest problem of his time [the threat of Quebec separation], which was a mortal threat to the country, and because there was no one else on the federal scene who would have been credible trying to do so, I think Trudeau must be judged as a successful, as well as an important prime minister, whatever his other policy shortcomings. Apart from that, I always found him a delightful conversationalist and a gracious host, though perhaps slow to reach for the bill in a restaurant, even when we were there on his invitation.[7]

Black was not alone in commenting on Trudeau's frugality, perhaps an extension of the ascetic side of his character, or simply another reminder of his self-determined right to do pretty much as he pleased.

Yet, for many other Canadians, who did not know him personally, Pierre Trudeau was more admired for his style and what he symbolized than for what he did or did not do. What he symbolized was a new Canada and a new way of being a Canadian:

> ... the remaking of a country where Anglophone prime ministers spoke no French, where public servants could not serve a quarter of the population in their own language, where politicians could not break from constitutional links with Britain, where courts shied away from activism, where foreign leaders were not challenged, where there were no separatists in the House of Commons, and where great existential challenges of the nation's future had not been faced for over a century.[8]

Even more basically, many Canadians loved the fact that Trudeau put Canada on the map. To them, he was perhaps the country's first enduringly famous citizen. They admired the man, even when they were uncertain about his policies and record. "He was our intellectual philosopher king, the millionaire socialist with glamorous women on his arm. ... He was fascinating, eccentric, and entertaining. We admired him for never backing down from a fight, or ducking for cover when under attack."[9] When he died, thousands flocked to the Hall of Honour on Parliament Hill in Ottawa to view his casket. Others gathered at Montreal's Notre-Dame Basilica and other meeting and grieving points across the country. Cardinal Turcotte, at Trudeau's funeral, covered all the bases by asking that "all that for him was great and holy [be] respected and preserved" and that "any evil he may have done be pardoned."[10]

Peter Lougheed also had his detractors, more than once having been called Canada's most selfish premier. Nonetheless, he was widely considered by political experts to have been one of Canada's best, if not the best, provincial premier of the second half of the twentieth century, and perhaps in Alberta's history as a province of Canada. At Lougheed's death, Prime Minister Stephen Harper opined that Peter Lougheed had been "a truly great man ... quite simply one of the most remarkable Canadians of his generation," continuing to praise Lougheed as "a master politician, gifted lawyer, professional-calibre athlete and philanthropist," and adding that "the former premier was instrumental in laying the foundation for the robust economic success that his cherished province of Alberta enjoys today."[11]

Lougheed's harshest critics argued that his legacy was tainted by relationships between his government and business interests that were too secretive and too cozy. They noted his opposition to freedom of information legislation and hinted at conflicts of interest. But, almost all observers agree that Lougheed succeeded in establishing:

> ... a lasting image of Alberta as the heart of the new West, a province with unlimited potential and one whose national weight exceeded that of the other three western provinces. His single-minded focus on economic diversification and modern economic infrastructure contributed to the wellbeing of future generations and built bonds between Albertans and their provincial

government. Without exaggeration, Peter Lougheed was seen as the principal architect of modern Alberta.[12]

As Trudeau did for many Canadians, Lougheed's lasting legacy for most Albertans was to make them proud to be who they were:

Albertans no longer look at themselves as simple prairie folks. ... They have felt the disapproval and the power of Ottawa, but, even in troubled times, there is an undercurrent of western confidence that Alberta will come back and will continue to play a role in a better and more flexible country. ... This is a new era for Albertans, who now have a real sense of destiny, and a new sense of pride. With other Canadians, they want a better nation, and they demand to be an important part of that fashioning. That in essence, is the Lougheed legacy.[13]

However their legacies are viewed, Pierre Trudeau and Peter Lougheed lived and led at a time that Canada came to maturity as a nation, independent and influential beyond its borders, and perhaps beyond reasonable expectations for a country of its population and geographic challenges. Their battles over (and contrary visions of) the very nature of Canadian federalism, especially with respect to the development of the country's vast natural resources, captured and set in place inevitable tensions in the political and sociocultural fabric of the nation—concerns that continue to challenge today's generation of Canadians and our provincial and federal leaders.

Questions such as which of them made the greatest and most lasting impact on Canadian society, exactly what made them so influential and memorable, and precisely how they were similar and different in ways that might carry implications for understanding political effectiveness more generally have been entertained herein, but remain far from resolved. Nonetheless, the stories of their lives contribute to a greater awareness of how our nation works and sometimes fails to work. Perhaps, in their stories there are hints of how the Canadian federation might continue to be fashioned and refashioned as circumstances demand. Will we ever see their likes again? In general, perhaps; in particular, definitely not, for both were embedded and bounded by their place and time. We can learn from their lives, battles, and visions, but as the world changes, and Canada with it, what makes sense and what might be the best paths to take also will inevitably be in flux—a fluidity that we will not be able to escape and must somehow manage.

Facing such challenges, and flourishing as a consequence of doing so, inevitably will require compromise. Perhaps the most important lesson that might be learned from a historical, biographical study of the lives and times of Pierre Trudeau and Peter Lougheed is that despite the extent and depth of their differences in background, life experiences and circumstances, and personal and political views and convictions, they retained sufficient respect and admiration for each other and their offices that they were able to compromise for the good of their country and its people.

One glaring example of interactions between Lougheed's provincial and Trudeau's federal governments during which possible compromise was itself compromised, by apparent insincerity and purposeful deceitfulness, occurred in the Spring of 1980. This sad event involved meetings and interactions between Marc Lalonde (Federal Minister of Energy, Mines and Resources) and Merv Leitch (Alberta Minister of Energy and Natural Resources) about federal taxes and provincial royalties on Alberta's petroleum resources. [At that time, Trudeau was fully engaged with the Quebec referendum on sovereignty association.] In these exchanges, Lalonde and officials in his department seem purposefully to have acted out a mere charade of negotiation, having already made up their minds unilaterally to impose the National Energy Program in the October 1980 federal budget announcement. This was a most unfortunate matter that almost had disastrous consequences, not only for the political careers of both Trudeau and Lougheed, but for Canada as a nation.

It does not take a great deal of imagination to understand the upset that Lougheed felt and displayed after learning of these events, which must have further ignited a smoldering resentment against the Trudeau government concerning its dealings with him and his province about Alberta's natural resources. Indeed, there is considerable evidence to support the view that much of the truculence Lougheed displayed in the first day or two of the November 1981 constitutional talks was directly traceable to his sense of having been betrayed and manipulated by Lalonde and Trudeau over the NEP, especially about the way in which it was unilaterally and deceitfully initiated. With Trudeau intent on finally achieving his goal of bringing home the Canadian constitution, with the inclusion of his Charter of Rights and Freedoms, and Lougheed committed to his life goal of protecting Alberta's resources for the benefit of Albertans, it was a very narrow thing that they still were able to reach a brokered compromise at the end of the constitutional talks. What would have happened if Trudeau and Lougheed had loathed each other to the extent that they had lost each other's respect and trust completely?

In the final analysis, faith in the integrity and trustworthiness of others and the cultivation of trustworthiness in oneself are the glue that holds all social, cultural, economic, and political transactions and practices together. If our self-interests and emotions cannot be considered and constrained in the light of the legitimate interests of particular others and people more generally, we are lost. In this instance, amidst feelings of betrayal and worries about political and personal failure, Trudeau and Lougheed retained sufficient understanding of, and respect for, each other and their country to avoid a potentially catastrophic outcome.

And yet, there must have been something else at play, especially for Lougheed, who admired and respected, but never felt that he could fully trust Trudeau.[14] In all probability, that extra ingredient was, for both men, a strong sense of duty—to live up to the obligations of their offices and the expectations of their citizens and electors. From an early age, they both had decided to devote themselves to public service at the highest levels of provincial and federal governance. In the final analysis, it is likely that an overriding sense of duty helped to overcome any lapses in trust occasioned by their many years of battling each other over their visions of Canada and what it could become.

In describing their different visions of Canada, Peter Lougheed, in a 2005 reminiscence of Pierre Trudeau, summed things up by saying that "most of my memories of my dealings with Mr. Trudeau are of a very serious nature, because we looked upon our country in two very different ways":

> I saw Canada then—and I see it now—as a federal system responding to the regions through its provincial governments, with all coming together on a unified basis for the benefit of all Canadians. Mr. Trudeau saw Canada differently. He visualized it as more of a centralized nation, less fractious, and presenting a more unified approach. Both of these views of Canada have validity, and I respected Mr. Trudeau's intellect and leadership very much.[15]

Mutual respect, personal decency, and somewhat tempered trust, buoyed by a sense of duty and obligation, combined to allow Peter Lougheed and Pierre Trudeau eventually to compromise on the major issues that divided them during their long tenures as Premier of Alberta and Prime Minister of Canada. As this story of their lives, characters, battles and visions ends, contemporary tensions between Alberta and Ottawa seem to be at an all-time high. Will the tenuous combination of sufficient good will, respect, trust, and sense of duty once again hold to keep the country strong and united? Will the convictions, life experiences, characters, and social, political contexts of contemporary Canadians and their leaders allow them to meet the challenge of forging and maintaining a common good? Probably, because most Canadian citizens continue to want their provinces and country to stay united and the Canadian experiment to continue. But tearing things down is always easier than building them up, and an increasing number of us seem to struggle to balance our self-interest with the interests of our fellow citizens and the country as a whole.

Pierre Trudeau died of cancer on September 28, 2000. Peter Lougheed died of natural causes on September 13, 2012. Their visions of Canada continue to be debated. Many readers will point to their weaknesses and failures, and question their motives and goals. Fair enough. There are and can be no ideal political aims, actions, or outcomes that will suit everyone. Contexts and people are extremely complex, ever changing, and challenges are great. However, agree or disagree with their actions and accomplishments, no one should question the commitment and effort expended by Peter Lougheed and Pierre Trudeau in the service of their country. Both have found a well-deserved place in the history of memorable Canadians, as men of dignity and integrity who served their country, fellow citizens, and successors to the best of their abilities, despite the imperfections and inevitable mistakes that mark any lives lived well and with purpose.

To date, no federal government of Canada has invoked the notwithstanding clause (NWC) as stipulated in section 33 of the 1982 Canadian Charter of Rights and Freedoms. On the few occasions on which it has been invoked by provincial governments, it has functioned pretty much as Merv Leitch told Peter Lougheed that it would—to ensure that duly *elected* representatives of the people have a slight upper hand over *unelected* judicial officials when it comes to making the laws of the land. Until recently, the very infrequency with which the NWC had been invoked, and then only by provincial governments, was consistent with the intent of those like Lougheed, Blakeney, and Lyon who insisted that it be included as part of the Charter during the November 1981 constitutional conference in Ottawa. Even when invoked on somewhat questionable grounds, as in 1988 by Premier Robert Bourassa's Quebec provincial government to override English language users' legitimate objections to the imposition of his "no English signage" legislation, the use of the NWC was not renewed beyond its initial 5-year period as specified in section 33 of the Charter. On this occasion, Quebec legislators came to their senses after having five years to reflect on what they had done, and changed the law to permit English signage if desired and if it accompanied and followed or did not otherwise overshadow its French equivalent. Thus, even when abused the NWC has so far functioned in a mostly non-extreme and potentially ameliorative manner in support of a parliamentary system of governance that somewhat privileges its legislative over its judicial arms. It was included in the Charter to enable a parliamentary check on the decisions of a fallible judiciary in determining the limits and bounds of our fundamental rights and freedoms, as a compromise between parliamentary and judicial supremacy. And, its inclusion helped to ensure that then Prime Minister of Canada Pierre Trudeau had the support of nine premiers so that he could take what turned out to be a successful constitutional package to London for patriation—an event that has allowed all Canadians to enjoy the protection and other benefits of a Constitution and Charter of our own.

This said, current uses of the NWC, such as by Premier Doug Ford and his Ontario provincial government to limit third-party election advertising and by Premier François Legault and his Quebec provincial government to pass its Bill 21 which prohibits civil servants from displaying religious symbols, raise legitimate concerns about whether or not the intent of the framers of the 1982 Canadian Constitution and Charter will survive more cavalier and frequent uses of the notwithstanding clause that might erode citizens' faith in the Charter rights and freedoms of minorities. As contemporary debate rages over parliamentary privilege and/or judicial assurance of minority rights, one cannot but be reminded of the efforts of those who participated in the 1981 Ottawa Constitutional Convention to "get things right," despite their different perspectives and visions. Peter Lougheed and Pierre Trudeau might be gone, but their legacies concerning inter-governmental relations and constitutional protections persist, and now are in the hands of contemporary Canadians and our elected representatives. Whatever we decide and do with respect to these and other matters near and dear to the hearts of our two protagonists and vital to our nation, it perhaps is helpful to know something about their lives, perspectives, and visions and how they contributed to our present situation.

Endnotes

Chapter 1

[1]   Chastko, P. A. (2004). *Developing Alberta's oil sands: From Karl Clark to Kyoto* (p. 155). Calgary, AB: University of Calgary Press.

[2]   Morton, D. (2017). *A short history of Canada (7th Ed.)* (p. 147). Toronto: McClelland & Stewart.

[3]   Ibid, p. 148.

[4]   Ibid, p. 166.

[5]   Words spoken by Bourassa supporter Armand Lavergne, as quoted in Morton (2017), p. 167.

[6]   Hustak, A. (1979). *Peter Lougheed: A biography* (p. 16). Toronto: McClelland & Stewart

[7]   Quoted in English, J. (2007). *Citizen of the world: The life of Pierre Elliott Trudeau (Volume One: 1919-1968)*, (p. 6). Toronto: Vintage Canada.

[8]   Graham, R. (2014). *The last act: Pierre Trudeau, the Gang of Eight, and the fight for Canada* (p. 51). Toronto: Penguin Canada.

Chapter 2

1   Clarkson, S., & McCall, C. (1990). *Trudeau and our times: The magnificent obsession* (p. 27). Toronto, ON: McClelland & Stewart.
2   English, 2007, p.13.
3   Trudeau, P. E. (1993). *Memoirs* (p. 10). Toronto: McClelland & Stewart.
4   Clarkson & McCall, 1990, p. 27.
5   English, 2007, p. 14.
6   Trudeau, 1993, p. 12.
7   English, 2007, p. 15.
8   Radwanski, G. (1978). *Trudeau* (p. 46). Toronto, ON: Macmillan of Canada
9   Quoted in Radwanski, 1978, p. 45.
10   Quoted in Radwanski, 1978, pp. 46-47.
11   Quoted in Radwanski, 1978, pp. 47-48.
12   Quoted in Nemni, M. & Nemni, M. (2006). *Young Trudeau: Son of Quebec, father of Canada, 1919-1944 (Trans. W. Johnson)* (p. 89). Toronto: McClelland & Stewart.
13   Ibid, p. 89.
14   Ibid, p. 42.
15   Clarkson & McCall, 1990, p. 34.
16   Radwanski, 1978, p. 55.
17   Nemni & Nemni, 2006, pp. 42-43.
18   Quoted in Radwanski,1978, pp. 56-57.
19   Ibid, p. 57.
20   Ibid, p. 58.
21   Ibid, p. 57.
22   All quoted material in this paragraph is from Nemni & Nemni, 2006, pp. 43-48.
23   All quoted material in this paragraph is from Nemni & Nemni, 2006, p. 57.
24   Ibid, pp. 79-80.
25   Trudeau, 1993, pp. 25-26.
26   Nemni & Nemni, 2006, p. 68.
27   Radwanski, 1978, p. 58.
28   Ibid, p. 59.
29   Quoted in Radwanski, 1978, pp. 59-60.
30   Trudeau, quoted in Radwanski, 1978, p. 60.

31   Quoted in Radwanski, 1978, p. 61.
32   Ibid, p. 61.
33   Ibid, p. 60.
34   English, 2007, p. 68.
35   Ibid, p. 68.
36   Radwanski, 1978, p. 63.
37   Jerome Kagan,(2000). *Three seductive ideas* (p. 138). Cambridge, MA: Harvard University Press.
38   Ibid, pp. 145-146.
39   Quoted in George Radwanski, 1978, p. 35.
40   Ibid, p. 35.
41   Quoted in English, 2007, p. 113.
42   Quoted in Clarkson & McCall, 1990, pp. 44-45.
43   Quoted in Nemni & Nemni, 2006, pp. 308-309.
44   Quoted in English, 2007, p. 125.
45   Quoted in English, 2007, p. 127.
46   Ibid, p. 128.
47   Ibid, p. 139.
48   Nemni, M. & Nemni, M. (2011). *Trudeau transformed: The making of a statesman 1944-1965* (Trans. George Tombs) (p 46). Toronto: McClelland & Stewart.
49   Quoted in English, 2007, p. 143.
50   Quoted in English, 2007, pp. 140-144.
51   Clarkson & McCall, 1990, p. 48.
52   Ibid, p. 56.
53   Ibid, p. 59.
54   Trudeau, 1993, pp. 39-40.
55   Trudeau, P. E. (1990). The values of a just society. In T. A. Axworthy & P. E. Trudeau (Eds.), *Towards a just society: The Trudeau years* (pp. 357-358). Toronto: Viking.
56   Quoted in English, 2007, p. 155.
57   Ibid, pp. 155-157
58   Ibid, p. 163.
59   Paul Fox, as quoted in English, 2007, p. 166.
60   Trudeau, 1993, p. 47.
61   Nemni & Nemni, 2011, p. 46.
62   Trudeau, 1993, p. 49.
63   Nemni & Nemni, 2011, p.154
64   Ibid, p. 155.

65 The Gateway (October 30, 1919). University of Alberta Student Newspaper. Edmonton, AB.

66 Hustak, A. (1979). *Peter Lougheed: A biography* (p. 23). Toronto: McClelland & Stewart.

67 Ibid, p. 26.

68 Quoted in Hustak, 1979, p. 28.

69 Ibid, p. 30.

70 Quoted in Wood, D. G. (1985). *The Lougheed legacy* (p. 28). Toronto: Key Porter Books.

71 Quoted in Wood, 1985, p. 31.

72 Ibid, p. 10.

73 Quoted in Hustak, 1979, p. 33.

74 Quoted in Hustak, 1979, p. 33.

75 Quoted in Hustak, 1979, p. 37

76 Ibid, p. 37.

77 Ibid, p. 43.

78 Quoted in Hustak, 1979, p. 37.

79 Quoted in Wood, 1985, p. 33.

80 Quoted in Hustak, 1979, p. 42.

81 Ibid, 41-42.

82 Quoted in Hustak, 1979, p. 38.

83 Quoted in Wood, 1985, p. 33.

84 Nelson Aldrich, Jr., American writer and editor, as quoted in Allan Hustak, 1979, p. 45.

85 Quoted in Hustak, 1979, p. 45

86 *The Paper Chase* takes place at an unnamed elite American university and focuses on the experiences of law students, but clearly is modeled on the Harvard Law School and its pedagogical practices, which are similar to those of the Harvard Business School.

87 Quoted in Hustak, 1979, p. 45.

88 Quoted in Hustak, 1979, p. 46.

89 Hustak, 1979, p. 47.

90 Quoted in Wood, 1985, p. 34.

91 Tupper, A. (2004). Peter Lougheed (1971-1985). In Bradford J. Rennie (Ed.), *Alberta premiers of the twentieth century* (p. 206). Regina, SK: Canadian Plains Research Centre, University of Regina.

Chapter 3

1   English, 2007, p. 196.
2   Trudeau, 1993, p. 64.
3   Ibid, p. 63.
4   Ibid, p. 64.
5   Ibid, p. 64.
6   Nemni & Nemni, 2011, p. 191.
7   Ibid, p. 193.
8   Ibid, p. 193.
9   English, 2007 pp. 224-225.
10   Ibid, p. 233.
11   Ibid, p. 234.
12   Ibid, p. 239.
13   Quoted in English, 2007, p. 243.
14   Radwanski, 1978, p. 77.
15   Quoted in Radwanski, 1978, p. 77.
16   Ibid, p. 78.
17   Quoted in English, 2007, p. 246.
18   English, 2007, p. 252.
19   Quoted in Radwanski, 1978, p. 79.
20   Pierre Elliott Trudeau (1968). *Federalism and the French Canadians* (p. 120). Toronto: Macmillan of Canada.
21   Radwanski, 1978, p. 79.
22   Quoted in Radwanski, 1978, pp. 81-82.
23   Quoted in Radwanski, 1978, p. 82.
24   English, 2007, p. 252.
25   Ibid, pp. 254-255.
26   Trudeau, 1993, p. 69.
27   English, 2007, p. 255.
28   Quoted in English, 2007, p. 257.
29   Kahn, E. (2019). *Been hoping we might meet again: The letters of Pierre Elliott Trudeau and Marshall McLuhan* (p. 65). Montreal: Novalis.
30   Quoted in Trudeau, 1968, p. xiii.
31   Radwanski, 1978, p. 84.
32   Clarkson & McCall, 1990, p. 70.
33   Ibid, pp. 71-72.
34   Ibid, p. 73.

35   Ibid, pp. 43-44.
36   Quoted in Clarkson & McCall, 1990, pp. 277-278.
37   Clarkson & McCall, 1990, p. 341.
38   Ibid, pp. 341-342.
39   Ibid, p. 383.
40   Ibid, p. 75.
41   English, 2007, p. 341.
42   Ibid, p. 342.
43   Pierre Trudeau & Jacques Hébert (1968). *Two innocents in Red China* (pp. 71-72). Vancouver, BC: Douglas & McIntyre.
44   See Aivalis, C. (2018). *The constant liberal: Pierre Trudeau, organized labour, and the Canadian social democratic left.* Vancouver: UBC Press.
45   Quoted in English, 2007, p. 363.
46   Quoted in English, 2007, pp. 373-374.
47   English, 2007, p. 379.
48   Ibid, p. 392.
49   Hustak, 1979, p. 47.
50   Hustak, 1979 p. 49.
51   Ibid, p. 50.
52   Marsh, J. H. (2006). Alberta's quiet revolution: 1973 and the early Lougheed years. In M. Payne, D. Wetherell, and C. Cavanaugh (Eds.), *Alberta formed, Alberta transformed* (p. 645). Edmonton, AB: University of Alberta Press & Calgary, AB: University of Calgary Press.
53   Hustak, 1979, p. 52.
54   Hustak, 1979, p. 52.
55   Both quotations in this paragraph are from Wood, 1985, pp. 35-37.
56   Quotations in this paragraph are from Wood, 1985, p. 36.
57   Hustak, 1979, p. 56.
58   Quoted in Hustak, 1979, p. 60.
59   Quoted in Hustak, 1979, p. 61.
60   Wood, 1985, p. 37.
61   Quoted in Hustak, 1979, p. 62.
62   Ibid, p. 62.
63   Ibid, p. 62.
64   Ibid, p. 63.
65   Wood, 1985, p. 38.
66   Hustak, 1979, p. 65.
67   Ibid, p. 67.
68   Wood, 1985, p. 39.

69   Ibid, p. 43.
70   Hustak, 1979, p. 69.
71   Ibid, p. 71.
72   Ibid, p. 73.
73   Ibid, p. 73.
74   Ibid, p. 76
75   Wood, 1985, p. 53.
76   Ibid, p. 55.
77   Hustak, 1979, p. 86.
78   Ibid, p. 87.
79   Wood, 1985, p. 52.
80   Ibid, p. 52.
81   Ibid, p. 53.
82   Hustak, 1979, p. 99.
83   All quotes in this paragraph are from Hustak, 1979, p. 100.
84   Wood, 1985, p. 56.
85   Ibid, p. 62.

Chapter 4

1 Clarkson & McCall, 1990, p. 93.
2 Ibid, p. 93.
3 Quoted in English, 2007, pp. 421-422.
4 Radwanski, 1978, p. 84.
5 Ibid, p. 85.
6 Quoted in Radwanski, 1978, pp. 85-86.
7 Quoted in Radwanski, 1978, pp. 86-87.
8 All material quoted or cited in this paragraph is from Radwanski, 1978, pp. 91-92.
9 Radwanski, 1978, p 92.
10 Ibid, p. 94.
11 Ricci, N. (2009). *Pierre Elliott Trudeau* (p. 33). Toronto: Penguin Canada.
12 English, 2007, p. 442.
13 Ricci, 2009, p. 35.
14 Ibid, pp. 36-37
15 Ibid, p. 69.
16 Trudeau, 1993, pp. 84-85.
17 Quoted in English, 2007, pp. 463-464.
18 Quoted in English, 2010, p, 20.
19 Quoted in English, 2010, p. 16.
20 Ricci, 2009, pp. 37-38.
21 Radwanski, 1978, p. 243.
22 Radwanski, 1978, pp. 255-256.
23 Quoted in Ricci, 2009, p. 116.
24 Quoted in Ricci, 2009, pp. 116-117.
25 Ricci, 2009, p. 122.
26 Clarkson & McCall, 1990, p. 123
27 Ibid.
28 English, 2010, p. 175.
29 Ibid, p. 176.
30 Ibid, p. 190.
31 Trudeau, 1993, p. 158.
32 Ibid, p. 159.
33 Ibid, p. 160.
34 Radwanski, 1978, p. 271.
35 Ibid, pp. 275-276.
36 Ibid, p. 282.

37   Trudeau, 1993, p. 160.
38   Quoted in Radwanski, 1978, p. 281.
39   Ibid, p. 285.
40   Trudeau, 1993, p. 172.
41   Radwanski, 1978, p. 295.
42   Trudeau, 1993, p. 197.
43   Ibid, p. 198.
44   English, 2010, p. 259.
45   Radwanski, 1978, pp. 307-308.
46   Radwanski, 1978, p. 291.
47   Clarkson & McCall, 1990, p. 126.
48   Trudeau, M. (1979). *Beyond reason* (p. 168). New York: Pocket Books.
49   Clarkson & McCall, 1990, p. 131.
50   Ibid, pp. 134-135.
51   Ibid, p. 135.
52   Ibid, p. 140.
53   Ibid, p. 142.
54   English, 2010, p. 299.
55   Quoted in English, 2010, p. 300.
56   English, 2010, pp. 292-293.
57   Clarkson & McCall, 1990, p. 301-302.
58   Clarkson & McCall, 1990, p. 310.
59   Ibid, p. 136.
60   Quoted in Richard Gwyn (1981). *The Northern Magus* (p. 337)
61   Gwyn, 1981, p. 337.
62   English, 2010, p. 408.
63   Parli. (2015). Head waiter to the provinces. In *The dictionary of Canadian politics.* https://parli.ca/head-waiter-provinces/.
64   Gwyn, 1981, p. 339.
65   Quoted in Gwyn, 1981, pp. 340-341.
66   Clarkson & McCall, 1990, p. 156.
67   Quoted anonymously in Clarkson & McCall, 1990, p. 163.
68   Quoted in Clarkson & McCall, 1990, p. 164.
69   Kotcheff, T. (2005). Canoe gang. In N. Southam (Ed.). *Pierre: Colleagues and friends talk about the Trudeau they knew* (p., 269). Toronto, ON: McClelland & Stewart.
70   Ibid, p. 270.
71   Ibid, p. 272.
72   Ibid, p. 272.

73 Trudeau, 1993, p. 264.
74 Clarkson & McCall, 1990, p. 165.
75 Trudeau, 1993, p. 264.
76 English, 2010, p. 433.
77 Clarkson & McCall, 1990, p. 166.
78 English, 2010, p. 435.
79 Trudeau, 1993, p. 265.
80 English, 2010, p. 435.
81 English, 2010, p. 435.
82 Slightly different accounts are given by Trudeau's biographers about exactly who requested and drafted the two speeches, but it is agreed that both Coutts and Axworthy were involved (cf. Clarkson & McCall, 1990; English, 2010).
83 Trudeau, 1993, p. 268.
84 Clarkson & McCall, 1990, p. 170.
85 Ibid, p. 170.
86 Ibid, p. 170.
87 English, 2010, pp. 436-437.
88 Clarkson & McCall, 1990, p. 173.
89 Quoted in Radwanski, 1978, p. 179, from a CTV "W5" interview on Dec. 21, 1973.
90 Radwanski, 1978, p. 313.
91 Ibid, p. 313.
92 Ibid, p. 314.
93 Ibid, p. 315.
94 Quoted in Radwanski, 1978, p. 317.

Chapter 5

1   Quoted in Hustak, 1979, p. 103.
2   Ibid, p. 104.
3   Quoted in Hustak, 1979, p. 106.
4   Wood, 1985, p. 64.
5   Frank Calder, quoted in Wood, 1985, p. 68.
6   Quoted in Marsh, J. H. (2006). Alberta's quiet revolution: 1973 and the early Lougheed years. In M. Payne, D. Wetherell, & C. Cavanaugh (Eds.), *Alberta formed Alberta transformed* (p. 644). Edmonton: University of Alberta Press and Calgary: University of Calgary Press.
7   Hustak, 1979, pp. 118-119.
8   Interview with Jim Foster, August 18, 2021.
9   Quoted in Hustak, 1979, p. 123.
10 Hustak, 1979, p. 124.
11 Ibid, p. 127.
12 Ibid, p. 130.
13 Ibid, pp. 131-132.
14 Wood, 1985, p. 95.
15 Interview with Jim Foster, August 18, 2021.
16 Ibid.
17 Quoted in Hustak, 1979, p. 145.
18 Ibid, p. 146.
19 Ibid, p. 147.
20 Allan Tupper (2004). Peter Lougheed, 1971-1985. In B. J. Rennie (Ed.), *Alberta's premiers of the twentieth century* (p. 212). Regina: University of Regina Press.
21 Ibid, p. 212.
22 Chastko, 2004, p. 155.
23 Tupper, 2004, p. 214.
24 All newspaper quotes in this paragraph from Hustak, 1979, p. 180-181.
25 Ibid, p. 181.
26 Ibid, p. 181.
27 Ibid, p. 183.
28 Ibid, p. 184.
29 Marsh, 2006, p. 651.
30 Pratt, L. (1976). *Tar sands: Syncrude and the politics of oil.* Edmonton, AB: Hurtig.
31 Marsh, 2006, p. 654.

32   Fraser, F. (2003). *Alberta's Camelot: Culture & the arts in the Lougheed years* (p. 9). Edmonton: Lone Pine.

33   Hurtig, M. (1996). *Mel Hurtig: At twilight in the country [Memoirs of a Canadian nationalist.]* (p. 199). Toronto: Stoddart Books.

34   Ibid, 1996, pp. 199-200.

35   Ibid, 1996, pp. 200-201.

36   Interview with Jim Foster, August 18, 2021.

37   Quoted in Graham, 2014, p. 17.

38   Quoted in Hustak, 1979, p. 221.

39   Quoted in Hustak, p. 224.

40   Ibid, p. 224.

41   Ibid, p. 226.

42   Ibid, p. 226.

43   Ibid, p. 227.

44   Ibid, p. 227.

45   Ibid, p. 228.

46   Marsh, 2006, p. 667.

47   Ibid, p. 667.

48   Raymaker, D. (2017). *Trudeau's tango: Alberta meets Pierre Elliott Trudeau, 1968-1972* (p. 279). Edmonton: Gutteridge Books.

49   Wood, 1985, p. 158.

50   Ibid, p. 159

51   Jim Seymour, as quoted in Wood, 1985, p. 159.

52   Quoted in Wood, 1985, p. 160.

53   Quoted in Wood, 1985, p. 160.

54   Interview with Jim Foster, August 18, 2021.

55   Quoted in Wood, 1985, p. 169.

56   Quoted in Wood, p. 169.

57   MacDonald, L. I. (2012). The best premier of the last 40 years: Lougheed in a landslide," *Public Policy* June 1. https://policyoptions.irpp.org/magazines/the-best-premier-of-the-last-40-years/the-best-premier-of-the-last-40-years-lougheed-in-a-landslide/

58   Cardinal, H. (1969). *The unjust society: The tragedy of Canada's Indians.* Edmonton, AB: Hurtig.

59   Hustak, 1979, p. 238.

60   Hustak, 1979, p. 241.

61   Quoted in Hustak, pp. 244-245.

62   Hustak, 1979, p. 243.

Chapter 6

1   Lalonde, M. (1990). Riding the storm: Energy policy. In T. S. Axworthy & P.E. Trudeau (Eds.), *Towards a just society* (p. 63). Toronto: Penguin Books Canada.

2   Government of Canada (1980). *The National Energy Program* (p. 22). Ottawa: Department of Energy, Mines and Resources.

3   Nemeth, T. (2006). 1980 duel of the decade (p. 686). In M. Payne, D. Wetherell, and C. Cavannaugh (Eds.). *Alberta formed Alberta transformed.* Edmonton: University of Alberta Press and Calgary: University of Calgary Press.

4   Lalonde, 1990, p. 66.

5   Quoted in Wood, p. 169.

6   Nemeth, 2006, p. 684.

7   Ibid, 2006, p. 685.

8   Ibid, 2006, p. 678.

9   Fraser, G. (2001). *René Lévesque & the Parti Québécois in power* (p. 207). Montreal & Kingston: McGill-Queen's University Press.

10   English, 2010, p. 448.

11   Quoted in English, 2010, p. 449.

12   Ibid, p. 449.

13   Ibid, p. 450.

14   Ibid, pp. 452-455.

15   Ibid, p. 459.

16   Burelle, A. (2005). *Pierre Elliott Trudeau: L'intellectuel et le politique.* Montréal: Éditions Fides.

17   Tupper, 2004, p. 216.

18   Wood, 1985, p. 175.

19   Nemeth, 2006, p. 689.

20   Ibid, p. 690.

21   Ibid, p. 691.

22   Fraser, J. (1980). PM to boost cash in Alberta offer, but no tradeoffs. *Globe and Mail* (front page), July 16.

23   English, 2010, p. 489.

24   English, 2010, pp. 491-492.

25   Trudeau, 1993, p. 290.

26   Graham, 2012, p. 24.

27	CBC Archives (1981, April 16). The "Gang of Eight" and Canada's Constitution, https://www.cbc.ca/archives/entry/the-constitution-the-gang-of-eight, retrieved on April 17, 2021.

28	Graham, 2012, p. 17.

29	English, 2010, pp. 493-494.

30	Graham, 2012, p. 40.

31	Government of Canada (1981, November 2-5). *Federal-Provincial Conference of First Ministers on the Constitution* (p. 3). Ottawa. [J. Martin, Trans.]

32	All quotes in this paragraph from Government of Canada (1981, November 2-5) *Federal-Provincial Conference of First Ministers on the Constitution* (pp. 5-11), Ottawa.

33	Ibid, 1981, pp. 67-68.

34	Ibid, 1981, pp. 74.

35	Ibid, 1981, p. 75.

36	Ibid, 1981, pp. 75-76.

37	Ibid, 1981, p. 77.

38	Sheppard, R. (2012). Patriation of the Constitution. In *The Canadian Encyclopedia Online.* Retrieved May 7, 2021 https://www.thecanadianencyclopedia.ca/en/article/patriation-of-the-constitution

39	Graham, 2012, p. 42.

40	Trudeau, 1993, p. 317.

41	Graham, 2012, p. 113.

42	Trudeau, 1993, p. 318.

43	Trudeau, 1993, p. 319.

44	Graham, 2012, p. 114.

45	Fraser, G. (2001). *René Lévesque and the Parti Québécois in power* (p. 296). Montreal: McGill-Queen's University Press.

46	Graham, 2012, p. 119.

47	Ibid, 2012, pp. 120-121.

48	Ibid, 2012, p. 121.

49	Graham, 2012, p. 138.

50	Ibid, 2012, p. 139.

51	Trudeau, 1993, p. 321.

52	Ibid, 1993, pp. 322-323.

53	Ibid, p. 324.

54	Ibid, p. 324.

55	Graham, 2012, p. 204.

56   Ibid, pp. 204-205.
57   Graham, 2012, p. 131.
58   Graham, 2012, pp. 131-132.
59   Ibid, p. 132.
60   Ibid, p. 215.
61   Ibid, p. 217.
62   Wood, 1985, pp. 230-231.
63   Graham, 2012, p. 220.
64   Ibid, p. 225.
65   Wood, 1985, p. 232.
66   Trudeau, 1993, p. 328.

Chapter 7

1   Christo Aivalis (2018). *The constant liberal: Pierre Trudeau, organized labour, and the Canadian social democratic left* (p. 181). Vancouver: UBC Press.

2   English, 2010, p. 606.

3   Ibid, 2010, p. 625.

4   Peter Lougheed (October 19, 1992). "Peter Lougheed Answers Pierre Trudeau." *McLean's Magazine.*

5   Laforest, G. (1995). *Trudeau and the end of the Canadian dream.* Montreal and Kingston: McGill-Queen's University Press.

6   Quoted in Plamondon, B. (2013). *The truth about Trudeau* (p. 332). Ottawa: Great River Media.

7   Conrad Black (2005). Longer views, differing angles. In N. Southam (Ed.), *Pierre: Colleagues and friends talk about the Trudeau they knew* (pp. 189-190).

8   English, 2010, p. 635.

9   Plamondon, 2013, pp. 343-344.

10   Quoted in English, 2010, p. 638.

11   Tim Rice (2012, September 12) "Lougheed Remembered." The Canadian Press.

12   Tupper, 2004, p. 227.

13   Wood, 1985, p. 244.

14   Interview with Jim Foster, August 18, 2021.

15   Peter Lougheed (2005). Notwithstanding everything and all of us. In N. Southam (Ed.), *Pierre: Colleagues and friends talk about the Trudeau they knew* (p. 177).

Index

A

B

C

T

THE AUTHOR

Jack Martin is Professor Emeritus at Simon Fraser University. After publishing a number of scholarly books throughout his career, in his retirement he has turned to writing nonfiction for a general audience. His first book of this kind was *Hometown Asylum: A History and Memoir of Institutional Care,* in which he tells the story of the large psychiatric hospital on the outskirts of his hometown of Ponoka, Alberta where his father was employed, his grandmother was a patient, and he worked as an institutional attendant while completing his degrees in psychology at the University of Alberta. *Peter & Pierre* is a dual biography of Peter Lougheed and Pierre Elliott Trudeau that draws on long-standing interests in psycho-biography and political history. Martin and his wife Wyn live in Tsawwassen, BC.